SAGE was founded in 1965 by Sara Miller McCune to support the dissemination of usable knowledge by publishing innovative and high-quality research and teaching content. Today, we publish over 900 journals, including those of more than 400 learned societies, more than 800 new books per year, and a growing range of library products including archives, data, case studies, reports, and video. SAGE remains majority-owned by our founder, and after Sara's lifetime will become owned by a charitable trust that secures our continued independence.

Los Angeles | London | New Delhi | Singapore | Washington DC | Melbourne

1962
BORDER
WAR

Thank you for choosing a SAGE product!
If you have any comment, observation or feedback,
I would like to personally hear from you.

Please write to me at **contactceo@sagepub.in**

Vivek Mehra, Managing Director and CEO, SAGE India.

Bulk Sales

SAGE India offers special discounts
for purchase of books in bulk.
We also make available special imprints
and excerpts from our books on demand.

For orders and enquiries, write to us at

Marketing Department
SAGE Publications India Pvt Ltd
B1/I-1, Mohan Cooperative Industrial Area
Mathura Road, Post Bag 7
New Delhi 110044, India

E-mail us at **marketing@sagepub.in**

Subscribe to our mailing list
Write to **marketing@sagepub.in**

This book is also available as an e-book.

1962
BORDER WAR
SINO-INDIAN TERRITORIAL DISPUTES
AND BEYOND

ISMAIL VENGASSERI

Los Angeles | London | New Delhi
Singapore | Washington DC | Melbourne

First published in 2021 by

SAGE Publications India Pvt Ltd
B1/I-1 Mohan Cooperative Industrial Area
Mathura Road, New Delhi 110 044, India
www.sagepub.in

SAGE Publications Inc
2455 Teller Road
Thousand Oaks, California 91320, USA

SAGE Publications Ltd
1 Oliver's Yard, 55 City Road
London EC1Y 1SP, United Kingdom

SAGE Publications Asia-Pacific Pte Ltd
18 Cross Street #10-10/11/12
China Square Central
Singapore 048423

Published by Vivek Mehra for SAGE Publications India Pvt Ltd. Typeset in 10.5/13 pt Berkeley by AG Infographics, Delhi.

Library of Congress Cataloging-in-Publication Data

Name: Vengasseri, Ismail, author.
Title: 1962 border war : Sino-Indian territorial disputes and beyond / Ismail Vengasseri.
Other titles: Sino-Indian territorial disputes and beyond
Description: New Delhi, India : SAGE Publications India Pvt Ltd; Thousand Oaks, California: SAGE Publishing, 2020. | Includes bibliographical references and index.
Identifiers: LCCN 2020034622 | ISBN 9789353885281 (hardback) | ISBN 9789353885304 (pdf) | ISBN 9789353885298 (epub)
Subjects: LCSH: Sino-Indian Border Dispute, 1957- | India—Military relations—China. | China—Military relations—India. | India—Military relations—China—Tibet Autonomous Region. | Tibet Autonomous Region (China)—Military relations—India. | China—Military relations—China—Tibet Autonomous Region. | Tibet Autonomous Region (China)—Military relations—China. | Borderlands—India. | Borderlands—China. | India—History—1947- | China—History—1949-
Classification: LCC DS480.85.V37 2020 | DDC 954.04/2—dc23
LC record available at https://lccn.loc.gov/2020034622

ISBN: 978-93-5388-528-1 (HB)

SAGE Team: Rajesh Dey, Sandhya Gola and Madhurima Thapa

Contents

List of Abbreviations

CCP	Chinese Communist Party
CGS	Chief of the General Staff
CIA	Central Intelligence Agency
COAS	Chief of the Army Staff
CPI	Communist Party of India
DBO	Daulat Beg Oldi
DGMO	Director General of Military Operations
DMI	Director of Military Intelligence
FP	Forward Policy
GOC	General Officer Commanding
IB	Intelligence Bureau
ITBP	Indo-Tibetan Border Police
LAC	Line of Actual Control
LBA	Land Boundary Agreement
MEA	Ministry of External Affairs
MFA	Ministry of Foreign Affairs
MIO	Military Intelligence Organization
NCNA	New China News Agency
NEFA	North-East Frontier Agency
PLA	People's Liberation Army
POK	Pakistan Occupied Kashmir
PRC	People's Republic of China
UN	United Nations

Foreword

In the context of India–China relations, 1962 has become the quintessential 'riddle wrapped in a mystery inside an enigma'. Seemingly in the past, it is still very much a part of our present situation, as we continue to have a disputed boundary, no mutually accepted Line of Actual Control, regular 'incursions' or 'intrusions' across the boundary as perceived by each side and, above all, as the author states in his preface, the 'ignominious military debacle' that India suffered in 1962 'continues to be a haunting memory of great concern and consternation…'. China's border incursions have dominated print and electronic media in India, and the strategic discourse has by and large focused on the existing situation without regard and sensitivity to complex historical legacies. This is not a desirable state of affairs, because while the leadership on both sides invariably applauds the 2,000 years of interaction between the two ancient civilizations, the colonial period during which the imperialist intrigues and manoeuvres between British India, Imperial China and Tibet hopelessly tangled the borders is routinely sidestepped.

Just as memories of 1962 begin to get less intense with the younger generations in both countries, the legacies of 1962 continue to shape our attitudes and perceptions. This was witnessed rather dramatically when the Galwan Valley clash took place between India and China in the summer of 2020. Among the number of lessons that it drove home, the most significant to my mind was the manner in which the complex and knotty 'historical' legacies resurfaced, and the extent to which confusions and obfuscations continue to cloud the average understanding.

It is therefore with great pleasure that I welcome this most timely and necessary book written by Ismail Vengasseri. By virtue of being a greatly respected faculty in the Department of History at the Lady Shri Ram College for Women in the University of Delhi, Dr Vengasseri brings to his writing an acute understanding of history and a teaching experience of nearly three decades. His current and continuing engagement with teaching and research on modern Indian history, the history of China and Japan, and issues in world history has added greater breadth and depth to his approach and led to a finely nuanced way of writing on these complex themes.

The fruits of Dr Vengasseri's labour during his postdoctoral research on the exploration of archival sources that could shed light on 1962 can be gathered from his review of the available literature in this book *1962 Border War*; the factors which led up to it, the historical records—all are critically discussed. And yet it is easy to navigate and bring out the complexities of the different theoretical approaches with lucidity and clarity. This should be of tremendous help to young scholars as they attempt to make sense of the profusion of writings, analyses and documentation, most of which are highly debatable and contested. More significantly, given its interdisciplinary nature, this book is likely to be equally beneficial to people of diverse backgrounds. Dr Vengasseri takes a critical view of the current dominant tropes and helps one think and rethink many of the extant interpretations that we accept as given and true.

Dr Vengasseri's work also brings into sharp relief how much more we have to travel to acquire a substantial and holistic grasp of the problem in their various dimensions. As he points out most correctly, the full record and official documents are still withheld from public scrutiny, which has also prevented a genuine scholarly assessment and therefore effectively blocked the proper assimilation of vital lessons regarding our own perceptions and handling of the 1962 crisis. He brings in not only the larger international backdrop of the Cold War but also the various ups and downs in the turbulent domestic politics of that time, which added to the complexity of the boundary dispute. This book points to the fact that, in many ways, we are still not out of the long shadows cast by 1962 and that a sense and awareness of history, which must be central to our understanding of this core problem in India–China relations, must be firmly grasped if we are to resolve this dispute and put 1962 firmly in the past.

I write this foreword with a deep sense of appreciation and gratitude to Dr Vengasseri for a work that will most certainly ignite a spirit of critical enquiry and equip young scholars and researchers with tools and a road map to explore this most momentous and troublesome episode in independent India's external relations. It is also my hope that this book will be picked up by the general reader, as China is looming larger and larger in many ways on the Indian horizon and consciousness. Hopefully, a better informed public will generate a need to move beyond emotive dimensions and support a political will to resolve this dispute and pave the way for a recasting of India–China relations, which would not only be of mutual benefit but will resonate in the region and beyond.

Alka Acharya
Professor, Centre for East Asian Studies,
School of International Studies
Jawaharlal Nehru University, New Delhi
(Honorary Fellow and Former Director of
Institute of Chinese Studies, New Delhi)

Preface

The ignominious military debacle at the heights of the Himalayas in the freezing winter of 1962 continues to be a haunting memory of great concern and consternation for New Delhi. The military fiasco, therefore, has been reflected upon in detail, repeatedly and exhaustively, in the post-war years, and the factors that dragged India and China to war have generated a heated controversy. The nature of the border dispute has been at the centre of the debate among national and international scholars, historians, political scientists as well as military strategists and diplomats ever since the beginning of bilateral relations between the two nations in the post-colonial days. Naturally, there have been a series of publications covering various aspects of this encounter in 1962, largely reflecting on the reasons that led to the war along the borders, the Tibet factor, the nature of the border dispute, issues in diplomatic relations, etc. However, the vaults of the archival documents pertaining to these issues have been kept closed for more than seven decades, and neither 'political aspirations' nor judicial interventions could uncover the enigma surrounding dozens of these documents, including several investigative reports by military officials and the Ministries of Defence, Home and External Affairs, in addition to documents on diplomatic dealings. In the aforementioned context, the new studies are very relevant. There is a level of curiosity among readers, as well as the scholarship, to look into the nature of the contents of those documents, raising a question as to why they continue to remain inside sealed vaults. This mysterious inaccessibility to such documents arouses pertinent doubts, prompting one to want to take a look at these concealed documents. *1962 Border War: Sino-Indian Territorial Disputes and Beyond* is the outcome of such an enquiry, based on some newly available classified and declassified archival data. This study, as part of my postdoctoral research work in contemporary history, therefore, looks not only into the historical antecedents for the origins and developments of the border disputes between India and China but also tries to determine the ulterior forces that proved to be a catalyst in propelling what seemed to be minor differences into something which gained such large dimensions that it ended up potentially spoiling the friendly bilateralism that existed.

Since time immemorial, these twin ancient civilizations of Asia shared a warm understanding on cultural, economic and spiritual realms, until the seeds of the dispute were sown between them by a colonial game played by the British during their imperialist 'extravaganza' in the subcontinent. The bilateral relations between these two millennium-old friends during the post-colonial days, therefore, had been decisively determined by the imperialist interventions of that time. The two major border issues between these neighbours, namely the territorial disputes of Aksai Chin in the west and the McMahon Line in the east, no doubt, have their origin in the colonial 'cartographic mischief', which has been extensively discussed in this study. Delving into the nitty-gritty of the Aksai Chin dispute and critically analysing the archival documents for the historical legitimacy of the McMahon Line, the work locates the crux of the disputes and the internal and external developments in both countries during the post-colonial days. The central theme of the thesis, therefore, is to focus on locating disruptive elements within India's post-colonial polity, as well as external forces that worked clandestinely to exacerbate the existing dispute, eventually leading to a massive military encounter in 1962.

These narratives are reliably and credibly sourced from a few recently declassified confidential reports, as well as rare and yet-to-be-declassified archival documents that throw light on the intriguing inter and intranational influences that were factored into the bilateralism between the two Asian giants. The striking significance and scope of the work is that it has extensively used for academic research two of the most controversial historical reports submitted more than half a century ago: 'Henderson Brooks–Bhagat Report', a highly confidential Indian Military Enquiry Commission Report of 1963, kept classified by the Government of India till date, but partially available in the public domain and the most secretive Central Intelligence Agency top Secret Staff study Reports of 1963–1964 on the Sino-Indian border dispute, declassified (2007) by the USA. This study, which is of an interdisciplinary nature, unravels the facts on some of the highly debated and much deliberated issues, such as the Tibet factor in the Sino-Indian border dispute and the pro-Rightist impact on India's internal politics, in addition to the influences and interferences of the USA and the Western powers in the decision-making process in New Delhi, bringing novelty to the nuanced interpretations of the issue.

As the title of the work suggests, this enquiry goes into identifying the most important factors that pushed these nations on the path towards a large-scale military encounter in 1962, swayed by factors beyond frontier issues. First, the Sino-Indian border dispute, one of the largest border disputes in the world, both in terms of its territorial size and its potential impacts, has historically been traced back with archival evidence of its origin in the colonial game theory as played out in the region. Second, the study answers one of the most pertinent questions: Why did these two newly created republics finally choose the path of armed conflict after 1959, even after discarding their ideological divergences and coming close for the sake of Asian unity on the foundation of Panchsheel, through the efforts of Nehru–Chou comradeship? The study identifies the forces and their motives that propelled nations from within and without, until the existing border issue got entangled with emotional issues like the Tibet factor, resulting in rivalry which finally culminated in the border war. It is also pointed out that such a looming potential boundary dispute could have been appropriately and affably settled by both nations, largely by ignoring their respective imperial legacies and through active negotiations on the basis of a 'give-and-take' formula with little resentment on either side. However, no constructive negotiation was possible, since certain forces played an ulterior role, undermining all the positive efforts made. The contribution of the Indian press, the political opposition and parliamentary deliberations have also been critically analysed here. Since the study proposes a thesis on these premises, the work provides enough scope for novelty in reading and presents interesting thoughts and reflections for political strategists to analyse and mull over.

Introduction

'Good fences make good neighbours', opines Robert Frost's neighbour. He insists that Frost mends the walls between them, as he believes this would buttress their relationship within the neighbourhood. Like Frost's neighbour, if the nations of the world were to succeed in mending walls with their neighbours and ensuring that their frontiers were stable, their bilateral relations would also be sustainable in the long term. History is testimony to the fact that uncertain border definitions have proved to be a hurdle in maintaining friendly relations across frontiers, and this, in turn, has created clashes and conflicts. This continues to be one of the greatest concerns between neighbouring nations—the 'tripwires of war'. Over the years, debates around frontiers have tended to trigger discord and disharmony, and even now border disputes have been the source of some of the major wars. The case has not been any different in Europe, but despite their experiments on 'withering walls', they have managed to define their borders by and large. Most of the major European wars in history were fought on the issue of territorial frontiers, and this might have prompted Lord Curzon to rightly observe, 'Frontiers are indeed the razor's edge on which hang suspended the modern issues of war or peace, of life or death to nations'.[1] In the premise mentioned earlier, India, which shares land boundaries with seven other countries, cannot continue to wait indefinitely for its walls to be mended with its neighbours. There are areas of unsettled disputes, both minor and major, with most of the neighbours, including those of a more significant magnitude with

---

[1] Lord Curzon of Kedleston, *Frontiers in Oxford Lectures on History 1904–23*, Vols. 1–58 (Oxford: Clarendon Press, 1924), 7. Quoted in Bardo Fassbender and Anne Peters, ed., *The Oxford Handbook of the History of International Law*, 240.

China and Pakistan. Disputes with Bhutan and Sri Lanka (Ceylon)[2] were of a minor nature, and most of these, by and large, were amicably resolved in the 1970s. Despite the nature of the territorial dispute with Nepal being comparatively smaller (520 sq. km), the buffer status of Nepal between India and China makes the magnitude of the Kathmandu–New Delhi dispute of greater significance.[3] The Nepalese government's release in May 2020 of a 'new political map laying claim over Lipulekh, Kalapani and Limpiyadhura has only further strained the situation'.[4] The porous nature of the India–Burma (Myanmar) border, along 1,472 km, is creating considerable ethnic tension in the area. Even when governments reiterated that there was no border dispute between the two nations, unsettled issues added to the border pressures in the Manipur region.[5] However, the success in the ratification of the Land Boundary Agreement (LBA) between India and Bangladesh in 2015[6] bears testimony to the fact that if the government

[2] India shares 699 km of border territory with Bhutan. There has been a dispute between the two nations involving several inconsistencies over this un-demarcated border. Similarly, India had a dispute with Sri Lanka over Kachchatheevu, a small island of about 235 acres. However, tensions within this region were reduced with the resolution of these two issues during Prime Minister Indira Gandhi's tenure through cordial dialogues with Bhutan (1973–1984) and the signing of agreements with Sri Lanka (1974–1976). Despite these efforts, minor issues, due to local dissatisfaction, are still pending in the region.

[3] The India–Nepal border dispute is mainly over Kalapani, a territory that extends over 400 sq. km, and over Susta, an area that extends over 140 sq. km. Most of the issues have still not been resolved. India's announcement of inauguration of a new road on 8 May 2020 to Manasarovar triggered a border tension.

[4] *The Diplomat* (22 May 2020), available at https://thediplomat.com/2020/05/amid-dispute-with-india-nepal-publishes-new-political-map-what-now/. *The Print* (21 May 2020), available at https://theprint.in/diplomacy/nepal-halts-distribution-of-new-text-book-with-revised-map-incorporating-indian-areas/508293/ (accessed on 20 October 2020).

[5] Minister of State for Home Affairs, Kiren Rijiju, in July 2018, stated in the Rajya Sabha that 'there is no Indo–Myanmar border dispute, we have an agreement. We have a complete understanding. It is only the demarcation of the pillars, total nine in numbers, that is to be settled'. *The Economic Times* (1 August 2018), available at https://economictimes.indiatimes.com/news/defence/no-border-dispute-between-india-and-myanmar-states-government/articleshow/65229882.cms?from=mdr (accessed on 20 October 2020).

[6] Sharing a land boundary of about 4,096 km, Bangladesh and India had been involved in disputes over 111 enclaves of 70 sq. km and 51 enclaves of about 28 sq. km. These territories, with a population of more than 5 million, border four north-eastern states of India. Problems of intrusion and border skirmishes have been rampant in these

and the opposition unite to resolve issues of national interest, going beyond their political ideologies, they can find resolutions to the most difficult issues. That said, however, it is important to note that New Delhi's existing border dispute with Pakistan and China is of a more serious and complex nature. These issues have been inherited as a legacy of the British colonial administration.[7] However, even after seven decades of independence, India's border disputes with these neighbours remain unsettled, though China has been successful in strategizing and tactfully handling such disputes with most of its neighbours, barring India.[8]

The burning nature of this dispute can be testified by the military face-offs between the two nuclear powers at multiple locations during the summer of 2020. These clashes in the Galwan Valley, Pangong Lake and Demchok in Ladakh and Nathula Pass near Sikkim in the eastern sector underscore the fact that border disputes are like dormant volcanoes that can come alive any time. After a gap of 45 years yet

regions. To avert frequent tension in the border region and to reach an amicable solution, feasible to the people who were living in a land locked within the territory of a foreign country, a historic LBA was signed between Indian Prime Minister Indira Gandhi and Bangladesh Founder Sheikh Mujibur Rahman, in 1974, by agreeing to swap these enclaves with each other. But the pact, which had to be ratified by both Houses of Parliament, could not be implemented for a long period, even after repeated attempts by the government, due to fierce resistance by the opposition parties, for the reason that the pact would end up giving up the territory of the nation to a foreign country. A final effort was made by the Congress government in 2013. However, this was also stalled in Parliament due to strong opposition by the Bharatiya Janata Party, the Trinamool Congress and the Asom Gana Parishad. Later, when the Modi government came to power in New Delhi on 7 May 2015, an agreement was signed for the mutual exchange of these enclaves. Although this resulted in a net loss of about 10,000 acres of the Indian territory, which falls on the opposite side of the international border, and was not accessible even by Indian officials, for all practical purposes, the exchange was a step in the right direction, decided upon many decades ago, but it had been in deadlock due to internal politics. Finally, with the support of the opposition, the Parliament ratified the decision for its implementation in a phased manner between 31 July 2015 and 30 June 2016. This agreement has brought about some much-needed solace and tranquillity to this region, also providing a precedent to the mutual exchange formula for other disputed areas as well.

[7] A. G. Noorani, 'The Truth about 1962', in *India–China Boundary Problem 1846–1947* (Oxford: Oxford University Press, 2011).

[8] China signed agreements to define its frontiers and resolved its differences with Burma on 28 January 1960, with Nepal on 21 March 1960, and with Pakistan on 2 March 1963. Joint committees were then set up to draw up a boundary treaty, to correct maps and to conduct surveys. Similar treaties were signed with Burma on 1 October 1960 and Nepal on 5 October 1961. Noorani, 'The Truth about 1962'.

again, the bloodshed in Galwan Valley in June 2020 escalates tension in the frontiers. These encounters along the border cannot be considered isolated incidents—they have frequently been reported in recent years. The 72-day Doklam face-off in June–August 2017 has become a lot more intensive and grave of late. During the 2018 Wuhan summit and the 2019 Mamallapuram meet, the Modi–Xi Jinping bonhomie has not in the least allayed the pressures at the frontiers.

Among other auxiliary factors, the Sino-Indian war of 1962 largely emanated from a boundary dispute,[9] and this border war has proved to have caused collateral damage to India's reputation in the international community. For the future 'prospect of a durable Sino-Indian strategic partnership the festering border dispute that calls immediate resolution can be a triggering factor for adverse Sino-Indian relations'.[10] In view of this, it is essential to recognize that the border dispute may well be the founding premise for any hostilities in the bilateral relations between these two emerging Asian powers.

However, there is no proper and pertinent information available to the public in India on the nature of the border dispute and the consequent war of 1962, even as voluminous documents pertaining to the issues are kept classified as 'top secret' with the different departments of the Government of India. 'The official documents of the Indian Foreign Affairs Ministry relating to the Sino-Indian frontier since 1914 are still classified, which has served to perpetuate ignorance about the true border legacy of the British Raj'.[11] Experts studying this say, 'Correct and full information is rather difficult to come by. The records of the period 1947–64 have not yet been made available to the public'.[12] It is a fact that a large bulk of the reports submitted

---

[9] Bhaskar Roy, *China Succinctly Broadening the Border Issue with India*. South Asia Analysis Group (Paper No. 5570, 29 September 2013). Available at http://www.southasiaanalysis.org/node/1366 (accessed on 20 October 2020).

[10] Subramanian Swami, 'Looking beyond the Border Issue', *The Hindu*, 18 June 2008.

[11] K. S. Subramanian, 'Looking Back to the Future: The Sino-Indian Border Dispute of 1954–1962', *Asia Times*, 6 June 2015. Available at https://asiatimes.com/2015/06/looking-back-to-the-future-the-sino-indian-border-dispute-of-1954-62/ (accessed on 20 October 2020).

[12] K. Subrahmanyam, 'Nehru and India–China Conflict of 1962', in *India's Foreign Policy, the Nehru Years*, ed. B. R. Nanda (New Delhi: Radiant, 1975), 1.

by the various commissions of enquiry and several diplomatic and military documents pertaining to the Sino-Indian border relations between 1950 and 1963 are inaccessible even for any scholarly reference purpose in India,[13] while China, the USA and a few Western powers have brought to light a large cache of documents pertaining to the same issue. The selected declassification or leakage of data by 'vested interests' at a time convenient for them makes one wonder why ambiguity still persists in the Indian stand on the issue.[14] The studies conducted, based on such selectively released data and available sources from other countries, makes room for more assumptions, speculations and rumours than for reaching any proper conclusion, putting in jeopardy the interests of the nations and their political stance. Hence, in the larger welfare of the nation and to respect the hopes and aspirations of its citizens, it is imperative that these data be made available for scholarly research. In the aforementioned context, the driving force behind this work is to understand the reasons for the ambiguity in the classification of documents[15] pertaining to the border dispute and the war of 1962.

The list of classified files in the Indian archives and the official shelves is quite lengthy. It includes dozens of military enquiry commission reports as well as several other official studies, recommendations

---

[13] A large volume of official correspondence between China and India since 1950 has been published in a series of Indian government white papers. However, certain relevant materials relating to the dispute have still not seen the light of day.

[14] Neville Maxwell has extensively written on the subject, and his magnum opus *India's China War* (1970) makes many revelations based on certain classified documents he accessed. However, the timing of Neville Maxwell's revelations has always had an intriguing proximity to the general elections in India. On 17 March, a few weeks before the 2014 general elections, Maxwell posted the first part of the 'Henderson Brooks–Bhagat Report' on his website. A few general elections earlier as well, Maxwell had been aggressively critical of the Nehru government. Immediately before the fourth general election in 1967, he wrote a series of articles fiercely attacking the Government of India. Nehru and the Congress government were always his targets. One can read his passionate anti-Delhi, pro-Peking arguments in most of his articles, more vividly apparent in an interview with Kai Friese published in *Outlook Special Issue* (17 December 2012).

[15] A change of government in New Delhi in 2014, to the Rightist opposition, had given some hope in this direction, as they had been demanding the declassification of these documents when they were in opposition. However, the issue went for a toss, with the new government also becoming silent and reluctant, adding more mystery to their situation.

and defence documents. In addition to the 'Henderson Brooks–Bhagat Report' (1963), a controversial military document substantiating the reasons for the reverses in the 1962 war, there are several documents directly pertaining to the border dispute, such as the Himmatsinhji Report (1951), the Kulwant Singh Committee Report (1952) and the Thorat Committee Report[16] (1952) in cold storage, all of which deal exclusively on the nature of the border. The Ministry of External Affairs (MEA) had prepared a comprehensive paper called 'Studies on the Northern Frontier' under the supervision of K. Zachariah, Director of the Historical Division. According to Noorani, this paper, based on archival documents, discussed the history and circumstances under which the different frontier lines were suggested. The content of the paper, however, is still kept secret from the public. The latest available information about these reports, if correct, is highly shocking. Claude Arpi says that Director, Vigilance, Ministry of Defence, issued a letter dated 12 October 2011, with the approval of the Defence Secretary, stating that

> none of the remaining (five) reports: (i) PMS Blackett Report 1948; (ii) Himmatsinghji Report, 1951; (iii) H. M. Patel Committee report on functioning of the Ministry of Defence,1952; and (vi) Sharda Mukherjee Committee report on restructuring Ministry of Defence 1967; ... are available in the Ministry of Defense.[17]

Arpi expresses apprehension whether these reports have lost forever. It is in such prevailing situations that Noorani says, 'the nation must be told the truth, the historical truth since 1842 and the truth about Indian diplomacy since 1947'.[18] Therefore, an enquiry into the archival documents on the Sino-Indian border relation becomes impera-

---

[16] Major General S. P. P. Thorat had submitted the findings of his study, on the situation in Nepal and border region, in August 1951. Later in 1959–1960, as Lt General and GOC in Charge of the Eastern Command, Thorat made an assessment of the magnitude of the Chinese threat to the Indian borders in the eastern sector.

[17] P. K. Gupta, Director, Vigilance, Ministry of Defence vide ref. CIC order file no. CIC/LS/A/2011/001106 issued letter dated 12 October 2011 in Claude Arpi, 'Himmatsinhji Committee Report' (10 August 2012). Available at http://claudearpi.blogspot.com/2012/08/the-himmatsinhji-committee-report.html (accessed on 30 July 2020).

[18] Noorani, 'The Truth about 1962'.

tive to bring to light the actual state of affairs, so as to get rid of the persistently haunting nightmare that has created a diplomatic deadlock for creative and constructive bilateralism in Asia. This study, therefore, is an attempt to appraise the nature and origin of the dispute and to trace the factors that later led to a border war.

Whether or not it was delimited by natural boundaries and mutually agreed upon by the customs and traditions at a historical period in the past, the fact remains that, after the emergence of India and China as modern states, with their resolve and self-determination to establish political sovereignty, there were efforts and initiatives taken, on several occasions, all of which made little progress. Despite their best efforts, time and again, to work towards peaceful coexistence, there were deadlocks from within and no tangible progress in this direction. No sooner would the negotiations begin than the media and political opposition would take up the issue and blow it out of proportion, searching for loopholes, grey areas and casting suspicion on each other. And so 'the border between China and India remains undefined (and it is) a constant source of friction between the world's two most populous countries'.[19] Intermittent border clashes, incited by claims and counterclaims over distant and desolate mountain peaks, have created much havoc in the country, compounded by frequent media wars. On several occasions, at the bureaucratic, ministerial and prime ministerial levels, discordant nations have tried to work out their differences, but to no avail. Already 21 rounds of border-related dialogues have taken place between New Delhi and Peking.[20] Yet the Doklam and Pangong Lake, and multiple other incidents, add to the uncertainty at the frontiers.

The focus of this volume is therefore not only to trace the historical origin and nature of the dispute (Chapters 2 and 3) but also to ascertain the factors which have contributed towards the complication of the issue. Hence, the discussions here revolve largely around

---

[19] Jaswant Singh, *The Invisible Border War* (Prague: Project Syndicate, 2013).

[20] The latest Sino-Indian border talk was held between Ajit Doval, the National Security Advisor of India, and Wang Yi, the Chinese Foreign Affairs Minister, in November 2018, in Sichuan Province, China.

three narratives: (a) the legacy of imperialist border devices during colonial and post-colonial days, and their impact on present-day border perceptions; (b) Tibet as a protruding ominous factor in the Sino-Indian border dispute and (c) internal as well as external factors that have triggered the border war. While substantiating the narrative, to the extent possible, an earnest effort has been made to balance the perceptions of both nations. The time frame of the study is limited to the period between 1949 and 1962, from the emergence of the People's Republic of China (PRC) to the Sino-Indian border war. The significance of this time frame is that it was only during this period that the dispute had been identified as an existing irritant, which further grew into a dispute, getting entangled with other problems. The basic structure of border alignment and the underlying issues pertaining to that have not changed even a little since then.

Literature and Historiography

The border dispute and the subsequent military face-off in the winter of 1962 has always been a subject of interest to historians, political scientists and military strategists; these topics have been discussed and debated at length within political and academic circles. Therefore, the wide range of literature existing in these areas of study necessitates a brief review of some of them in order to identify the various schools of historiography in these writings. This literature is, for the most part, based on research conducted in the 1960s and 1970s, a larger chunk of which is from the Western scholars with a few by Indian authors. Some of the earliest notable accounts on the subject have been penned down by military generals and defence personnel, who have experienced the war first-hand, in addition to contemporary journalists like D. R. Mankekar.[21] Writers such as B. M. Kaul,[22] Brigadier J. P. Dalvi,[23]

---

[21] D. R. Mankekar, *The Guilty Men of 1962* (Bombay: Tulsi Shah Enterprises, 1968). Mankekar was a contemporary journalist who had direct access to the people and events of the time to narrate the issues as a critical appraisal.

[22] B. M. Kaul, *The Untold Story* (New Delhi: Allied Publishers, 1967).

[23] Brigadier J. P. Dalvi, *Himalayan Blunder, The Curtain-raiser to the Sino-Indian War of 1962* (Dehradun: Natraj, 1969).

S. S. Khera,[24] B. N. Mullik,[25] S. P. P. Thorat [26] and Major General D. K. Palit[27] have presented an insider's view of the Indian armed forces. With the exception of Dalvi and Mankekar, most of them have endeavoured to portray a bright picture within the defence establishment. Although these accounts are largely confined to narratives on armed forces and military encounters at the frontiers, they provide materials for further enquiry into the dark and unexplored areas of the dispute and the border war.

The second group of early writers, who narrated extensively on the predicaments at the border, includes Western scholars such as Margaret W. Fisher, Leo E. Rose, Robert Huttenback,[28] John Rowland,[29] Dorothy Woodman,[30] Alastair Lamb,[31] James Barnard Calvin[32] and Steven A. Hoffmann.[33] The writings of these scholars are largely in the context of a political narrative during the international Cold War era. Western scholars of the 1970s and 1980s have invested immensely in this area of study and their political analysis of the subject. In particular, the

---

[24] S. S. Khera, *India's Defence Problem* (Hyderabad: Orient Longman, 1968).

[25] B. N. Mullik, *My Years with Nehru, The Chinese Betrayal* (New Delhi: Allied Publishers, 1970).

[26] S. P. P. Thorat, *From Reveille to Retreat* (New Delhi: Allied Publishers, 1986).

[27] D. K. Palit, *War in High Himalayas, The Indian Army in Crisis, 1962* (London: C. Hurst & Co. Publishers, 1991).

[28] Margaret W. Fisher, Leo E. Rose, Robert A. Huttenback, *Himalayan Battleground: Sino-Indian Rivalry in Ladakh* (New York, NY: Praeger, 1963).

[29] Robert John Rowland, *A History of Sino-Indian Relations: Hostile Co-existence* (Princeton, NJ: D. Van Nostrand Co., 1967).

[30] Dorothy Woodman, *Himalayan Frontiers: A Political Review of British, Chinese, Indian, and Russian Rivalries* (London: Cresset Press, 1969).

[31] Alastair Lamb, *The China–India Border: The Origins of the Disputed Boundaries* (London: Oxford University Press, 1964); Alastair Lamb, *The McMahon Line: A Study in the Relations between India, China and Tibet, 1904–1914*, Vol. 21 (Toronto: University of Toronto Press, 1966), 966; Alastair Lamb, *Britain and Chinese Central Asia: The Road to Lhasa, 1767 to 1905* (London: Routledge, 1960); Alastair Lamb, *The Sino-Indian Border in Ladakh* (Canberra: Asian Publications, 1973); Alastair Lam, *Tibet, China, and India, 1914–1950: A History of Imperial Diplomacy* (London: Roxford Books, 1989).

[32] James Barnard Calvin, *The China–India Border War* (Bloomington, IN: MCCSC, 1984).

[33] Steven A. Hoffmann, *India and the China Crisis* (Berkeley, CA: University of California Press, 1990).

writings of Alastair Lamb have provided the largest bulk of primary reading for the understanding of this subject. These texts were the foundations on which most of the later academic discourses on the subject were formulated, both by India and by other writers, especially at a time when archival documents were inaccessible. Naturally, their narrative too could not escape the influence of Western imperialist interpretations. Shanti Prasad Varma,[34] G. S. Bhargava,[35] S. R. Johri,[36] Mohan Ram,[37] Parshotam Mehra[38] and a few other Indian writers come first in this series of authors. However, scholars such as Karunakar Gupta,[39] A. G. Noorani,[40] Neville Maxwell,[41] S. P. Sen[42] and John Lall[43] have carried out extensive archival research in this field.

Let us now take a look at the nature and contributions of some of the works that have come out in recent years. A majority of these publications deal with diplomacy and bilateralism in the modern era. Anna Orton[44] provides a diplomatic account of the bilateral relations and warns of the dangers posed by an aggravating dispute between two

---

[34] Shanti Prasad Varma, *Struggle for the Himalayas: A Study in Sino-Indian Relations* (New Delhi: University Publishers, 1965).

[35] G. S. Bhargava, *The Battle of NEFA—The Undeclared War* (Bombay: Allied Publishers, 1964).

[36] S. R. Johri, *Chinese Invasion of Ladakh* (Lucknow: Himalaya Publications, 1969).

[37] Ram Mohan, *Politics of Sino-Indian Confrontation* (Noida: Vikas Publishing House Pvt Ltd, 1973).

[38] Parshotam Mehra, *An 'Agreed' Frontier, Ladakh and India's Northernmost Borders, 1846–1947* (Oxford: Oxford University Press, 1993); Parshotam Mehra, *Essays in Frontier History: India, China, and the Disputed Border* (New Delhi: Oxford University Press, 2007).

[39] Karunakar Gupta, *Spotlight on Sino-Indian Frontiers* (Calcutta: New Book Centre, 1982).

[40] A. G. Noorani, *India–China Boundary Problem 1846–1947, History and Diplomacy* (New Delhi: Oxford University Press, 2011).

[41] Neville Maxwell, *India's China War* (London: Pantheon Books, 1970).

[42] Siba Pada Sen, *The Sino-Indian Border Question: A Historical Review* (Calcutta: Institute of Historical Studies, 1971).

[43] John Lall, *Aksai Chin and Sino-Indian Conflict* (New Delhi: Allied Publishers, 1989).

[44] Anna Orton, *India's Borderland Disputes: China, Pakistan, Bangladesh, and Nepal* (Aurangabad: Epitome Books, 2010).

nuclear powers. While concluding that 'boundaries are manifestations of national identity, and it could be trip-wires of war', she suggests some diplomatic solutions to this complicated issue. John Garver provides an exclusive account of the half-a-century-strained Sino-Indian relations on the basis of the literature available in Chinese as well as interviews with people who have direct information on the area.[45] Most Indian authors, such as M. L. Sali,[46] R. K. Tiwari,[47] Gautam Das,[48] Shiv Kunal Verma[49] and Raghava Saraṇa Sarma,[50] also narrate the dispute from a conventional Indian standpoint. However, an insider's account of the Indian Army is available in the works of D. K. Palit,[51] Jaidev Singh Datta[52] and D. K. Khullar[53] and is highly revealing and resourceful for corroborating accounts. Although Palit presents a detailed narration of the circumstances that led to a disastrous military campaign which in turn led to the Chinese invasion of the lands along the Indian border, J. S. Datta, Brigade Major of the 62 Infantry Brigade, provides a similar factual military account in the North-East Frontier Agency (NEFA). Although a great deal seems to have been written in the justification of military actions, Khullar also narrates the intricate situation of the military forces in the NEFA during the war. An account of the strategies and planning of the armed forces on the other side of the

---

[45] John W. Garver, *Protracted Contest: Sino-Indian Rivalry in the Twentieth Century* (Seattle, WA: University of Washington Press, 2001).

[46] M. L. Sali, *India–China Border Dispute: A Case Study of the Eastern Sector* (Ladakh: APH Publishing, 1998).

[47] Ravi K. Tiwari, *Line of Actual Control: Contesting Boundaries between Nations* (New Delhi: Bio Green Books, 2015).

[48] Gautam Das, *Understanding the Sino-Indian War, 1962* (New Delhi: Hindustan Publishing Corporation, 2013).

[49] Shiv Kunal Verma, *1962: The War That Wasn't: The Definitive Account of the Clash between India and China* (New Delhi: Brilliance Publishing, 2016).

[50] Raghava Saraṇa Sarma, *The Unfought War of 1962: An Appraisal* (Abingdon: Routledge, 2017).

[51] Palit, *War in High Himalayas.*

[52] Jaidev Singh Datta, *Recollections of the Se La-Bomdila Debacle, 1962* (New Delhi: KW Publishers, 2013).

[53] D. K. Khullar, *When Generals Failed: The Chinese Invasion: Abdication from Battle, Tawang, Sela, and Bombdia 1962* (New Delhi: Manas Publications, 1999).

border against India, as perceived from the Indian side of the border, is narrated by a group of military officers in the book *1962: A View from the Other Side of the Hill*.[54] However, Brigadier Dalvi (referred to earlier) had written one of the earliest Indian narratives covering the major aspects of the situations that led to the war, which created huge controversies in the political and defence circles.[55] Dalvi has pointed out several fallacies in the Indian border policy, especially military blunders. There are a number of essayists, such as K. Subramanyam, Mohan Guruswamy and Zorawar Daulat Singh[56] and Bertil Lintner,[57] who throw light on the latest observations.

Despite the existence of a vast collection of Western literature pertaining to the Cold War and other later discussions by scholars on this topic, a comprehensive account of the disputes, including the origin and development of Aksai Chin and NEFA, two of the world's major territorial disputes in the colonial era, their transformation into a highly volatile frontier situation during the post-colonial days, and the factors that led to the military encounter in 1962, has not been written in the light of newly available sources. The present work, therefore, not only provides an account of the trajectory of pre-colonial developments but also analyses the internal and external factors that pushed the two nations to the war front in the post-colonial period (1950–1962) and is a comprehensive account. The contents of the text are based on some of the revelations in lately declassified and classified documents.

It is still observed that Indian testimonies to the dispute are inadequate and therefore 'everything is dominated by the West'. 'Published work of any kind on China or on Sino-Indian relations by Indian scholars and analysts is to be welcomed…because they are not produced as often enough as the importance of China for this country

---

[54] Bhavna Tripathi, Vinay Shankar, G. G. Dwivedi, Bharat Kumar, P. J. S. Sandhu, *1962: A View from the Other Side of the Hill* (New Delhi: Vij Books India Pvt Limited, 2015).

[55] Dalvi, *Himalayan Blunder*.

[56] Mohan Guruswamy and Zorawar Daulat Singh, *India China Relations: The Border Issue and Beyond* (New Delhi: Viva Books, 2009); Mohan Guruswamy, *Emerging Trends in India–China Relations* (Gurgaon: Centre for Policy Alternatives, 2006).

[57] Bertil Lintner, *China's India War, Collision Course on the Roof of the World* (New Delhi: Oxford University Press, 2018).

deserves'.[58] It, therefore, does not come as a surprise that there is a dearth of Indian publications in this area, since a sizeable proportion of reports and government diplomatic documents pertaining to the dispute are kept concealed in official vaults. However, even in the absence of such reliable data, scholars such as Neville Maxwell and A. G. Noorani, among others, launched an all-out attack on Nehru and his China policy, when he was prime minister of India and also the external affairs minister. In Maxwell's magnum opus, published in 1970, it is observed that he had 'woven a string of half-truth and misinterpretations around a pre-conceived conclusion'. 'Bias and distortions are so blatant throughout the book'.[59]

Scholars like A. G. Noorani have studied the archival documents exhaustively.[60] Tracing the origins and developments of the boundary dispute during the British Raj, Noorani has exposed the claims of both parties on the basis of history or tradition. Examining the internal diplomatic negotiations and debates between the British bureaucracies and their conflicting policies, Noorani presents a thesis that history has had a direct impact on shaping the Sino-Indian conflict. This diplomatic historian primarily focuses on exploring a possible diplomatic solution to the exasperating border issue and analyses the failure of independent India to arrive at a final resolution. But in this effort to come to a decision on the dispute, he failed to delve into the underlying factors that existed in the post-colonial phase of native and international politics, which had disallowed the Nehru government from arriving at a suitable proposition. Hence, Noorani squarely lays the blame on the Nehru–Menon duo. But Noorani, like most other scholars, has not given due emphasis to the Right-wing impact on the post-partition Indian politics. The Right-wing impact played a role not only in opposition politics but also within the ruling Congress. When such is the nature of a larger chunk of the literature in the area of study, the present work is relevant, as it is based on recently declassified sources.

[58] Jabin T. Jacob, Book Review of *India China Relations: The Border Issue and Beyond* (New Delhi: IPCS, 2016). Available at http://www.ipcs.org/ipcs_books_selreviews.php?recNo=245 (accessed on 30 July 2020).

[59] K. Subramanyam, *Hindustan Times, Weekly Reviews* (18 and 25 October 1970).

[60] Noorani, *India–China Boundary Problem*.

The official Indian version of the dispute by scholars and bureaucrats is available in works such as that of K. Gopalachari,[61] Major General D. K. Palit,[62] Kalha[63] and a few others. This school of Indian writers is associated with the official Indian perspective of the dispute. Being an Indian diplomat for several years in East Asian nations and having been directly involved in India–China boundary negotiations, Kalha presents an insider's view of the border issue rather than giving an objective analysis of the facts, including a view from the other side of the border. Guruswamy and Singh in their work[64] not only try to contextualize the border dispute in the present India–China relations and as rising powers in the world but also to deal with the impact of the origin of the disputed border on account of Russo-British expansionism in the 19th century. The work largely laments that despite increased interaction in trade and other activities between the two, everything is mired in mistrust and suspicion. However, the work does not explore the political pressure on India from inside and outside the establishment as a dominant factor during the Nehru era. Rather than exploring the historical past, the work of Guruswamy and Singh focuses on the present and proposes possible solutions for the future. They suggest the 'book to be viewed as a policy relevant document rather than an abstract historical research paper'. This demands a further comprehensive analysis of all the influential and detrimental factors during the colonial and post-colonial days that shaped the Sino-Indian relations and calls attention for further enquiry. I believe that the research paper presented here would bear effort in this direction.

A few official investigations[65] were also conducted to explore the immediate reasons that provoked war in the winter of 1962, though most of these are yet to see the light of day. Although there were sev-

---

[61] K. Gopalachari, 'The India–China Boundary Question', *International Studies* 5, no. 1–2 (1963): 10.

[62] Palit, *War in High Himalayas*.

[63] R. S. Kalha, *India–China Boundary Issues: Quest for Settlement* (New Delhi: Institute of Peace and Conflict Studies, 2014).

[64] Guruswamy and Singh, *India China Relations*.

[65] Himmatsinhji Report (1951), Kulwant Singh Committee Report (1952), Thorat Committee Report (1952) Henderson Brook and Bhagat Report (1963), etc., are still laying in cold storage.

eral studies by individual officials such as B. N. Mullik,[66] S. P. Sen[67] and S. S. Khera,[68] among others, who have had hands-on experiences in the area, they were largely seemed to have been written either on a personal defensive nature, to ward-off attacks on their alleged guilt during their service, or to have been influenced, if not always, by other inclinations of personal or factional feud. In addition to these, certain official documentations, such as that of the History Division, Ministry of Defence, were available.[69] However, these were of a peripheral nature without going to the crux of the matter, or were purportedly to justify the official actions.

The topic, however, has been extensively deliberated upon in Western print media, and the causes and impacts of the conflict have been thoroughly investigated by the Central Intelligence Agency (CIA) and other secret services in the West.[70] Scholars from the post-imperialist Western world had shown an overzealous interest in the dispute and this was apparent in their investment in defence and political literature. On the other hand, a few pages over the issue have been inked in Communist China, but there has been no elaborate official probe undertaken in their military, academic or political circles. Peking has literally 'forgotten' the military feat, and neither any commemorative events nor any deliberations, in the defence or academic circles, have been observed so far.

As we can see, there is a wide array of literature available on the study, predominantly brought out by scholars in the East as well as in the West. The historiography of the Sino-Indian military encounter and its related issues, therefore, can be broadly divided into three major schools of scholars: (a) Western colonial writers; (b) Marxist and Chinese historians and (c) native Indian scholars and bureaucrats, in

[66] Mullik, *My Years with Nehru*.

[67] Sen, *The Sino-Indian Border Question*.

[68] Khera, *India's Defence Problem*.

[69] P. B. Sinha and Col. A. A. Athale, *History of the Conflict with China 1962*, ed. S. N. Prasad (New Delhi: History Division, Ministry of Defence, Government of India, 1992), 22.

[70] CIA, 'Sino-Indian Border Dispute, 1963', Sections 1–3 and Wilson Centre Digital Archives, International History.

addition to a coterie of Rightist writers. Of these, the Western colonial historiography was dominant in the early 1960s and 1970s[71] and, with a few exceptions, was apparently influenced by the political strategy of the Cold War era and focused on the theory of belligerent militarism in the PRC. These writings, evidently influenced by a residual colonialist instinct, were distinctively noticed as being pitched in an anti-communist perspective. The scholars of this disposition largely comprised political scientists from the USA and the UK and a few European nationals. Pakistan, while maintaining a strained relation with New Delhi, came closer to Peking and evinced interest in bringing out some literature in the area that was highly critical of the Indian view.[72] The Western scholarship had significantly invested in the area of study, primarily during the Cold War, in which the narrative was based on an emerging aggressive Chinese militarism in the region and their efforts for an extended sphere of communist influence. A few Western scholars had expressed apprehensions about Nehru's China policy as being inclined towards the socialist block. However, the work of the West was not always of an imperialistic nature and had, by and large, presented a balanced approach in many instances.[73] After the Cold War era, Western scholarship showed lesser interest in publishing in this sphere of study, and recent literature from the West, therefore, is quite insufficient.

The Marxist school of thought has not been very active, neither in the early years nor even later, and this was primarily because Communist China did not attach much significance to the 1962 war and showed least interest in the interpretation of what prompted the nation to adopt a belligerent posture in the border region that led to a military clash. To the PRC and its historians, the 1962 military clash seems to be more of a timely matter in response to the Anglo-American

---

[71] Fisher et al., *Himalayan Battleground*; W. F. Van Eekelen, *Indian Foreign Policy and the Border Dispute with China* (The Hague: Springer, 1965); R. J. Rowland, *History of Sino-Indian Relations*.

[72] Nadeem Shafiq Malik, *India vs China: A Review of the Aksai Chin Border Dispute* (Islamabad: Knowledge Bylanes, 2015).

[73] Alastair Lamb, *British India and Tibet: 1766–1910* (New York, NY: Routledge, 1960); Alastair Lamb, *Asian Frontiers: Studies in a Continuing Problem* (London: Pall Mall, 1968); Lamb, *The China–India Border*; Lamb, *The McMahon Line*.

adventurism pitched against Communist China and also as an indirect blow to the USSR for anti-comradeship. It might also be due to the fact that Peking, being the first to strike during the winter war, did not want to deliberate on its guilt. However, the Marxist school of narrative was represented by scholars from various social backgrounds, irrespective of national or regional considerations.[74] Therefore, the Chinese version of the narratives on the border dispute or 1962 war is limited and largely confined to only the official view. Xuecheng Liu in his book *The Sino-Indian Border Dispute and Sino-Indian Relations*[75] gives an insight into the arguments of the other side of the border, especially during the Mao era. However, the effort, like that of Chinese scholar Liu, provides no revelation of any special significance different from those already existing in the public domain. The central theme of Liu's work is that Sino-Indian relations were intricately interwoven with Indo-Pakistan enmity and American-Soviet-Chinese triangular rivalry. Another notable work, by Chinese author Chih H. Lu, provides a detailed historical account of the contact of China with Tibet since the 7th century and explores the roots of the dispute and proposes a settlement that could possibly be acceptable to both countries.[76] The Marxist school of historians, whose interpretation of the developments is largely an attempt to justify a belligerent Chinese military exploit in 1962, suggests that the imperialist game theory is still active in the subcontinent, even in the post-independence era, as a residual imperialist legacy reflecting in Indian narratives. They argue that the Western imperialist intervention in the subcontinent had created a profound impact that New Delhi could not resist even in the later years as it had reflected in the Tibetan policy. However, on the other hand, the Swedish author Bertil Lintner, in his recent work, suggests that it was not Nehru's forward policy (FP) that triggered the war; in fact, Mao declared war on India not only to strengthen its geopolitical

---

[74] Karunakar Gupta, *Hidden History of the Sino-Indian Frontier* (Calcutta: Minerva Associates, 1974); Neville Maxwell, *India's China War*; Xuecheng Liu, *The Sino-Indian Border Dispute and Sino-Indian Relations* (Lanham, MD: University Press of America, 1994).

[75] Liu, *The Sino-Indian Border Dispute and Sino-Indian Relations*.

[76] Chih H. Lu, *The Sino-Indian Border Dispute: A Legal Study* (Westport, CT: Praeger Publishers, 1986).

status among the nations of the world but also to internally stabilize the nation due to the disastrous result of his Great Leap Forward launched in 1958.[77]

The third school of writers includes a cross section of ideologues from among native bureaucrats and military strategists, in addition to native Indians, academics and political advocates. However, even when a nationalist fervour is common in their writings, two opposing subdivisions of writers are apparent among this category. An intensely obsessive category of writers among them is 'vigorously active' in national politics and is intricately involved with the bureaucrats and military officials, who later emerge as a firebrand of Indian Rightist writers.[78] They are markedly active in partisan politics and are largely focused on social media. Their focus was muddled with the idea of an emerging 'Red phobia' in the Southeast Asian region in general and anguish over India's China policy as 'Nehruvian follies' in particular. The Indian Rightist argument of a Sino-phobic perspective largely emanated from domestic partisan advocacy, which tried to pin the blame on Prime Minister Nehru. The narrative of this school tends to strengthen the imperialist stand and they blame the Nehru government for failing to retain the imperialist privileges that British India enjoyed in Tibet during its colonial days, even after India's independence.[79] There are a few other native writers who, taking cue from the Rightist narrative, are critical of the Indian official version[80] to put blame squarely on Nehru and V. K. Krishna Menon.[81] There are a few writers who take the middle path; some of the latest publications of Guruswamy and

---

[77] In 1961, several million (estimated between 17 and 45) people had died due to famine as a result of this policy. Lintner, *China's India War*.

[78] Mehra, *Essays in Frontier History*.

[79] There was wide propaganda, in circulation at present, that Nehru was responsible for giving up all the rights that India enjoyed in Tibet during the colonial days. This cannot be denied, especially because Nehru was eager to renounce the colonial privileges enjoyed by British India in Tibet, as both these nations, India and China, had struggled under the yoke of imperialism for a couple of centuries. Hence, for Nehru, to retain such privileges, was seen as a matter of immoral action.

[80] Official Indian narrative as seen by Sarvepalli Gopal, *Jawaharlal Nehru: A Biography*, Vol. III (New Delhi: Harvard University Press, 1984); K. Subrahmanyam, 'Nehru and India China Conflict of 1962', 102–130; R. S. Kalha, *India–China Boundary Issues*.

[81] Noorani, *India–China Boundary Problem*.

Singh reflect this. However, these works also do not escape the influence of the Western narratives, as the authors themselves have noted.[82]

A few lately published studies about the border war and related aspects have brought out issues which did not play a dominant role in earlier discussions. The US factor in the war and dispute is one such significant aspect. Even when the US factor in the Sino-Indian relation is quite apparent and dominant, the reference to these significant pieces has been relatively distant and discarded in the larger part of the historiography. However, the recently published works by Atul Bhardwaj[83] and Rup Narayan Das[84] have made efforts in this direction. But a revealing first-hand narration of the role of the Kennedy government in the USA comes from Bruce Riedel.[85] He suggests that even though the Cuban Missile Crisis of 1962 was examined in detail, the vital role played by the USA and the CIA in the Sino-Indian border war was largely neglected. Furthermore, the question as to how the CIA and its policies got a safe abode on Indian soil is a relevant one. The present work will delve into these aspects in the light of the newly declassified and available documents, which could explain the intricate internal political connections to it.

This study has been primarily sourced from documents preserved in various departments of the Government of India and foreign countries. Some of the major primary sources used for the work include the following.

1. *The Henderson Brooks–Bhagat Report Part I*[86] is a secret controversial military document to arbitrate many contentious issues of discus-

---

[82] The authors state that their analysis of the dispute owes a great deal to the works of prominent Western scholars of the dispute. Guruswamy and Singh, *India China Relations*.

[83] Atul Bhardwaj, *India–America Relations (1942–62) Rooted in the Liberal International Order* (New York, NY: Routledge, 2019).

[84] Rup Narayan Das, *The US Factor in Sino-Indian Relations: India's Fine Balancing* (New Delhi: IDSA, 2015).

[85] Bruce Riedel, *JFK's Forgotten Crisis: Tibet, the CIA, and the Sino-Indian War* (Ingelheim am Rhein: B I Press, 2015).

[86] Government of India, 'The Henderson Brooks–Bhagat Report', Part I (New Delhi: Ministry of Defence, 1963). Cited on Neville Maxwell's website (hereafter, HBR NM).

sion in the study. This report is a two-volume, top-secret document kept classified by the Government of India till date. However, during the period of discussion, Neville Maxwell, an acclaimed Australian journalist and New Delhi correspondent of *The Time*, had unauthorized access to the report and had widely published on the issue, after repeated unsuccessful attempts for permission from the Indian authorities to publish the documents. In March 2014, Maxwell released the first volume of the report in his blog,[87] and the author was able to consult on the work.

2. *The Official History of the Conflict with China, 1962*, brought out by the History Division, Ministry of Defence, Government of India, is an equally worthy document which provides credibility to the topic of the discussion here.[88] The work published in 1993[89] highlights the political, strategic and tactical failure of the country in the 1962 border war and, therefore, its availability was restricted to limited circles within the military and defence sectors, with the aim of providing to the military planners and technical advisors some lessons emerging from this study. Although its authors claim that it is an unbiased and balanced version without involving individual comments, this official history is largely an attempt to 'whitewash' government and higher officials in the Ministry of Defence and the higher circles in the government. Since written with nationalistic fervour, most references to the Chinese are evidently clear to the reader as unrealistic, justifying the activities of one side against the other. However, the editorial conclusion of S. N. Prasad seems to be, by and large, balanced. The authors of the official history, which was prepared during the period 1986–1990, state that they

[87] All references to the report in this book are available in the public domain and are based on the content of the websites of Maxwell and the Indian Defense Review (IDR). Available at (http://www.indiandefencereview.com/wp-content/uploads/2014/03/TopSecretdocuments2.pdf) (accessed on 10 October 2020). The authenticity of this partially published first volume has not been officially verified. Based on the report, a large number of articles have been published in India and Maxwell himself has provided a detailed account of the report in the E&PW (*Henderson Brooks Report: An Introduction*, E&PW, Vol. 36, April 14–20, 2001). However, the Government of India has not raised any objection to the reference of the website in any of these publications.

[88] Sinha and Athale, *History of the Conflict with China 1962*.

[89] The footnotes were deleted from the report in order to protect the secrecy of the source of the content, except for the master copy available with the Ministry of Defence.

had access to the classified document 'Henderson Brooks–Bhagat Report' for the first time ever.[90] This official history, primarily prepared on the basis of the voluminous records preserved with the Indian Army, the Air Force and the Ministry of Defence, in addition to interviews with several officials involved in the Sino-Indian disputes and the 1962 border war, is a highly dependable source of material for this work.

3. Volumes I–III of *The Sino-Indian Border Dispute*,[91] a top-secret CIA report on this border dispute, submitted between March 1963 and May 1964, and other documents pertaining to the dispute and related issues declassified (2007) by the USA, are of significant relevance for reference. The major part of the report in three volumes discusses the issues exclusively in the period 1950–1962. Besides this, the CIA has declassified more than a dozen related documents on the issue. The contents of these documents, prima facie, cannot be taken as final and authentic, as they are not absolutely free from bias and judgements from the US point of view, especially since the USA had active interest in the issue as a consequence of the international political equations in place at the time. According to the CIA analysis, the developments between 1950 and late 1959 were marked by Chinese military superiority, which, combined with 'cunning diplomatic deceit', contributed to nine years of New Delhi's reluctance to change its policy from friendship to open hostility towards the Peking regime. However, these documents are the primary resource of the data referenced for various aspects of this study.

4. Documents included in the *Digital Archives, International History, Woodrow Wilson International Centre* for scholars, Washington, DC, have provided invaluable references for this study. These documents are mostly minutes of meetings and interactions among the leaders and officials of nations, including India, China, the USSR, the USA, etc., in addition to notes sent from embassies to other countries, letters of a personal and official nature, etc. This reliable source has been used here to corroborate the claims made.

---

[90] Neville Maxwell published his masterpiece *India's China War* in 1970, which was largely based on the top-secret 'Henderson Brooks–Bhagat Report'. He claimed that he had unauthorized access to the document for the first time.

[91] CIA, *Sino-Indian Border Dispute*.

5. Documents with the MEA, Government of India, on treaties and agreements between the governments of India, China, Tibet, Kashmir, Nepal and the UK, and the notes, memoranda and letters exchanged and agreements signed between the Governments of India and China, the *White Papers* published by the MEA, etc., are direct sources of material for this work.[92]

6. Documents pertaining to the Simla Agreement of 1913–1914 and British diplomatic relations with China are available in the Indian Office Record.[93] The National Archives, New Delhi, has offered a trove of documents pertaining to the topic. These, along with the proceedings of the Lok Sabha and the Rajya Sabha, the *Selected Works of Jawaharlal Nehru* and other published literature—books, articles in periodicals and newspapers and reliable online commentaries—have been referred to extensively.

The *present* study has been organized in a chronological sequence and the dispute has been analysed on a sectoral as well as an issue-specific basis. Therefore, even when the chapters are organized as a part of the whole book, each chapter has a body of its own, and efforts have been made to avoid repetition. Chapter 2 discusses the historical origin and developments of the dispute in the western sector since the British annexation of Kashmir between 1846 and 1947, during which time they had experimented on nearly half-a-dozen borderlines. The priority of the British to defend its Indian colonial frontiers with China is explained in the backdrop of their Russo-phobic strategic game. It is argued that this elasticity in the nature of the colonial borders has brought about much ambiguity in the post-colonial period, adding to the indecision in defining the borders. Further, after locating the reasons for the origin of the Aksai Chin dispute, the chapter not only discusses this logjam in the post-colonial period but also suggests possible solutions to disengage from this dispute.

---

[92] These documents were published by the MEA for official reference as part of the notes and documents exchanged between India and China during the bilateral discussions on the dispute.

[93] References from the India Office Records were quoted from the work of Karunakar Gupta, *Hidden History of the Sino-Indian Frontier.*

The focus of Chapter 3 pivots around three narratives: (a) the British imperialist designs in Tibet and the background that led to the British convening a tripartite Simla Conference in 1913–1914; (b) the developments that led to the breakdown of the conference and (c) the role of a few British officials in fraudulent documentation and distortion of facts in tune to their imperialist designs. This chapter also underlines the fact that the Sino-Indian tension is not exclusively about strips of soil in the Himalayan mountains; it rather emanates from the PRC's loathing of all colonial vestiges, while independent India was willing to accept colonial legacy. Chapter 4 discusses the early stage in the perception of the border on each side and the efforts to validate their claims in Aksai Chin and NEFA by Peking and New Delhi, respectively. This period is therefore identified as a quiet but active phase of expansion by both nations. The chapter also narrates the background behind an emerging Red phobia in India, which forced the Government of India to show renewed interest in a new 'map-manship'. Chapter 5 presents the theory that Tibet was a dominant and determining factor in the straining of bilateral relations between the two countries, adversely impacting the coexistence idealized in the Panchsheel principles. The Tibet factor created the first tussle in Sino-Indian relations, and this became even more apparent once a noticeable faction in India 'empathized' with the Lama and Tibetan rebels in 1959. The overreach of the Government of India and the overreaction of the Indian public, press and Parliament had justified the Chinese border outrages in the same year. Chapter 6 traces the reasons behind the emergence of NEFA as a crucial factor after 1959, with the third wave of the Tibet uprising. It was noticed that after the asylum given to Dalai Lama and the Tibetan rebels in March 1959, and his political statement in Tezpur that the rage in bilateral relations had become discernible.

The central theme of the work is discussed in Chapters 7 and 8. 1959 was the most eventful year in Sino-Indian relations, as Peking had become offensive in the Longju and Kongka Pass. It was after 1959 that the internal and external forces propelled the nation towards a military face-off. The chapters outline the reasons for the failure of the New Delhi dialogue, the rejection of the mutual exchange formula of the two sectors and Nehru's enforced 'no negotiation' attitude. The chapter identifies an emotionally motivated partisan political force as well as vested bureaucratic interest groups within the government and the opposition. The involvement of the CIA is vividly portrayed as a decisive factor in the dispute that pushed the nation towards a military clash. The developments post-1961 were marked by the most controversial and misguided FP as the road to the 1962 border war, and what happened in Dhola was nothing less than deliberate. The concluding remarks in the last chapter highlight the damages incurred as a result of the dispute and a proposal for a possible solution to this complicated issue.

Before entering into a discussion of the dispute on a sectoral and issue basis, it is imperative to get a general overview of the nature and topography of the frontier in all the three sectors, an overall picture about the border perceptions of both the parties and the nature of the Line of Actual Control (LAC) during the period of the discussion.

Topography of the Borders

Running through the high altitude of the Himalayas, the Sino-Indian border begins in the west at the north-western tip of Jammu and Kashmir (in Pakistan Occupied Kashmir [POK]) and reaches the north-eastern point of Arunachal Pradesh (NEFA) in the east. The total length of the Sino-Indian border falls under the Sinkiang and Tibetan regions of China in the northern side, while it traverses the south through six Indian states, including Ladakh (a union territory), Jammu and Kashmir, Himachal Pradesh, Uttarakhand, Sikkim and Arunachal Pradesh. For administrative convenience, this length of the border is divided into three sectors: western, central and eastern.

The major portion of the borders remains formally un-demarcated, but follows certain geographical watershed principles. The border alignment, which falls entirely on the Himalayan terrain, is hardly habitable, badly accessible and not human-friendly for settlements. The loss of life of armed personnel in these terrains is quite frequent and is several times higher than the casualties on account of border clashes.[94] A neighbour that you are on friendly terms with and who respects a properly delimited territorial frontier would, in itself, be the solution to prevention of the loss of human lives, in addition to the larger relief from a financial burden to the public exchequer. As per the perception of New Delhi, the total length of its northern border is approximately 3,488 km[95] and shares territorial borders in the north with Pakistan and Afghanistan (both in POK),[96] China, Nepal, Bhutan and Burma. The actual disputed area in these three sectors approximately covers 125,000 sq. km as per the Indian version. But for Peking, according to the latest (2010) available data in the Chinese media, including the state-owned Xinhua, Global Times and *People's Daily*, the total length of the Sino-Indian border is just 2,000 km (Figure 1.1). This contradiction with the Indian figure (3,488 km) is due to the latter's claim of an extended circular border through the Kunlun range.

In the western sector, the total length of the border, according to New Delhi, is approximately 1,770 km, which begins from the tri-junction of Afghanistan, China and India (in POK) and joins the central sector at Uttarakhand. As per the Indian claim, the disputed area in this sector has been traditionally carried over for centuries, reaffirmed through treaties by local rulers, having finally been ratified by the Treaty of Amritsar by the Government of British India. Therefore, the boundary, according to New Delhi, in the west begins from the west of the Karakoram ranges (and east of the Durand Line) to run in a circular route through the far north through the Kunlun ranges, passing through Khurnak Fort, and comes near Demchok.

---

[94] Media reports show that there have been more than 2,000 human casualties on the Siachen Glacier, where soldiers stay day and night at temperatures that reach −50 °C. Human life cannot survive in such a dangerous situation, and soldiers are forced to serve in the name of border protection. It is high time that the deployment of troops in such harsh environments be replaced by robots or other suitable technologies.

[95] According to the data available in 2010, the Chinese media, including the state-owned Xinhua, *Global Times* and *People's Daily*, claim that the total length of the border is 2,000 km, which contradicts the Indian figure.

[96] This territory between India and Pakistan is under dispute and is under Pakistan's control. Pakistan, through an agreement, had ceded a large part of it to China in 1961.

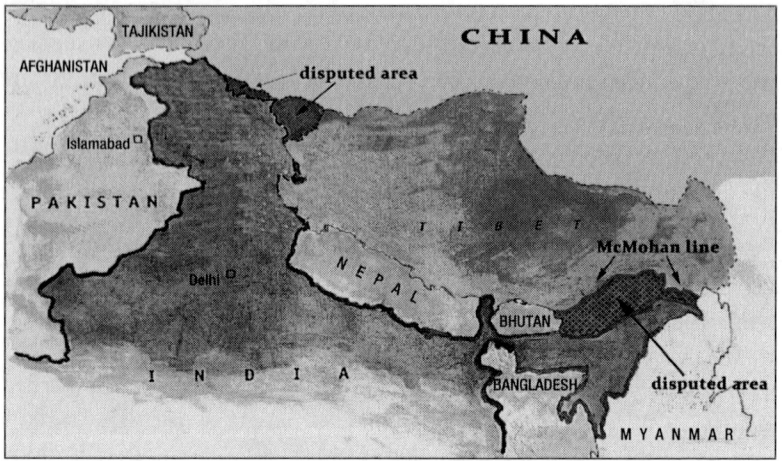

Figure 1.1 *Disputed Territories of Sino-Indian Border Including POK*

Source: Author.

Disclaimer: This figure has been redrawn and is not to scale. It does not represent any authentic national or international boundaries and is used for illustrative purposes only.

It is sufficiently demarcated by geographical and natural features, and therefore a new delimitation during the post-colonial days was not a necessity unless to rectify a few issues in certain pockets. The Indian narrative also tries to emphasize that the colonial definition of the Sino-Indian border in this sector was finalized as per the aforementioned perception.

The disparity in the Chinese version presumably begins here. Peking claims that the nature of the pre-colonial Sino-Indian border in the western sector was largely notional, and the series of treaties and agreements by the local rulers of this period, which New Delhi points out to make its claim, were not meant to define or delimit any border; rather they were meant for trade and commercial agreements. Peking suggests that they had denied the initial joint boundary commission, set up by the British in 1847, to formally fix the Ladakh–Tibet boundary between British India and China, with a Tibetan representative, in the early years of colonial intervention in the region. Later in the last quarter of the 19th century, several cartographic experiments were explored by British India in the region.[97] Peking had expressed strong reservations against such imperialistic adventurism. However, despite their disavowal, Peking remained largely averse to these imperialist ventures. Thanks to the political turmoil in the Middle Kingdom at its terminal stage, they had also not accepted any further colonial intervention of the British in the region. Aksai Chin, the north-eastern portion of Ladakh bordering Tibet (China), which is the central axis of the whole Sino-Indian border debate, actually emerged as a matter of contention due to these colonial excesses. The issue, however, did not come to the fore immediately until other issues cropped up in post-independence India.

Due to the unfriendly nature of the terrain with steep creeks and deep valleys, it was left remote and unattended to by independent India, until the PRC began to construct a road through the region connecting its Sinkiang and Tibet provinces, over which New Delhi became alert. So the Aksai Chin area in the Ladakh region of Jammu and Kashmir state came under China's control, and it further extended its control further south after 1959, from the Karakoram Pass in the north to the south Khurnak Fort and beyond, crossing the Spanggur Lake near the Himachal Pradesh border, running along 600 km, and occupying a land area of about 33,500 sq. km.[98] In addition, when Peking and Islamabad signed an agreement on 2 March 1963 delineating the border of POK, a large area of this disputed territory in northern Kashmir had been transferred by Pakistan to China.

The *central sector* begins from the Gya peak in Ari district of the Nagri prefecture of Tibet and the northern point of Himachal Pradesh, and extends to the tri-junction of Tibet, Bhutan and Sikkim in the east. The disputed areas in this sector are comparatively smaller and lie scattered across pockets, measuring only about 2,000 sq. km. Divided by Nepal and Bhutan, this frontier is located in two segments. In this

---

[97] For further details, read Chapter 2.

[98] Hongzhou Zhang and Mingjiang Li, *Sino-Indian Border Dispute* (Milano: Italian Institute for International Political Studies 2013). Available at https://www.ispionline.it/en/pubblicazione/sino-indian-border-disputes-8070 (accessed on 30 July 2020).

sector, China has maintained resentment over the status of Sikkim as well. It was on the basis of a referendum among the people that Sikkim joined the Indian Union on 16 May 1975.[99] But China had strong reservations on these actions.[100]

In the central sector, the terrain is relatively hospitable and is therefore not only populated but also a hub for trade and commercial activities between people on both sides of the border, using different passes to travel across the Himalayas. As per the Indian claim, the treaties and agreements of 1684 and 1842 between Ladakh and Tibet included the area of the western central sector[101] and, therefore, there is no need for a dispute on this part of the border. However, the borderline in Barahoti area of Uttarakhand was a disputed region at an early stage itself. The first border dispute in this sector occurred in 1954, when China objected to the establishment of Indian posts, as the area belongs to them. Several diplomatic correspondences have been exchanged between India and China on the Barahoti dispute. In the eastern part of this sector, the Doklam Plateau, a newly emerging sensitive area, is infamous for its 72-day military stand-off between the two nations in 2017, situated in the eastern side of the finger-pointed Tibetan region.

The *eastern sector* boundary begins at the Bhutan–India–China tri-junction in the west and runs for about 840 km to reach the Burma–India–China tri-junction in the east near the Diphu Pass. The

---

[99] In 1947, when India became independent, a referendum was held to determine whether or not Sikkim joins the Indian Union. The people of Sikkim rejected the referendum, but maintained a special status of protectorate under the Government of India by controlling its external affairs, defence, etc., and more closer links were established in 1954. Later, in 1975, in a politically turbulent situation within the kingdom, the prime minister of Sikkim requested the status of a state under the Government of India. Hence, in April 1975, the Indian Army took over the city of Gangtok. A referendum was held which favoured the abolition of the monarchy by 97.5 per cent of the votes. Sikkim became the 22nd state of the Indian Union 16 May 1975 and the monarchy was abolished.

[100] The maintenance of India's defence and external affairs of Bhutan, which shares a border with China, was also a matter of resentment for China.

[101] Government of India, 'Report of the Officials of Govt. of India and PRC on the Boundary Question' (New Delhi: MEA, 1961), 84.

border alignment mostly runs along the crest of the Himalayan ranges, dividing southern Tibet (China) from Arunachal Pradesh (India).[102] Even though China suggests that an area of about 90,000 sq. km in this sector is disputed territory, it presents one of the most feeble disputes in this sector due to a complex political situation under imperialist intervention.[103] Henry McMahon had secretly 'drawn up' an 890-km borderline dividing Tibet and British India. Independent India considered this line to be the actual border limits between India and China, while China refused to accept this line, instead raising concern about the nomenclature (McMahon Line) as a vestige of British imperialism. When India became independent in 1947 and confederated several princely states into the Indian Union, China waged a civil war to define its nation's future destiny. The timing was not conducive for either party to define the borders, but to accept the existing status. So the McMahon Line became India's north-east border,[104] inherited from the British as the 'legitimate' border. However, when the newly established PRC took over Tibet in 1951, it was not willing to recognize the British legacy as a tag on its borders. However, though disputed on the validity of the McMahon Line, the LAC in this sector also runs along the same alignment.

[102] It was named NEFA after the promulgation of the North East Frontier Areas (Administration) Regulation of 1954.

[103] For further details, see Chapter 3.

[104] Neville Maxwell, 'Sino-Indian Border Dispute Reconsidered', *Economic & Political Weekly* 34, no. 15 (1999): 905–918.

Aksai Chin Dispute

Colonial Cartographic Extravaganza on the Legendary Frontiers

Two oriental civilizations, neighbours India and China, had been maintaining a friendly relationship and peacefully coexisted for more than a couple of millenniums, sharing their spiritual and material wealth and experience. There had rarely been any confrontation between the two during the period, either territorially or ideologically, until the late 19th century. Despite sharing a legendary border in the Himalayan ranges for centuries, there had never been any territorial claims or counterclaims between these nations during the pre-colonial period. This legendary boundary, working as a LAC between the two, 'had taken final shape on the basis of the extent of each other's administrative jurisdiction over a long course of time'.[1] However, these borders were drawn more from the zonal perception than from any specific demarcation or delineation in the modern sense. Therefore, the roots of the origin of these existing disputes, largely emanating from the border issue between these two 'giants', do not go very deep into the past and can be traced back to the middle of the 19th century, when the British Indian territorial frontiers came closer to the Chinese borders.

It was in 1846 that, for the first time, the British gained entry into the territories of the Sino-Indian border in the western sector by annexing Kashmir as part of its colonial territorial conquest. This was also the beginning of a period of uncertainty about the existence of this

[1] Xuecheng Liu, 'Look beyond the Sino-Indian Border Dispute', Research Gate (November 2011). China Report 47 (2): 147–158. Available at https://www.research-gate.net/publication/254082638_Look_Beyond_the_Sino-Indian_Border_Dispute. SAGE Journals, available at https://doi.org/10.1177%2F000944551104700207 (accessed on 20 October 2020).

part of the border, because the colonial strategies of expansion and defence were subjected to changes, from time to time, in keeping with their international aspirations. The uncertainty in the 19th century was a consequence of the colonial game theory.[2] Deciding whether or not to defend or annex, countries pushed the border forward and backward, in pursuance of their immediate interests. As a result, the total length of this western border had 'never been formally delimited by any mutually-accepted treaty'.[3] So the legacy left behind by the British imperialist interventions in this region was that of creating uncertainty, not only in the nature of the existing legendary borders but also in generating mutual distrust and disagreement about the real nature of the frontier. Almost a century later, when the state of Jammu and Kashmir was acceded to the Indian Union in 1947, this territorial uncertainty was inherited. The issue was lying in a latent state until 1956, when it got entangled with the Tibetan crisis, bringing in a potential undesirable dimension to the bilateral issue.

By the middle of the 20th century, when both nations took on their political mantle, a 'classic pattern for a boundary dispute present between these two nations' was noticed by scholars.[4] But by ignoring these imperial legacies, this looming potential boundary dispute could have been resolved amicably, benefitting both sides for a long-lasting favourable relationship between the neighbours. It could have been further possible to resolve the issues through active negotiations on the basis of a 'give and take' formula with minimum feelings of resentment on both sides. Scholars and strategists had suggested that 'it was pre-eminently susceptible to a solution'.[5] However, before 1956, no consistent and concerted efforts were made by both parties to work out their differences for a lasting solution.

---

[2] The rival interest of the industrial–capitalist Britain and the Tsarist Russia in the imperialist expansion in Asia prompted them to defend their rich Asian possessions by creating buffer zones in Tibet, Afghanistan and other regions.

[3] Liu, 'Look beyond the Sino-Indian Border Dispute'.

[4] Robert Trumbull, 'India Assumes Defense of Sikkim, Strategic Principality in Himalayas; Treaty Grants to New Delhi Military Rights in Key Link to Tibet, Nepal', *the Times of India*, 7 December 1950.

[5] A. G. Noorani, 'Facing the Truth', *Frontline* 23, no. 19 (2006).

The larger concerns of New Delhi, during the early years, were focused on the status of Tibet under the Communist Republic and the possible communist menace in the neighbourhood. India, at this early stage, put very little effort on the border issue and a large part of its attention was focused on the status of Tibet and its benefit to India. Even when official diplomatic efforts were underway to work towards a cordial bilateral relation with the PRC, the Indian press and a section of the political leaders found the presence of an 'unreliable' communist neighbour dangerous to India. This emerging communist phobia within the Indian public created an uneasy environment in the diplomatic circle. On the other side of the border, despite the cordiality in relations in dealing with international affairs, due to the warmth in the Chou–Nehru camaraderie, the conservative circle of Mao's China viewed New Delhi in the prism of an inheritor of the British colonial legacies. Because of mutual distrust and suspicion, the diplomatic efforts initiated by both governments drowned in internal political controversies, disallowing any conclusive and fruitful negotiation on the existing border issue. So the early days of friendship between the new republics did not bear any fruit, and the stalemate with the Tibet issue continued, with US interventions aggravating the situation. In the meanwhile, constructing a road through the Aksai Chin plateau, the PRC slowly but steadily took control of the region and, after 1959, once the Tibet crisis became a burning issue, the PRC pushed the LAC farther south. However, in the early 1950s, New Delhi had shown little interest in taking possession of this far-off Ladakh region, despite its later claims.[6]

Therefore, the entire length of the Sino-Indian border, which is one of the longest interstate borders in the world, remains 'not defined, let alone demarcated, on maps or delineated on the ground'.[7] Neither

[6] Immediately after the Panchsheel agreement in 1954, India had brought out a map in which an apparent extended western sector was notified. However, the first Indian claim in this sector was emphatically made only on 21 August 1958. Refer to Note No. 95 (July 1958) the Government of India to Embassy of China, MEA.

[7] M. Malik, 'India–China Competition Revealed in Ongoing Border Disputes', Power and Interest News Report (PINR, 7 October 2007). Available at http://www.worldse-curitynetwork.com/China-India/Malik-Dr.-Mohan/India-China-Competition-Revealed-in-Ongoing-Border-Disputes (accessed on 30 July 2020).

the history of friendship shared over the course of millenniums nor a series of constructive and creative negotiations between the premiers or officials could work towards bringing about a lasting solution. So 'at the root of the rift between India and China was the boundary question'[8] and it was inherited as a legacy of British imperialism, and this issue, which could otherwise have been solved, soon got entangled with complex factors during the post-colonial days.

The focus of the present chapter is therefore to identify the real nature of the border in this sector, as left behind by the colonial government, and also to identify the reasons as to why it remains ambiguous. This narrative of the colonial period would give the readers a clear understanding about the nature of the colonial border, so as to gain the right perspective about the nature of the dispute as well.

Company to the Kashmir Borders

In a series of territorial annexations by the English East India Company government in various parts of the country, the First Anglo-Sikh war (1845–1846) and the Treaty of Lahore on 9 March 1846, the province of Kashmir was taken over. However, the Company did not take over the political control of this region and subsequently, on 16 March 1846, the Company ceded this newly acquired Kashmir region to Gulab Singh.[9] The terms of the Treaty of Amritsar specified that all the territories of Jammu, Kashmir and Ladakh would be handed over to Gulab Singh for a sum of ₹7.5 million. Singh not only acknowledged the suzerainty of the Company but also placed the external affairs of his government under the Company's authority.[10] Any modification to the boundaries of Kashmir was to be determined by a Joint Frontier Commission.[11] However, British relinquishing responsibility of ruling

---

[8] Noorani, 'The Truth about 1962'.

[9] Gulab Singh was the founder of the Dogra dynasty of Jammu and Kashmir, a princely state in colonial India. His allegiance to the British in the First Anglo-Sikh war against the Sikh force made him dear to the colonial government, which made him ruler of the province of Kashmir for a sum of ₹7.5 million.

[10] Noorani, 'Facing the Truth'.

[11] Lamb, *Britain and Chinese Central Asia*, 73.

Kashmir was not only merely in terms of strategic ambivalence in the Anglo-Sikh war but was rather considered more viable for their own mercantile interest[12] as well as other concerns.

Hence, even when Gulab Singh was enthroned as the maharaja, the British had larger control over its affairs[13] and assumed responsibility for the protection of its border because they were concerned with the security of the Kashmir borders with Sinkiang and the Tibet provinces of China. Virtually, this brought the 'British borders' closer to the frontiers of the Middle Kingdom. Since the British were very concerned about their rich colonial possessions remaining unaffected in India, they were also looking out for a buffer zone in this region. Naturally, this prompted the British to experiment with several border strategies in this region, opening up a new phase in its boundary problems, which, so far, were unknown in history. This trajectory in the border experiments undertaken during the period 1846–1947 will be discussed here in order to understand if there was any finality in the decision regarding this part of the border and, if not, why there was an 'elastic' nature to the British borders in the Kashmir region.

Colonial Interventions Upset the Bilateral Relations

In the pre-colonial period, territorial borders in this region were decided on the basis of natural geographic demarcations, and they were legendary boundaries lacking intricate modern cartographic delineations. However, despite lacking such demarcations, there was an understanding on a certain definition of the boundary on a zonal basis. Hence, until the colonial period, there was no area of contest and confrontation to determine territorial limits. However, prior to awakening to the dawn of the new republics in the mid-20th century, both nations had undergone a bitter phase of imperialist intervention. While India was under the direct colonial administration of the British Crown, Manchu China was subjugated to unequal treaties by Western

[12] For details, see Christopher Snedden, *Understanding Kashmir and Kashmiris* (London: Oxford University Press, 2015).

[13] C. U. Aitchison, *A Collection of Treaties, Engagements and Sanads Relating to India and Neighbouring Countries* (Charleston, SC: Nabu Press, 1909), 247.

financial imperialists, and Britain was prominent among them.[14] During this colonial tenure, the centuries-old friendly relationship that the two nations shared was totally upset and, in the last quarter of the 19th and the early 20th century, it became worse. In fact, during the colonial period, instead of a definite and lasting understanding of the borderline being created, what was already in existence, as per the traditions and customs, became further complicated and contradicted.

The British Indian officials were concerned with the nature of the territorial frontiers with Ching China. Hence, their attention was turned to the cartographic specifications of their border with the Tibet-Sinkiang provinces of China. But the nature of these efforts varied from time to time, as it was influenced by the impact of international political equations. It meant that despite the efforts made to define the border with China on various occasions, none of these were permanent and stable—most of the decisions were subject to change in the subsequent years due to international geopolitical reasons. Hence, during the British administration in India, its northern 'borders were either never clearly demarcated or established. Lines kept shifting on maps as political contingencies arose'.[15] What was the reason for this unstable nature of the British Indian border in the north? Why were these multiple cartographic efforts left inconclusive in the region between 1846 and 1899? A study on the 19th-century international geopolitical equation in the Asian region would answer these questions. At this juncture, a brief account of the Russo-phobic British game plan is imperative to comprehend the developments.

Impact of Colonial Geostrategic Game in Asia

The answer to the question as to why ambiguity persisted in the nature of the territorial boundaries in the province of Kashmir is explained by the 'colonial game' theory that dominated international relations in

---

[14] Tan Chung, *China and Imperialism: During the Nineteenth Century* (New Delhi: Gyan Publishing House, 2013); Dong Wang, *China's Unequal Treaties, Narrating National History* (Lanham, MD: Lexington Books, 2008).

[15] Mohan Guruswamy, 'India–China Border, Learning from History', *Economic & Political Weekly* 38, no. 39 (2003): 4101–4103. Available at http://www.jstor.org/stable/4414072 (accessed on 30 July 2020).

Asia in the 19th century. There is no doubt that the history of the Sino-Indian border dispute is closely intertwined with the 'colonial game' due to the ambitions of other 'empires'—the expansionism of the imperialist Britain and the Tsarist Russia—in Central Asia.[16] The quest to protect the interests of their colonial empire in Asia prompted the British to chart out a geostrategic 'game' against Russia. The industrial–capitalist Britain was very concerned about the economics of imperial defence, and the focus of this game was to avoid any threat to their rich Indian colonial possession. The British wanted to halt the Russian south-ward expansion, well before they reached beyond the Himalayas.[17] The diminishing vigour of the Middle Kingdom in Peking in the last quarter of the 19th century, the political uncertainty in the status of Tibet in relation to the Manchu dynasty and the uncertain nature of Chinese cooperation in the wake of any Russian southward adventure were the reasons that prompted British India to think of making their borders stable. This prodded Britain not only to actively consider a buffer zone in this region but also to make efforts to decide on a stable cartographic border definition.

London's obsession with the thought that Russia might move towards India was therefore a decisive factor in determining the nature of its northern borders with China as well as its Tibet policy.[18] Despite being a decisive power in the region, China's political instability and the question of its political morale for an effective stalling of the Russian menace disturbed Britain. They were of the view that a weak China could no longer exercise power on its southern province of Tibet and, therefore, the British must pay serious attention to Tibet. The British presumed that the perceived Russian threat to Tibet would jeopard-ize their interest in the region and that China could never be able to protect Tibet from Russian intrusions.[19] This provoked the British to remain engaged in these Himalayan frontiers. Hence, the creation of a 'buffer zone' in Tibet was found to be the most economical strategy

---

[16] Liu, 'Look beyond the Sino-Indian Border Dispute'.

[17] See Figure 2.1 for the expansion of the Russian empire.

[18] Maxwell, *India's China War*, 40–41.

[19] Wendy Palace, *The British Empire and Tibet, 1900–1922* (London: Routledge, 2004), 2–3.

Figure 2.1 *Russian Expansion and the British Indian Possessions in the 19th Century*

Source: Author.

Disclaimer: This figure has been redrawn and is not to scale. It does not represent any authentic national or international boundaries and is used for illustrative purposes only.

for this objective,[20] and this was seen capable of stalling any serious menace to British India.[21] Therefore, in their subsequent dealings with Tibet, Chinese sovereignty over this territory was not duly respected, and Britain even encouraged Tibetan resistance against Peking.

[20] The idea was, 'We do not want to occupy it, but we also cannot afford to see it occupied by our foes'. Mehra, *Essays in Frontier History*, 88–92.

[21] Guruswamy and Singh, *India China Relations*, 10.

Naturally, Peking, which had had a bitter experience with the imperialist West in its eastern coast during the post-opium war, viewed these developments in their southern borders with much suspicion and apprehension. Lhasa had already developed an anti-Manchu strategy, which they feared, under the patronage of British imperialism, would create more annoyance to the Middle Kingdom. Amid these uncertain relations, when the British suggested several proposals for border delimitations between British India and China (in Tibet), Peking was least interested in these negotiations, as most of the efforts were seen to serve the economic aspirations and to protect the imperialist interests of the British. Hence, most of the proposals by the British officials for border demarcations were responded by a studied negligence from Peking.

Moreover, the cartographic proposals of the British were not static and stable, as these were subject to change, now and then, in keeping with the international political equations of the time. The territorial interests that British evinced were not limited to some acreage of barren land in eastern Ladakh. They had set their sights on the Hunza Valley far away, for active military defence of its rich possessions in the south. It was apparent that a couple of cartographic proposals made by British officials in 1865 and 1897[22] for an extended border at the Kunlun range, including eastern Ladakh, and the whole of Aksai Chin as part of Kashmir, were not accepted by their home government as final. Subsequently, when the British transferred power to India in 1947, there remained enough scope for a dispute between the two over Aksai Chin as it was left 'undefined' and no boundary was specified even in the existing official maps. So, in the post-colonial era, when independent India and the PRC entered a period of self-determination and political stability, they could not refrain from the contradictions arising from the 'colonial game'. So a detailed discussion on the story of the interventions on the Sino-Indian borders in the western sector during the British period since the mid-19th century is of importance here.

---

[22] See Figure 2.2 for the Johnson Line and the Johnson–Ardagh Line.

British Cartographic Extravaganza in the Kashmir Borders

In an effort to come to a final cartographic understanding between China and British India, colonial officials in the Himalayan ranges invested considerable time and energy. But contrary to the existing perception that borders were demarcated more accurately during then, no definite and final demarcation was left behind in the western sector. The fact remains that 'Aksai Chin, was pretty well ignored by most settled surrounding powers in India and China'[23] and no definite territorial borders were finalized before the departure of the British in 1947. We can thus analyse how those cartographic explorations undertaken by British officials in the second half of the 19th century further complicated and convoluted what was historically in existence.

Failed Border Commissions of 1847

Soon after conferring political control over Kashmir to Gulab Singh and ensuring British political suzerainty over the foreign affairs of the province, the Company was determined to demarcate the Kashmir borders with China, and a border commission was appointed in 1947 for the purpose.[24] The surveyors, who were mandated with the task of demarcating the boundary between Ladakh and Tibet, were advised by Henry Lawrence to strictly abide by the territorial limits of Ladakh and work on defining the borders in consultation with Tibet and its Chinese suzerain in Peking. This underlined the fact that a clear and well-defined boundary was the basic intention of the British and not any larger part of the territory.[25] But the commission could not consult

---

[23] David Scott, 'Sino-Indian Territorial Issues: The "Razor's Edge"?' in *The Rise of China: Implications for India*, ed. H. Pant, 197–220 (New Delhi: Cambridge University Press India, 2011), 6.

[24] There were two commissions. The first one, entrusted with the task of defining the internal boundary between the territory of the raja and of the British, submitted its report in May 1847. Noorani, 'Facing the Truth'.

[25] John Lall, 'The Sino-Indian Border Problem as a Leftover of History', in *Indian and Chinese Foreign Policies in Comparative Perspective*, ed. Surjit Mansingh (New Delhi: Radiant Publishers, 1998), 445.

with the government in Peking and was not able to complete the task for various technicalities. The commissioners were not able to reach the Tibetan border, and the demarcation of the boundary had to be abandoned due to the rebellion in the area. While the British dispensation of a 'ghost ruler' in Gulab Singh was abhorred by the people,[26] the British presence in the tribal zones was seen with suspicion by the local people who resisted any intervention in the region. So the first attempt by the British to test its cartographic feat was not successful, and the failure of this commission is also attributed to the lack of interest on the part of the Manchu dynasty to define its border with imperialist Britain.[27] The forceful opening of the Middle Kingdom by British gunboats in the First Opium War (1839–1842) and subsequent unequal treaties at Nanking had already taught Peking a lesson. The Forbidden City was quite apprehensive of any dealings with the 'barbarian' West,[28] and they distanced themselves from any effort to open up their territorial borders from the south-west as well.

In the middle of the 19th century, when the Manchu imperial authority was at the height of its glory and had extended its political power far south to Tibet and north Magnolia, the then Viceroy, Lord Hardinge, had preferred to write directly to the authorities in Tibet on 4 August 1846, informing them of the treaty between the Company government and the raja of Kashmir. He requested them 'to settle definitely the boundaries to the eastward' of Kashmir—the northern part adjoined Xinjiang—'in order that hereafter no questions or disputes may arise concerning their exact limits'. Even though necessary arrangements had been made to secure the cooperation of Chinese officials, the authority at Peking was negligent of the proposal[29] and did not turn up to sign any agreement with the British. The Sino-centric Middle Kingdom was least interested in any diplomatic deal with the Western 'barbarians' whom

---

[26] Rao Farman Ali, 'Kashmir: A Century Struggle (1846–1948)' (2015). Available at https://www.researchgate.net/publication/279314623 (accessed on 30 July 2020).

[27] Guruswamy and Singh, *India China Relations*, 12.

[28] Chinese Confucian philosophers considered Western culture dangerous to China and, therefore, used the term 'barbarian' as a misnomer to denote the cultural defence.

[29] Guruswamy and Singh, *India China Relations*, 12.

the Confucian scholars viewed with suspicion. The Chinese disregard of the British proposal was also seen in the light of an already existing legendary borderline and the absence of any kind of uncertainty in this matter at the time (the 1840s). Vans Agnew, one of the commissioners, also pointed out that the line was 'already sufficiently defined by nature, and recognized by custom, with the exception of its two extremities'.[30] However, despite the failure, later, in the second half of the 19th century, British efforts for demarcation of the boundary of Kashmir with China were further pursued.

Whitehall Disowns the Johnson Line of 1865

The earliest successful cartographic work in defining the British Indian border with China at the heights of the Himalayas was carried out by W. H. Johnson in 1865. He had travelled extensively in the difficult terrain of the Himalayas and had acquired experience in surveying the regions of Punjab, Nepal, etc. Due to his expertise in the topography of the area, his report was one of the earliest detailed accounts of the Aksai Chin region. According to the terms of the Treaty of Amritsar, it was the prerogative of the British to conduct a survey of the border between Kashmir and China. Accordingly, the work was undertaken by British Officer Johnson, with whom Gulab Singh shared a close bond. In the absence of any concrete proposal on delimitation from the British authority, his efforts were, by and large, independent and as per his vision. When Johnson embarked on the task in May 1865, he had a clear objective about the nature and extent of the territory he had to bring under the survey. Since the region was desolate and distant from New Delhi as well as Peking, and no Tibetan official had shown any special interest in this matter, Johnson was absolutely free to work at his discretion. He thus fixed the limits of the Kashmir boundary along the remote Kunlun range, making the entire Karakash Valley part of the territory of Kashmir.[31] He tried to link Demchok in the south with the Karakoram Pass in the north through a circuitous route, and

---

[30] Quoted in Noorani, 'Facing the Truth'.

[31] Virenrda Sahai Verma, 'Sino-Indian Border Dispute at Aksai Chin, a Middle Path for Resolution' (May 2010). Available at http://chinaindiaborderdispute.wordpress.com (accessed on 30 July 2020).

this alignment ran between Ladakh in the southern side, including the whole Aksai Chin in the territory of Gulab Singh, and placing Tibet and Sinkiang on the other side beyond the Kunlun Mountains.[32]

However, despite having completed an advanced survey of this remote and difficult terrain, Johnson's efforts could not lead to any final conclusion because of the various other controversies in which he was involved. The proposal of this British civil servant of the Trigonometrical Survey of India became controversial for multiple reasons and, therefore, his survey was not recognized as final. Since his report had placed the Aksai Chin plateau in Kashmir, it was rejected by the Chinese government as well, with the result that his report and demarcation 'remained nominal rather than implemented'.[33] His overenthusiasm is reported to have invited a censorship of his service, as he had crossed the borders without permission and later alleged that he was forcibly taken.[34] The Surveyor General, Colonel Walker, criticized his survey in 1867 for its inaccuracies and errors. However, using Johnson's report as the basis, with a few minor corrections, a map was published, soon known as the 'Johnson Line'.[35] This advanced boundary line drawn by Johnson was rejected by most Western and Chinese scholars and cartographers, and it still continues to be a controversial one. Actually, 'this line was based on the Kashmir maharaja's outpost at Shahidullah, making the Kunlun watershed as the divide and not the Karakoram Range'.[36]

There is supposedly a reason for Johnson showing interest in bringing an extended territory under the kingdom of maharaja. It is suggested that Johnson colluded with raja's Ladakh wazir, who generously supported him for the safe conduct of the work.[37] According to many scholars,

[32] This controversial line on the alignment of Kunlun is the basis for the claim of independent India in Aksai Chin. Guruswamy, 'India–China Border'.

[33] Scott, 'Sino-Indian Territorial Issues', 6.

[34] Peter Hopkirk, *Foreign Devils on the Silk Road: The Search for Lost Treasures of Central Asia* (London: John Murray, 1980), 42–43.

[35] Verma, 'Sino-Indian Border Dispute at Aksai Chin'.

[36] Gangesh Sreekumar Varma, 'Reading between the Lines: Understanding the India–China Border Dispute'. *Fair Observer* (November 2012). Available at https://www.fairobserver.com/region/central_south_asia/reading-between-lines/ (accessed on 20 October 2020).

[37] Lall, *Aksai Chin and Sino-Indian Conflict*, 141–142.

there were personal reasons behind Johnson's drawing of an advanced borderline, thus expanding the size of the maharaja's domain, incorporating Aksai Chin, which he found to be to his advantage as well.[38] The ambition he nurtured for better prospects in the future of the services is said to have been the basic reason behind him for drawing an extended line in the survey.[39] This was proved by subsequent developments. When Johnson's survey got entangled in controversies, and when he was denied promotion, he resigned from the British service in the Survey of India. He was re-employed in 1869, after severe condemnation, and in 1872 he joined the services of the Kashmir maharaja and became the governor of Ladakh.[40] This service history of Johnson justifies the fact that his actions were unauthorized. Hence, even though the 'Johnson Line' was a British initiative, it was not conducted as per the interests of the British India government; it instead promoted the aspirations of the Kashmir raja for an extended territory. In the subsequent years, the line remained unaccepted by the British government, primarily because Shahidullah, in the far-off Karakash Valley, could not be defended from the outsider threat. The joint commissioner of Leh, Ney Elias, an expert on the trans-Karakoram territories, who had extensively explored the Himalayan ranges, advised the British government against the endorsement of the Johnson Line as it was unwise and practically hard to defend. According to him, it would be very difficult to claim Shahidullah, as per the Johnson Line, in the remote Karakash valley, situated about 400 km from Leh. Alastair Lamb has considered Johnson 'a very real political surveyor', whose survey was 'incredibly inaccurate' and 'patently absurd'.[41] While Mehra argues that Johnson's survey is rated as 'valuable and important' in the official report of the Great Trigonometrical Survey of India, he agrees that the latter's survey certainly invited heavy criticism.[42] It is also alleged that Johnson was on 'a major intelligence

---

[38] Guruswamy, 'India China Border'.

[39] An advanced borderline to the territory of raja, based on his survey, rewarded him with the position of Ladakh governorship. Guruswamy and Singh, *India China Relations*, 12–13.

[40] Ravina Aggarwal, *Beyond Lines of Control: Performance and Politics on the Disputed Borders of Ladakh, India* (Durham, NC: Duke University Press, 2004), 34.

[41] Lamb, *The China–India Border*, 43, 83–84.

[42] Mehra, *Essays in Frontier History*, 288–293.

mission' in which the Survey of India was directly involved.[43] But even when he was on an intelligence mission for the British government, he proceeded to 'show more than the usual zeal' for the cause of his future employer, the maharaja of Kashmir.[44]

Independent India's claim to the entire Aksai Chin plateau is based on Johnson's map. This boundary line was first notified in 1868 in the map of the Survey of India and the Kashmir Atlas boundary.[45] The Viceroy of India, Lord Elgin, had rejected Johnson's proposal, as he feared that it would strain relations with China and would also precipitate Russian advances in the region. Director General of Military Operations (DGMO), D. K. Palit, said, 'There was much controversy about every aspect of Johnson's geographical and other claim right up to Kunlun range and beyond'.[46] To look at this fairly, Johnson's intention of a farther border delimitation through the Kunlun range might have been to keep the Russians as far away as possible from British India proper. However, later, the British commander-in-chief also called it 'militarily unsound'. Foreign Secretary W. J. Cunningham noted that the proposed 'Kunlun Line would be unwatched or cost of watching would be tremendous'. In short, the Johnson Line of 1865 neither provides any credential for cartographic authenticity nor does it have any historical validity. Neither the governments of British India nor the Chinese authority accepted this line. So the major British efforts, both in 1847 and 1865, failed to produce a permanent border demarcation.

The Foreign Office Line of 1873

Subsequent to the dropping of Johnson's Kunlun line proposal, further efforts to draw up the frontiers continued. The British Foreign Office at London therefore entrusted the Governor of Leh, Frederic Drew, with the responsibility of demarcating a border on the basis of his explorations of the region. As a result, his team drew up a line starting from Lanak La in the south-east and moving north-west to finally join the

[43] Ibid.

[44] Lall, *Aksai Chin and Sino-Indian Conflict*, 142.

[45] Guruswamy and Singh, *India China Relations*, 12.

[46] Palit, *War in High Himalayas*, 31.

Karakoram range. This was called 'the Foreign Office Line' of 1873 (Figure 2.2). Starting from the south at Lanak La, this line ran parallel, but far south of the Laktsang range, leaving a larger portion of Aksai Chin in Chinese territory and later joining partially to the Karakoram range, according to the Macartney–MacDonald Line of 1899, which was drawn later. Hence, the 1873 line had included a larger portion of the Lingzi Tang plains on the Chinese side. While the Johnson's line had proposed to include territories farthest to the north-east, including

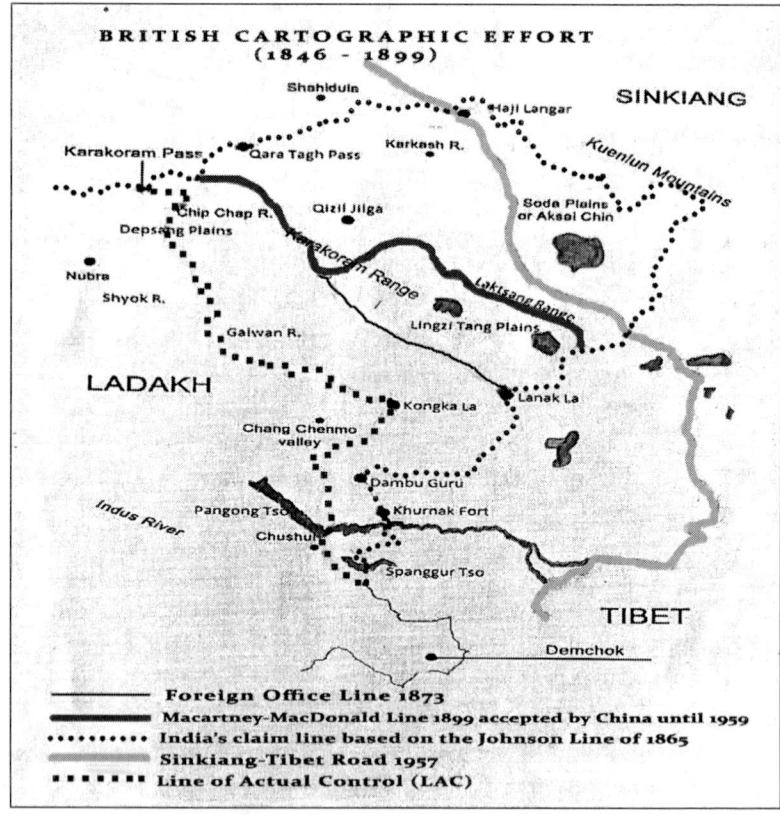

Figure 2.2 *British Cartographic Efforts in the Western Sector*

Source: Author.

Disclaimer: This figure has been redrawn and is not to scale. It does not represent any authentic national or international boundaries and is used for illustrative purposes only.

the whole of Ladakh in British India, the 1873 Foreign Office Line proposed to include a larger part of Ladakh on the Chinese side. This Foreign Office Line is actually closest to the LAC that the PRC gradually occupied from 1959. But this too was not final and the British uncertainty and indecisiveness over the border continued further. The wide variations in these demarcations by British officials were on account of their priority for defence at that particular time. The British military establishments had alerted the government on the need to defend such far-off borders at the chilling height of the Himalayas.

Britain's obsession with the border continued, but it was settled neither in favour of the Johnson Line nor the Foreign Office Line. Frequent but inconclusive correspondence between Whitehall and the Government of British India continued with additional efforts. The general view from Whitehall was that 'it is unnecessary to trace the voluminous consultations between London and Calcutta and within the Government of India',[47] because the need of the international power equation was the decisive factor. So even when most of the official responses to the farthest Johnson Line were not encouraging, the military considerations of the British officials began to dominate their decision-making, and the conclusion of the Director of Military Intelligence (DMI), Sir John Ardagh, was in favour of an advanced forward line.

The Johnson–Ardagh Boundary of 1897

After two decades, yet another cartographic venture was in consideration and the DMI, Major General Sir John Ardagh, took the initiative in 1897. He was much concerned with the security of the British India. The military general's concern arose from a possible Russian expansion at the weakness of Peking, which prompted him to propose a boundary north of the Yarkand River.[48] Colonel John Ardagh, private secretary to the Viceroy and later DMI, therefore, recommended an advanced boundary alignment, similar to Johnson's proposal in 1865, along the crest of the Kunlun mountain range. This proposal, in tune

[47] Noorani, 'Facing the Truth'.

[48] Woodman, *Himalayan Frontiers, 101.*

with the Johnson Line at the crest of Kunlun range,[49] was largely due to the geostrategic consideration of military intelligence. Hence, Colonel Ardagh, once again, brought back the proposal of Sir W. H. Johnson, now called the 'Johnson–Ardagh Line'. Colonel Ardagh had incorporated the upper reaches of the Yarkand River, its tributaries and the Karakash River within British territory. By a strategic adaptation of Johnson Line of 1865, he 'closed the gap between Pangong lake and Karakoram pass and extended the line from Shahidullah, along the Kunlun Mountains'.[50] In January 1897, Sir Colonel John Ardagh wrote a memorandum[51] in which he justified the British claim for its boundary alignment 'at the crest of the Kunlun range' and the upper reaches of the Yarkand River, its tributaries and the Karakash River, as well as the whole Aksai Chin plateau placed within British territory.

But even before Whitehall could make up his mind on these advanced lines under British possession, the Chinese had already occupied Shahidullah in 1890.[52] The Secretary of State for India therefore observed, 'We are inclined to think that the wisest course would be to leave them (China) in possession as it is evidently to our advantage that the tract of territory between the Karakoram and Kunlun mountains be held by a friendly power like China'.[53] However, despite the fact that the idea of drawing such a line far to the north was to keep Russia away, it was against the majority view of the government.[54] On the basis of Captain Younghusband's report, this line was actually a departure from the general consensus at all levels, which was largely in favour of a boundary along the Karakoram watershed. Therefore, the suggestion was rejected and the authority in London was not inclined to the idea of extending its territory in India beyond the Aksai Chin plains on

---

[49] Mohan Guruswamy, 'The Great India–China Game' (23 June 2003). Available at https://www.rediff.com/news/2003/jun/20spec.htm (accessed on 31 July 2020).

[50] Varma, *Understanding the India-China Border Dispute*.

[51] John Ardagh, *The Northern Frontier of India, From the Pamirs to Tibet* (Oxford: Oxford University Press, 1897).

[52] Guruswamy, *Emerging Trends in India–China Relations*, 216.

[53] Guruswamy, 'India–China Border'.

[54] Noorani, 'Facing the Truth'.

account of security. In the meanwhile, between the two extremes of border proposals, there was a suggestion to divide Aksai Chin between India and China along the Laktsang range.[55] This seemed to be a fair balancing of the region on either side leaving south-western Aksai Chin in Ladakh and the north-eastern Aksai Chin in Tibet based on the Laktsang range demarcation.

The Macartney–MacDonald Line (1899)

The tenure of Lord Curzon, who had taken charge on 6 January 1899 as the new British Viceroy, was noted for British India's frontier policies. As the 1897 proposal was rejected, Curzon apprised the government on the urgency of a frontier convention in which the sources of discord could be removed by the 'adjustment of rival interests or ambitions at points where the territorial borders adjoin'.[56] In the absence of any general consensus and clarity on the specifications on the lines so far suggested, Curzon, who had shown great zeal in the Tibetan policy, was encouraged to arrive at a finality on the nature of British India's border with China. Emphasizing the significance of borders in bilateral relations, Curzon had concluded that 'frontiers are indeed the razor's edge on which hang suspended the modern issues of war or peace, of life or death to nations'.[57] Repeated and prolonged efforts for a stable and lasting solution to the Aksai Chin frontiers continued to be pursued in order to arrive at a final demarcation, and the motivation was nothing less than the safeguarding of British Indian possessions.

In the meantime, as a result of continuous explorations and observations, by the end of the 19th century, the Foreign Department of the Government of British India had observed the existence of two distinct and separate parts in Aksai Chin. It was noted that the north-eastern Aksai Chin had been merged with Tibet's Changtang and was now part of China's domain, and a distinct part of Aksai Chin, on the western Lingzi Tang plain, was part of the Ladakh region of Kashmir. These

---

[55] Verma, 'Sino-Indian Border Dispute at Aksai Chin'.

[56] Scott, 'Sino-Indian Territorial Issues', 1.

[57] Lord Curzon of Kedleston, *Frontiers in Oxford Lectures on History 1904–23*.

two areas were divided by the Laktsang range.[58] Accordingly, on 20 July 1898, a borderline depicted on the crest of Karakoram, heading south-east on the Laktsang range until it reached the eastern boundary of Ladakh, a little east of 80° longitude, was in consideration.[59] Subsequently, a final proposal was submitted by Macartney and MacDonald in early 1899 for redrawing the borders on these lines.[60] The new proposal by Macartney–MacDonald was, more or less, on the same principle of the existence of two regions of Aksai Chin. Hence, the Government of British India was considering abandoning earlier advanced boundaries along the Kunlun range for various reasons.[61] Whitehall gave consent to the proposal, placing north-east Aksai Chin in Chinese territory and western Aksai Chin or the Lingzi Tang plain in Ladakh. Accordingly, on behalf of the home government, Lord Salisbury forwarded the proposal to Sir Claude MacDonald, the British Ambassador to Peking, on 14 March 1899, with a note addressed to the Chinese government. MacDonald soon communicated Macartney's alignment to China. In so modifying the existing boundary, in 1899, a new map was drawn through the Karakoram range and was called the 'Macartney–MacDonald Line' after Sir George Macartney, the British representative at Kashgar, and Sir Claude MacDonald, the British Ambassador to China. This was the last and final of the border delimitation proposal considered by the British government in India and submitted to the Peking authority.

So the Macartney–MacDonald Line put forth a less ambitious territorial claim by the British north of the Karakoram ranges. East of the Karakoram Pass, it left to China the whole of the Karakash Valley and almost all of Aksai Chin proper. It was through this north-east Aksai Chin that the PRC later constructed the Xinjiang-Tibet road.

---

[58] Mehra, *Essays in Frontier History*, 288–290.

[59] For details, refer to Figure 2.2.

[60] Curzon had reservations about the Macartney–MacDonald Line as he was in favour of Ardagh's boundary. Lord Curzon of Kedleston, *Romanes Lecture on the Subject of Frontiers* (1907). Available at http://wwwibru.dur.ac.uk/resources/docs/curzon1.html (accessed on 31 July 2020).

[61] This was motivated by the news of a Sino-Russian understanding in April 1898 to fix the frontier in Turkistan. So this suggestion was accepted in order to discard any possible Russian threat.

It followed the Laktsang range, the Lingzi Tang salt plains and the whole of the Chang Chenmo Valley, as well as the Chip Chap river further north. Shahidullah, Suget and the Aksai Chin plateau, north of Lingzi Tang, were conceded to China. The Lingzi Tang plain or southern Aksai Chin was considered a part of Kashmir, and China had not encroached upon this territory until 1959, when border preparedness from both sides intensified.

This historic British borderline proposal based on the watershed principle on the Karakoram range[62] notifying only north-east Aksai Chin to China was submitted to the Zongli Yamen, the Chinese Department of Foreign Office, on 14 March 1899, by British Ambassador Sir Claude MacDonald.

> The note intimated to the Peking government had stipulated inter alia that in return for the Chinese renouncing their 'shadowy' claim to suzerainty over Hunza, a little principality lying north of the Karakoram pass, the British would be willing to offer 'a large tract of country' hitherto 'outside' the Chinese domain, namely, western Aksai Chin.

However, there was no response from the Chinese government apart from a verbal assurance that a reply would be sent after receiving the views of the Governor of Sinkiang. But there was no further follow-up on this by either government.[63] 'There was little doubt that the line suggested in Aksai Chin along Laktsang range was tacitly acceptable to the Chinese', but their reservation was about wording of 'extra territorial rights over the Hunza area'.[64] Purshotam Mehra says:

> archival records reveal that British-India's major objective was to end China's suzerain rights over Hunza, which, it was feared would play havoc with Indian security if the Russians marched into Kashgaria, as was then widely feared. The British concern, was not the merit or otherwise of the surrender of Aksai Chin.[65]

[62] Karunakar Gupta, 'Distortions in the History of Sino-Indian Frontiers'. *Economic & Political Weekly* 15, no. 30 (1980): 1265–1270. Available at http://www.jstor.org/stable/4368898 (accessed on 31 July 2020).

[63] R. Huttenbach, 'A Historical Note on the Sino-Indian Dispute over the Aksai Chin', *China Quarterly* (1964): 201–207.

[64] Verma, 'Sino-Indian Border Dispute at Aksai Chin'.

[65] Mehra, *Essays in Frontier History*, 288.

The British anxiety was, in large part, about the closing of the Afghan and Chinese boundaries on the Pamirs to block a possible Russian menace, for which they were more than willing to surrender their well-established claims to Shahidullah.[66] It was in such a context that the earlier viceroy, Lord Lansdowne, noted in the minutes on 28 September 1889:

> The country between the Karakoram and Kuenlun ranges…is of no value, very inaccessible and not likely to be coveted by Russia. We might, I should think, encourage the Chinese to take it, if they showed any inclination to do so. This would be better than leaving a no-man's land between our frontier and that of China. Moreover, the stronger we can make China at this point, and the more we can induce her to hold…the whole Kashgar-Yarkand region, the more useful will she be to us as an obstacle to Russian advance along this line.[67]

But even when both the British authorities in India and at home were committed to the new line, 'no further attempt was made to secure a Chinese "definition" of Kashmir's northern boundaries'.[68] On 24 March 1904, Viceroy Curzon said, 'in the absence of reply, the Government of India took it that the proposal had been accepted and they, for their part, would proceed to act as if it had'.[69] And so, this line holds the significance of being the only line that the British formally notified to the Chinese government,[70] even when they did not await any response from Peking, which showed an undue delay in giving a response, and no reply was received at all. Although the British tried to get the Chinese to sign an agreement to this effect, the latter did not respond to these moves.[71] Lord Curzon wanted to end this uncertainty in the border issue and therefore concluded that their silence could be taken as acquiescence and decided that henceforth this should be considered the border.[72] Writing to the Secretary of State, John Brodrick, Curzon,

---

[66] Guruswamy and Singh, *India China Relations*, 12–18.

[67] Minutes of Viceroy Lord Lansdowne, 28 September 1889, quoted in A.G. Noorani, 'Facts of History', *Frontline* 20, no. 18 (2003).

[68] Lamb, *The China–India Border*, 105–107.

[69] Quoted in Lall, *Aksai Chin and Sino-Indian Conflict*, 195.

[70] Lamb, *The Sino-Indian Border in Ladakh*, 15–16.

[71] Varma, *Understanding the India-China Border Dispute*.

[72] Guruswamy, 'India–China Border'.

on 24 March 1904, stated that since the Chinese had not shown any reason for disagreeing with the proposals, it was assumed that it had their concurrence.

But later, on 10 August 1905, he proposed 'a modification of the 1899 offer so as to include fertile tracts of Raskam north of the Shimshal Pass in Hunza. The Aksai Chin part of the offer remained unaffected'.[73] Accordingly, on 1 August 1907, the secretary of state directed that the map of the border between China and Kashmir 'should indicate the frontiers as following the line described in Note of 1899 to China'.[74] Aksai Chin was made part of Tibet, and the British government held on to the 1899 proposal as being final. The maps accompanying the Simla Convention of 1914 also showed Aksai Chin as part of Tibet. However, the British Indian colonial government was not satisfied with the nature of the border definitions with Peking, as the latter had not acknowledged any of these proposals, and the latest one of 1899 was also unsuccessful. Since these trial and error experiments had not yet brought about a lasting solution, the British Indian officials were prompted to ascertain the stability of their Indian possessions by charting out a larger ambitious plan venturing into the Tibetan province of China.

Fall of Imperial China and the British Ambivalence

1911 was a major milestone in the history of China. The fall of the Ching (Manchu) dynasty as a result of the Republican Revolution of 1911 not only brought to an end the two millennium-old dynastic political traditions but also destabilized the political power centre in Peking. This political uncertainty prompted the British to further reassess the northern frontier of Kashmir, because they feared that the political anarchy in the larger parts of the distant Chinese provinces would encourage the Russians to move to the peripheries of China. Consequently, once again, the Johnson–Ardagh Line began to be considered the frontier, and the maps published by the *Times Atlas* and *Oxford Atlas* included Aksai Chin as part of British territory.[75]

---

[73] Noorani, 'Facing the Truth'.

[74] Quoted in Lall, *Aksai Chin and Sino-Indian Conflict*, 196.

[75] Verma, *Sino-Indian Border Dispute*.

The major takeaway from the discussion until now is that the Kunlun or Karakoram-Laktsang range that the British suggested were 'not because they felt that China had a claim over that region, rather it was to make China strong in Kashgar-Yarkand to become an obstacle to Russian advance in this line'.[76] However, these unilateral border definitions by British India had the least respect to the sentiments of Peking. One of the British internal notes to Whitehall in April 1917 emphasized the fact that the 1899 line was drawn 'not as the result of any treaty or engagement with China, nor as finally and definitely marking the bounds of our (British) spheres of influence, nor altogether as forming a scientific or strategic border'. 'It could not in any sense be regarded "as a fixed or final international boundary" nor could India regard itself "as absolutely bound" by a border which it had itself laid down, without the concurrence of any other party concerned'.[77] The British took advantage of the political turbulence in China and Peking's apparent disinterest in border negotiations to effect minor changes in the alignment, first in 1905 at the west of the Karakoram Pass, then in 1907 and 1912 in Aksai Chin to their favour, finally placing it once again in Ladakh. This ambivalence in the British border policy was characteristic of their colonial ambitions. Their strategic game continued further until 1949.

Even though the intensity of Anglo-Russian colonial rivalry had begun to subside in the early 20th century,[78] this 'geo-political and geo-economics competition for influence in China continued right up to the formation of the People's Republic of China in 1949'. After the fall of its Manchu dynasty in 1911, China was nominally a Republic and had little control over the distant provinces of Sinkiang and Tibet. While Sinkiang was ruled by a Russian puppet warlord,[79] Tibet had,

---

[76] Ibid.

[77] Mehra, *Essays in Frontier History*, 290–293.

[78] During the 1907 convention, they signed an agreement by the terms of which both the powers decided 'not to enter into negotiations with Tibet, except the knowledge of Chinese Government'. Lamb, *The McMahon Line*, 251–255.

[79] During this time, Russians showed interests in creating a buffer in western China, and they had placed Sheng Shih-tsai (1933–1944) as a puppet ruler in Sinkiang. Mark Dickens, 'The Soviets in Xinjiang: 1911–1949' (1990), Available at http://www.oxuscom.com/sovinxj.htm#sheng (accessed on 31 July 2020).

by and large, declared its independent status under the spiritual leader Dalai Lama. In 1940, the British had once again reversed the alignment to the Johnson–Ardagh Line.[80] But the principality of Hunza in the north continued to be under the authority of Peking, which the British considered 'harmless' in Chinese hands. However, they neither published any official maps nor attempted to demarcate the border. Neither any 'posts were established in Aksai Chin, …nor were any expeditions sent to show the flag. For all practical purposes, the Raj ceased at the Karakoram Range'.[81] Hence, the legacy of the British colonial aspirations had left a profound impact on the nature of the border for certain 'renewed perceptions', which previously only had legendary zonal frontiers. The PRC had viewed this British Indian border strategy to annihilate its internal stability and obstruct its political integrity in the province of Tibet. In such a context, when the PRC showed much aversion to accept the legacies of British imperial devices, independent India was eager to recognize its borders with China as having been inherited from the British. The displeasure that arose from this uncertainty on the borders soon began to metamorphose into a border dispute.

Crux of the Issue in the Kashmir Sector

What was the post-colonial scenario of the existing dispute in this sector, specifically before 1957? Actually, 'the Kashmir section of the northern boundary is the heart of India's boundary dispute with China',[82] because the Chinese interest in this region is primarily to link two of its most turbulent provinces, namely Sinkiang and Tibet, through this territory. New Delhi considered it quite significant for the strategic defence of its northern frontiers. Two-thirds of the total length of the boundary in this sector are shared with the Tibet–Ladakh borders, while the remaining is shared with the

---

[80] When the British intelligence learned of a Russian survey of Aksai Chin for the pro-Soviet Sinkiang government, they pushed the border again to the Kunlun ranges. Guruswamy and Singh, *India China Relations*, 19.

[81] Guruswamy, *Emerging Trends in India–China Relations*, 217.

[82] Guruswamy and Singh, *India China Relations*, 8.

Sinkiang–Kashmir (PoK) borders. Peking has virtually taken control of a larger share of this region and has built a road traversing the disputed territory of Aksai Chin.

The major area of the dispute in this sector revolves around Aksai Chin, which is debated as being part of the Sinkiang–Tibet provinces of China, against a part of Ladakh, the new Union Territory of India. Other than acceptance of the two ends, at Karakoram Pass in the north-west and Demchok in the south-east, a proper border alignment between these two extremes is absent and this creates disparity about the nature of 'how the line traversed between the two points'.[83] The PRC holds that the border alignment on this sector has not been delimited and that this part of the Aksai Chin territory traditionally belongs to China. The border alignment according to the PRC runs along the Karakoram range, placing the whole territory of Aksai Chin, including a large portion of Ladakh, in its jurisdiction. However, Peking has no documentary or historical backing for this proposition of an extended claim beyond north-eastern Aksai Chin. Initially, a dispute in this sector was not apparent, though it was silently active from the perception of both nations. But, by 1957, Peking quietly built a road and later pushed the LOC farther, possibly expecting a favourable mutual settlement.

New Delhi, on the contrary, specifies the details of the boundary alignment from their perspective as being traditionally handed over and confirmed on the basis of the watershed principle. The Indian claim of the borderline is that it runs along the crest of the Kunlun range, including the whole of Aksai Chin within its territory. The Indian narrative is largely based on treaties and agreements signed between the Kashmir rulers and the Tibetan or Chinese authorities during the pre-British and British periods. New Delhi has also published a series of White Papers narrating the nature of its claims and has also brought out a few reports by the History Division of the Ministry of Defence. These documentations propose a theory of the natural and geographical watershed principle, focusing its credibility

---

[83] Mohan Guruswamy, 'The Battle for the Border' (2003). Available at https://www.rediff.com/news/2003/jun/21spec.htm (accessed on 31 July 2020).

on the basis of treaties signed by the local political entities, primarily during the pre-colonial days.

However, one can notice disparities and contradictions in what has been published in the White Papers[84] and documented by the History Division of the Ministry of Defence[85] as well as other government documents. The Indian claim of an extended Kunlun range is in contrast to the documentary evidence available. These claims of New Delhi do not provide any reasonable corroborative evidence regarding proper delimitation. The treaties and agreements signed by the Kashmir and Tibetan authorities during the pre-British and British periods were largely of the nature of trade and mutual cooperation and did not provide for any territorial demarcation of their political jurisdictions.[86] The maps published in the 1920s and 1930s by the Survey of India under the British government had not specified any boundary alignment in the northern and eastern frontier of Kashmir and a large tract of land area between the Kashmir and Sinkiang–Tibet border regions were left undefined.[87] After an exhaustive research in the archival documents preserved in the India Office Library, Karunakar says that the Survey of India maps published during this period neither indicated any boundary alignment nor showed any colour difference in this area, and wide spaces between Kashmir and Sinkiang (Xinjiang) and Tibet were shown blank.[88] When the Simon Commission wished to include a map of India in its 1929 report, it could find nothing in the India Office to justify the line on the Kunlun range, as shown on some maps. The Commission accordingly adopted a line, roughly along the crest of the Karakoram range, excluding the Aksai Chin area.[89] In

---

[84] MEA, Government of India, 'Notes, Memoranda and Letters Exchanged and Agreements signed between the Governments of India and China', *White Paper* IV (1960): 100.

[85] Sinha and Athale, *History of the Conflict with China*, 1–2.

[86] MEA, Government of India, *Agreements between the Governments of Tibet, Kashmir and the British in the Years 1842, 1852, 1865, 1876, 1886, 1890, 1893 etc.*

[87] Gupta, 'Distortions in the History of Sino-Indian Frontiers'.

[88] Gupta, *Spotlight on Sino-Indian Frontiers*, 82.

[89] Karunakar Gupta, 'Myths about a Frontier Dispute', *The Statesman*, 29 November 1978.

1931, the official records published in the Aitchison Treaties reported, 'The Northern as well as the Eastern boundary of the Kashmir state is still undefined'.[90] Official maps and records available before 1947 more or less followed the same border description as in the Aitchison Treaties, making it evident that the borders of the Kashmir state were left undefined.[91] Nehru himself once stated that 'it is a matter of argument as to what part of it (Aksai Chin) belongs to us and what part of it belongs to somebody else'. This means that there has never been any delimitation in that area, and it has been a challenged area. Indian Foreign Secretary Louis Dane, in his letter to the Indian office, stated that Aksai Chin was in Chinese Xinjiang.[92] But it was in 1945, under the guidance of the then Foreign Secretary of India, Sir Olaf Caroe, that the Survey of India maps began to show Aksai Chin by a colour wash with the words 'boundary undefined' marked on it.[93] Even after independence, when the Survey of India issued a map of the political divisions of the country in 1950, it depicted its borders with China merely by a colour wash and denoted as 'boundary undefined'.[94] Similarly, in February 1951, K. Zachariah, Director of the Historical Division, MEA, informed Himmatsinhji[95] that there was no well-defined boundary along the northern and eastern frontier of Kashmir.[96] In 1947, the Indian Army in its 'top-secret' message to the British Cabinet Mission had also accepted the Karakoram range as the northern boundary of India in the western sector.[97] It was on account of the existence of these contradictory versions that, on 28 August 1959, after the border dispute pronouncedly came up between India and China, Nehru had stated in the Lok Sabha that 'this was the

[90] Aitcheson, *A Collection of Treaties*, 5.

[91] Gupta, 'Distortions in the History of Sino-Indian Frontiers'.

[92] Lamb, *Tibet*, 390.

[93] Gupta, *Spotlight on Sino-Indian Frontiers*, 82.

[94] Manoj Joshi, 'Lesson from an Unsettled Boundary', *The Hindu*, 27 April 2013.

[95] Prime Minister in Parliament, *Sino-Indian Relations*, Vol. 1 (New Delhi: Government of India, 1961), 251.

[96] Gupta, 'Distortions in the History of Sino-Indian Frontiers'.

[97] Gupta, *Spotlight on Sino-Indian Frontiers*, 24.

boundary of the old Kashmir state with Tibet and Chinese Turkestan. Nobody had marked it'.[98]

But post-independence years of the People's Liberation Army (PLA) storming into Tibet and an active presence of Communist China in the frontiers had awakened New Delhi to make clarity about the nature of the frontiers. Doubts were expressed about Peking's perception of the border, and it became necessary to clarify the nature of the frontier.[99] Meantime during 1950–1953 period, several border committees were appointed to study and report about India's frontiers with China, Nepal and Bhutan, and these reports enlightened the need to strengthen the border and to establish border posts.[100] It was based on this context and pending these proposals that, immediately after the signing of the 1954 Panchsheel agreement, Nehru directed to clarify the border. Subsequently, the new Survey of India maps began to show an international boundary in this sector running along Kunlun range. The reasons for placing the whole Aksai Chin area within the Indian territory was no doubt taken as per the directions of these expert proposals. This shows that the issue of a border dispute had not yet been clarified and that it had emerged quite late in the background of other related issues. Till that time, it was either pending or had been ignored until that got attention later. Actually, even when Peking had suggested a border settlement in the early 1950s, New Delhi adopted a stand of the borders being sufficiently demarcated by natural delimitations. However, there was neither any properly demarcated boundary in this sector nor had the British government recognized any as being conclusively demarcated.

Even when most scholars working in this area of study suggest that no such definite Sino-Indian boundary has ever existed in the west, and the available source of evidence does not provide any sound and

[98] PRC, *The Sino-Indian Boundary Question* (Peking: The Foreign Languages Press, 1962), 56.

[99] Kuldip Nayar, *Between The Lines* (New Delhi: Konark Publishers, 1969), 139. Nayyar quotes Indira Gandhi's doubt as expressed in 1954 about Chinese border understanding.

[100] Reports were submitted by Himmatsinhji Committee (1951), Kulwant Singh Committee (1952), Thorat Committee (1952) and H. M. Patel Committee (1952).

solid basis for either nation's border alignment, both parties later came up with their claims on the basis of tradition and geography. But historical facts show that, for centuries, large parts of these wide desolate tracts were not frequently explored and, in the absence of any possible specific demarcation of this Himalayan terrain, boundaries evolved more on the basis of legends, while administrative jurisdictions were more or less on a zonal basis. Therefore, 'the Sino-Indian border dispute has been a dispute on the "zone" rather than a "line."'[101] The LAC was also notional and has not been put down on any mutually agreed upon map.[102]

The PRC pointed out that it was necessary to demarcate the borders as they had been subjected to colonial manoeuvres. But it was an opportunity missed by New Delhi to come to a decisive and lasting agreement with the PRC. Even when there were prime ministerial-level efforts for diplomatic solutions by rectifying anomalies, it did not get the attention it deserved due to internal political dissent and discord. No sooner would the issue be taken up than it would be stretched out of proportion leading to repercussions in New Delhi until it got entangled with the issue of Tibet. Since there is an inherent natural division within Aksai Chin, it is also not impossible to reach a negotiable settlement without hurting either side. But the hurdle to any amicable solution would emerge from the willingness of either side to accept or reject the vestiges of the 'colonial game'. Even though it is not easy to arrive at a solution, either arbitrarily or amicably, there is enough scope for a settlement on a mutual give-and-take formula, provided the nature of dispute and the priorities of both nations are taken into account in the right context. So, despite there being ambiguity and confusion about the nature of the frontiers, one can explore the possible solutions to getting out of this quagmire created by imperialist interventions. A proper perception of the topography of the Aksai Chin region and a clear understanding of pre-colonial history and tradition would enlighten us with a solution from within.

[101] Liu, 'Look beyond the Sino-Indian Border Dispute'.

[102] Joshi, 'Lesson from an Unsettled Boundary'.

Neither Kunlun nor Karakoram, But Solution within

The post-colonial differences between Peking and New Delhi are regarding claims over two extremely distant borderlines at the Karakoram and Kunlun ranges respectively, but an amenable solution is a possibility. There is a middle ground that can be reached for a final resolution that balances the interests of both the parties, with due respect for geographical and historical aspects, as well as for political and geostrategic reflections. The topography of Aksai Chin itself reveals that there was a natural division within the plateau, and this division partitions the disputed territory into two Aksai Chin areas. Considering the pre-colonial position as well, there is little scope for discrepancy and debate, and if the colonial vestiges are relinquished, there are sufficient grounds for conformity and cooperation to settle any dispute that could arise later. Once you discard the colonial cartographic 'mischief', you can observe that there is a definite border as per the geography of the land and customs handed down.

But in the post-1959 period, when the dispute intensified into the war of 1962, the LAC underwent tremendous changes and did not meet any of these divergent claims of either party. Beginning in the north at the east of Karakoram Pass, the LAC moves far south on the Karakoram range, east of Daulat Beg Oldi (DBO), through the Depsang Plains, near Kongka Pass and Chushul, finally joining Demchok, grabbing an extended area from the Indian territory. The present position, therefore, is not based on any proper geographical or historical considerations. It necessarily would not be either at Shahidullah and Hajji Langar, covering the far north-eastern ranges of Kunlun, as claimed by New Delhi, nor at far south in the Karakoram ranges at DBO, Depsang Plains, Galwan Valley, Hot Spring, Chushul, Kongka La, as claimed by Peking. The LAC, therefore, runs through a far extended line south of all colonial dispensations and even beyond the original claim of Peking (see Figure 2.2). After 1959, Peking appropriated an extended territory in Ladakh, which cannot be justified either by pre-colonial traditions or by any colonial dispensations.

Aksai Chin proper is a high-altitude plateau 15,500–18,000 ft above sea level, enclosed largely by the great Karakoram ranges in the west and the mighty Kunlun range in the north, covering a total area of about 33,000 sq. km. Geographically, this plain lies divided into two unequal portions by a ridge called Laktsang, which runs from a little north-west of Lanak La towards Karakoram, making it two distinct areas of Aksai Chin, belonging to both sides. The Laktsang ridge is a watershed that divides the entire plateau into two regions—the northern part drains into Karakash, moving north to Chinese Xinjiang, while the southern part, between Laktsang and Chang Chenmo, drains into Shyok and later joins Indus in the south and south-west.[103] Several explorers of the 19th and 20th centuries have documented the existence of Laktsang ridge as a natural division of the plateau.[104] The existence of such a ridge can be clearly noticed from Google's satellite imageries. The 1899 Macartney–MacDonald Line, by and large, followed this alignment. But contesting this, New Delhi maintains that 'Laktsang is not a regular or even identifiable range.... The definition of the boundary mapped out in October 1898 dispatch, which later formed the basis for MacDonald line (1899), restricted on a faulty or even wrong premise'.[105] 'New Delhi maintains that the Qaratagh and Kunlun ranges form a "continuous watershed" and also have geographical continuity from Karakoram pass to Kuenlun ranges'. However, the fact that when Kunlun forms a major watershed in the region, 'the existence of Laktsang as a water parting of Karakash and Shyok rivers and their feeder rivulets is also true'.[106] Since the dispute in the western sector is largely involved in the Aksai Chin area, the existence of such a major natural range dividing the Aksai Chin into two distinct areas has much relevance.

When dividing the entire Aksai Chin plateau into two regions, there is an Aksai Chin for China in the north-eastern side of the Laktsang ridge, and there is a southern Aksai Chin (part of the Ladakh region of Kashmir) as part of India in the south-west. But the colonial geo-political exercise neglected the fact that these natural borders had

---

[103] Verma, 'Sino-Indian Border Dispute at Aksai Chin'.

[104] Ibid.

[105] S. Gopal's letter to the editor, *The Times Literary Supplement*, 6 February 1964.

[106] Verma, 'Sino-Indian Border Dispute at Aksai Chin'.

always existed. The post-colonial period was influenced by colonial reminders. While Peking had developed an aversion to these colonial vestiges, New Delhi had a persistent inclination towards them. This was the major area of contention in the bilateral relation between the neighbours. In short, the boundary in the western sector kept moving forward to Kunlun or retreated to Karakoram during the colonial period,[107] and this elasticity over the possession of Aksai Chin by the British and the Chinese in the late 19th and early 20th centuries caused enough damage to their post-colonial bilateralism. What is interesting is that between 1917 and 1933, Kunlun was shown as the boundary by the 'postal atlas of China'. Similarly, Sir Arthur Hirtzel, a British civil servant in India Office, commented on 10 January 1924, 'So far as we know there is no officially recognized boundary, though obviously the main Muztagh-Karakoram divide would constitute a natural frontier'.[108]

Later the Second World War, and its impact, turned attention away from these borders until India and China awoke to a new dawn of self-determination and political stability. Independent India and the PRC inherited a bilateral relation that was largely influenced by colonial legacy, but differently. They could have easily discarded any such legacy that would have influenced their bilateral relations. While China showed a kind of extreme loathing towards anything related to its 'imperialist' days, India, on the contrary, tried to have an intense passion to hold on to anything left over as an imperial legacy. When New Delhi chose to remain silent over its frontiers for a while, either relying on traditional certainty or believing in colonial dispensation, it was creating avenue for a major bilateral tussle. Having no definite boundary demarcated by the British in the Kashmir sector, what was left behind were legal claims on the presumptions and the aspirations of both sides for territorial gain. However, after the recognition by both parties of the existence of a border dispute, Peking's suggestion for border delimitations could have been accepted by New Delhi for a lasting solution to the issue.

---

[107] Ibid.

[108] Sir Arthur Hirtzel, Indian Office to V. Wellesley, the Foreign Office, dated 10 January 1924 quoted in Noorani, 'Facing the Truth'.

Even later, an overall mutual settlement of all sectors could have been possible if a determined political authority had worked passionately, keeping partisan political objectives aside. Agreeing on a division of Aksai, at the Laktsang range wherein the Sikiang–Tibet road traverses China and the withdrawal of the Chinese forces from a larger part of the Ladakh territory, which Peking has occupied since 1959, in favour of India, seems to be a possible and viable suggestion that China recognizes as a final solution. However, despite considering all these, the present position in 2020 is far different and distant away from all these thinking. Possessing the whole of Aksai Chin, China is now venturing further south in addition to the recurrent rhetoric regarding the non-recognition of McMahon Line.[109]

---

[109] Peking has been repeatedly protesting any official visits by the Government of India to Arunachal Pradesh (NEFA).

McMahon Line

History of the Mystery

Shrouded in mystery, for a long period of time, the history of the origin of the McMahon Line has continued to elude cartographers, social scientists and political strategists. Even at the time of its inception, there were deliberate attempts to conceal facts and distort the truth of its actuality by the parties involved in the work itself. Even after independence, a conspicuous lethargy was apparent in certain politico-bureaucratic circles in New Delhi in trying to ascertain the real facts behind the line and, therefore, the archival data pertaining to the issue were either kept suppressed or removed from access. Although the records relating to the mysterious origin of the line remained accessible in the archival documents of the British Museum, London, the evidence was discarded by the Indian officials deputed for the purpose of consulting on them. Consequently, the opportunity to unveil the mysterious origin of the border and thereby eliminate any precarious situation arising out of lack of consensus on the 'grey areas' between nations that had shared a two millennium-long friendship was broken.

However, after the Sino-Indian war of 1962, serious efforts were taken to unearth the cartographic riddle involving the McMahon Line. Largely initiated by the Western scholars, along with a few Indians, efforts to ascertain the nature of its origin finally attained success. These enquiries exposed the role and motives of a few imperialist cartographers and civil servants of British India between 1913 and 1949. However, the takeaway from these studies has not benefited either India or China till date for any amicable solution to the existing dispute. There is enough evidence, therefore, to assume that when the leaders of these two nations went to the negotiation table between 1954 and 1962, neither had they done their homework nor did they have any clarity of thought and relevant knowledge about the mystery behind the dispute. It was in this context that historian Karunakar Gupta, after an exhaustive study of the documents pertaining to this in the British archives stated, 'Neither Nehru nor Chou-Enlai seemed to have any knowledge of the mystery surrounding the origin of the McMahon Line'.[1]

The origin of this international borderline between north-eastern India and China (Tibet) is attributed to the Simla Conference of 1913–1914. Even when the professed aim of convening the conference by the government of British India was to reach a tripartite agreement on the Sino-Tibetan territorial limits, the ulterior motive behind such a convention was to fix the status of Tibet in such a way that it benefitted British interests. Positioning Tibet as a buffer state between India and China was envisaged as being advantageous to the British imperialist aspirations in South Asia, ensuring that any future Chinese expansionist venture beyond the Himalayan borders was averted. Hence, an autonomous Tibet with minimum Chinese influence was the most favourable option targeted by the conference.[2]

What did Sir Arthur Henry McMahon, the foreign secretary to the Government of India, target in Simla? Before going into a detailed analysis of the whole process, let us briefly understand what the objective was and what happened in Simla. In the process of determining the status of provincial Tibet in relation to China and the recognition of territorial demarcations between the two countries, the conference focused on drawing two lines on the Chinese map: (a) a red outer line between China and Tibet demarcating the total expanse of the Tibetan province distinct from China, and (b) a blue inner line demarcating the Tibetan autonomous region exclusively from the total territorial Tibet. The red line in the first category, therefore, identified the Tibetan territory as distinct from China, while the blue line was a zonal division within Tibet to identify its autonomous status as being from the Chinese-controlled area of the province. The red line naturally covered only the area where the Tibetan territory met

---

[1] Gupta, 'Distortions in the History of Sino-Indian Frontiers', 1265–1270.
[2] Refer to Chapter 1 for the buffer zone strategy.

China. It began in the far west, near Sinkiang–Tibet–Kashmir (India) tri-junction, moved eastwards covering the whole of Tibet, until the Burma–China–India (AP) tri-junction. The work should have finished here. But from here, it further moved westwards, partially demarcating the British India border with Tibet (China) covering present-day Arunachal Pradesh as well (actually, the map drawn at the conference did not demarcate all sides of the whole Tibetan borders, but only with China, and therefore, the larger part of its borders in the south-west, with Kashmir, Nepal, Sikkim[3] and Bhutan were left un-demarcated). However, this red line was extended to cover a part of present-day Arunachal Pradesh in India. What did it mean to McMahon to extend the line up to the area covering Arunachal Pradesh? If the red line was to demarcate Tibet from China, why was a larger line drawn at a single stretch extending partially bordering India?[4] The lines drawn on plain paper at the official British summer resort station in Simla, without incorporating the cartographic intricacies of the actual site, naturally fell short of geographical and natural specifications. The line in the far south, therefore, ended up un-specifically before reaching the border of Bhutan. Hence, it seems that a border definition between India and Tibet in the north-east frontier was not the professed aim of the convention, albeit McMahon had covertly attempted for this to happen. There is enough ambiguity in this action, which will be debated in the following pages.

As far as Tibet was concerned, a more specific border demarcation, distinguishing its territory from China, as well as the extent of the Tibetan autonomous region from Chinese sovereignty as a 'blessing' from the British, was the avowed aspiration of these sittings. The demarcation of a borderline between India and Tibet was neither the professed aim of the tripartite Simla Convention, nor was it a concern for either Tibet or China, and therefore the red outer line did not go into the nitty-gritty of the border between India and Tibet. But McMahon and the team had secretly made efforts for an

---

[3] Sikkim, a princely state under British India since 1890, was a protectorate under independent India and, finally, on the basis of a referendum, the monarchy was abolished. It became part of the Indian Union on 16 May 1975 as its 22nd state.

[4] This red line did not include the areas bordering present-day Uttarakhand and Himachal Pradesh in the central sector and Jammu and Kashmir in the western sector.

Indo-Tibetan border for which official sanction from Britain had never been obtained. The tripartite convention, therefore, went down in history as abortive, because China refused to sign the draft convention on the grounds of unacceptable border delimitation. However, whatever McMahon attempted to put in the papers of the draft convention and attached maps in Simla went to his credit, and the border was called after his name—the McMahon Line. Since his clandestine efforts to draw an Indo-Tibetan line had ultimately failed and it was neither sanctioned by the British authority nor signed by China, there were further 'successful' efforts by British officials later to sanctify that line on record. Actually, it was Olaf Caroe, the deputy secretary, Foreign and Political Department, who, later in 1936–1937, succeeded in obtaining the official sanction to the Indo-Tibetan border by suppressing the truth and distorting the facts in the official records. The McMahon Line, therefore, does not deserve to be named after Sir Arthur Henry McMahon; instead, a better nomenclature to this border would be the Olaf Caroe Line.

So a failed covert attempt by McMahon was later established on record by Olaf Caroe and still demarcated the border between north-eastern India and China (Tibet). While independent India recognizes the McMahon Line as a legal borderline, China disputes its validity as an imperialist devise, but the PRC accepts it as the LAC. Hence, this chapter not only discusses the failed colonial attempt to draw a Sino-Indian borderline in the north-east but also delves into the fraudulent means that they later adopted to establish such a line.

British in the 'Forgotten Frontiers'

In a series of British expansionisms in South Asia, the north-eastern tribal dominant frontier regions of India were not that easily viable for the colonialists. The colonial powers had never been that ambitious about these 'forgotten frontiers',[5] not just because of the difficult ter-

---

[5] Geoffrey Tyson, *Forgotten frontier* (Calcutta: W. H. Targett, 1945); Jonathan Glancey, *Nagaland: A Journey to India's Forgotten Frontier* (London: Faber, 2011) tell the story of the tea planters of north-eastern India and neglect of this remote region by government in New Delhi.

rain, but rather due to the difficulty in overpowering its tribal population. In the early decades of the 19th century, when the 600-year-old Ahom dynasty began to exhibit weakness due to internal rebellions and Burmese invasions (1817–1826), the British took the opportunity to invade this region.[6] Finally, after the Anglo-Burmese war (1824–1826) and the subsequent treaty (February 1826), the British acquired a larger share of Assam that extended up to the Lohit Valley (NEFA), but essentially not beyond the Brahmaputra Valley.[7] It was yet another half a century later (1886) that they were able to penetrate the hill tracks of the NEFA. Hence, most of the tribal areas of the NEFA remained autonomous until they were brought under independent India.

Gradually, even when the boundaries of the British Raj began to expand, the tribal areas of Assam and the NEFA were not accessible to Indian or British official tax collectors, and 'the British were in most places the first ever to come in contact with the aboriginal tribesmen'.[8] Colonial administrative dispensations into these outer Himalayan tribal regions from Calcutta were based on the Bengal Eastern Frontier Regulations, 1873. This regulation divided the territorial jurisdiction of these regions into two zones, namely the inner and outer lines. When the outer line or an international boundary[9] defined the actual extent of the British territory in principle, the inner line demarcated their revenue territories from the non-revenue ones.[10] The inner line had been laid down in detail and demarcated for some length[11] to prevent any

[6] Assam was under Ahom dynasty between 1228 and 1826. Records show that during their administration, except for a few pockets of Tibetan influence in the north-west, the rest of the state, particularly those bordering Myanmar in the east, was under the control of the Ahom dynasty until the advent of the British in Assam. Pranjit Agarwala, 'Is Arunachal Pradesh Part of China?' The Shillong Times, 10 January 2014.

[7] Maxwell, *India's China War*, 39.

[8] Lamb, *The China–India Border*, 130.

[9] A. G. Noorani, 'Perseverance in Peace Process', *Frontline*, 29 August 2003. Available at https://frontline.thehindu.com/world-affairs/article30218522.ece (accessed on 2 August 2020).

[10] Pradip Phanjoubam, 'How McMahon Drew His Line and Why China Wants It Changed', *The Wire*, 20 May 2015. Available at https://thewire.in/diplomacy/how-mcmahon-drew-his-line-and-why-china-wants-it-changed (accessed on 2 August 2020).

[11] Maxwell, *India's China War*, 39.

unlicensed travellers from venturing into the hills. Since the encroachment of the non-tribal community on the tribal hills was faced with stiff resistance, the British had undertaken several frequent punitive expeditions into the hills.[12] However, they were cautious enough not to resort to any provocation, and a general policy of non-interference with local tribal communities was followed.[13] So the legitimacy to assert any traditional and historical right on these Himalayan terrains populated with tribal communities in the 1950s or earlier cannot be made either by China or India. The British, if could claim any relation with the region, than others, is nothing but for their punitive expedition.

Did China Reach the Area beyond the Himalayas?

A question as to whether the Chinese had a presence in the southern part of the Himalayas at any point of time is a pertinent one. The fact is that, except for a short expedition in 1910, the Chinese had never been to the region, and no documentary evidence has suggested otherwise, and the 'Chinese assertive claim to Arunachal Pradesh is relatively recent'.[14] The last years of the Manchu dynasty (1905–1911) were marked by sudden military activism in the southern frontiers, and a very aggressive FP was followed in Tibet exercising full control over it in 1910. Britain's policy of keeping the Russians out had been rendered an anachronism.[15] And so the Chinese dominated Tibet and even established a strong presence along the Tibetan side of the Assam Himalayas.[16] After entering Lhasa, before its ultimate fall, the Chinese started probing the neighbouring principalities of Sikkim, Nepal and Bhutan.[17] Zhao Erfeng, one of the Chinese warlords, undertook an

---

[12] Phanjoubam, 'How McMahon Drew His Line and Why China Wants It Changed'.

[13] The British had undertaken punitive expeditions against tribal communities, including Khasis, Garos, Nagas, Monpas, Mishmis and Manipuris, among others.

[14] Phanjoubam, 'How McMahon Drew His Line and Why China Wants It Changed'.

[15] Maxwell, *India's China War*, 41.

[16] Hoffmann, *India and the China Crisis*, 18.

[17] Sikkim was a British protectorate. Nepal had a strong government, but it was only Bhutan that the British were worried about. Phanjoubam, 'How McMahon Drew His Line and Why China Wants It Changed'.

expedition to the region north of the Brahmaputra Valley and reached as far as Walong. Claude Arpi observes

> during the last two millennia, the Chinese have never set a foot in Arunachal Pradesh...except for one short visit in one particular location in 1910. Some Chinese officials posted near Rima, went as far south as Walong in Indian Territory where they planted boundary flags, in a place called Menilkrai.[18]

Moving into the tribal belt, the Chinese posed a threat to Assam, and they ordered the cutting of a road through the tribal belt to Assam.[19] Whether this brief incursion is enough evidence of Peking's claim to establish legitimacy over the NEFA is not even a relevant question.

Although brief, this Chinese intrusion beyond the Himalayas no doubt alarmed the British and the consequence of this was renewed urgency to create a buffer between China and the precious British investments in Assam.[20] The British apprehension was that the Chinese might challenge the influence of the British in Nepal and Bhutan, and that they might undermine the security of a long Indo-Tibetan border that had to be properly defined. The Chinese moves during the period seemed to underline this apprehension.[21] This Chinese forward movement was construed as a political and military danger to British India, which, in turn, invited countermeasures, accompanied by programmes of explorations and surveys in border regions.

British Himalayan Interest in the 'Roof of the World'

Was the Middle Kingdom powerful enough to pose a threat to the aspirations of British India beyond the Himalayas? Whether Manchu 'dynastic cycle' was in the descending order of its decay? Both these questions were immaterial for the British to explore the possibilities

---

[18] Arpi Claude, 'The McMahon Line Is Legal' (28 January 2015). Available at http://claudearpi.blogspot.com/2015/01/the-mcmahon-line-is-legal.html (accessed on 2 August 2020).

[19] Sir Robert Reid, *History of the Frontier Areas Bordering on Assam* (Shillong: Bhabani Books, 1942), 217.

[20] Guruswamy, *The Great India–China Game*.

[21] Lamb, *Tibet*, 9–10.

of venturing into Lamist Lhasa, a political hotbed for China, because Russo-phobia was still a factor in determining the British Tibet policy.[22] As early as 1886 itself, British Indian officials recommended to their home government to build a road to Tibet.[23] But such an indispensable punitive expedition, due to the hostile population, the huge expenditure that would be incurred in building a road in the region, etc., had dissuaded the home government from such a venture.

In the meantime, as a policy of its geopolitical strategy, Britain had concluded treaties with China to define Peking's border sharing with Burma (1886) and Sikkim (1890) as its protectorates. But when Tibet refused to recognize these boundaries, running through Tibetan frontiers, as defined by its Chinese suzerain, British India undertook its first expedition to Lhasa under Sir Francis Younghusband (December 1903–September 1904). After the success of this military feat, Britain imposed a treaty on Lhasa, by which diplomatic relations were established and the border disputes between Tibet and Sikkim were settled. On the basis of his research of the British archival documents, Atul Bhardwaj writes, '1904 was a watershed year in Tibetan history. It introduced a decade of large scale loot, violence and imperial lust to an otherwise tranquil land'.[24] This treaty bound the Tibetans to refuse entry of any foreign representatives other than that of Britain's.[25] So the 'British government established some kind of British protectorate over Tibet'.[26] Even when the Anglo-Chinese Convention of 1906 defined Tibet as a region belonging to China 'with restricted rights', and the Anglo-Russian Convention of 1907 took an undertaking to respect Tibet's territorial integrity[27] virtually, Britain retained certain special privileges as per the 1906 agreements with the Chinese.[28] Again, in 1908, Britain obtained a new trade regulation to govern the British

[22] Maxwell, *India's China War*, 40–41.

[23] Lamb, *The McMahon Line*, 315–317.

[24] Bhardwaj, *1914*.

[25] Maxwell, *India's China War*, 41.

[26] Guruswamy and Singh, *India China Relations*, 24.

[27] Maxwell, *India's China War*, 41

[28] Lamb, *The McMahon Line*, 255.

commercial contact with Tibet. Thus, British efforts through the period were not only to confirm Chinese suzerainty over Lhasa 'in principle' but to also ensure entry of no foreign powers into the region. This actually created the way for direct Anglo-Tibetan relations. A kind of 'active neutrality' adopted by Britain not only brought Tibet closer to them but also created a fissure between Lhasa and Peking. By 1909, the dissent of the Tibetans against Chinese authority began to gain strength, leading to a more deteriorated stage. Although Peking suppressed it ruthlessly as a result of the 1910 uprising, the 13th Dalai Lama took asylum in Darjeeling, British India. Even though this helped China to reassert power in Tibet, which hitherto had not been possible since the 1880s,[29] the Tibetan autonomy was getting strengthened under the patronage of the British Indian authority.

The British were of the view that, in the absence of a firm border-line with China, a buffer between China and their precious Indian possession was desirable. Further, British explorations and surveys in border regions were carried out with this objective. The British 'forward school' also argued for firm British control over the north-east in anticipation of further Chinese moves.[30] Thus, during 1911–1913, there were several explorations that strengthened British knowledge of the region's topography and population patterns. 'The Assam Lieutenant Governor, the Army General Staff, and senior officials in the administration were in essence, probing for the contours of a boundary line from which the Tibetans and Chinese could be kept out'.[31] Despite the new Viceroy Lord Hardinge's reservation against the proposition of the forward school,[32] the Noel Williamson incident of 1911 forced the British to move a punitive expedition against the tribal region. The expedition team was also instructed to obtain the requisite information for a suitable boundary between India and China. Now Hardinge

---

[29] Ibid., 226–227.

[30] Maxwell, *India's China War*, 42.

[31] Guruswamy and Singh, *India China Relations*, 25.

[32] Sir Robert Reid, *History of the Frontier Areas Bordering on Assam*, 222. In 1911, despite the government's refusal to approve patrolling across the outer line, a British official, Noel Williamson, crossed the outer line to explore the extent of Tibetan influence in the area and was murdered by tribesmen.

announced a policy reversal to ensure 'a sound strategic boundary between Tibet and the tribal territory'.[33] Meanwhile, the Qing dynasty came to a permanent end in 1911, and this new environment renewed British interest in the border region of India as well, and a military expedition was sent to the area in 1912–1913. Later, in 1914, incorporating the tribal majority area of British Assam, a new administrative set-up was created, namely the North-East Frontier Tracts. After ensuring internal political consolidation in the tribal region, after reaching agreements with tribal leaders who controlled a major part of the territory, British India turned its attention towards stabilizing the international front and determining the status of Tibet.

Lhasa's Call for Autonomy under British Backing

The diminishing vigour of the Middle Kingdom had serious impact on the peripheries of China, and they were largely buttressed by the imperialist interventions from both sides.[34] The British strategy in Tibet had been devised to accommodate a kind of anti-Peking euphoria that provided enough scope and space for the political ambition of Lhasa. Naturally, when the Republican Revolution of 1911 in Nanking pulled down the Manchu dynasty, it had a strong impact in Lhasa as well. In November 1911, Tibet revolted against the Peking agent (Amban) in Lhasa, asserted their autonomy and insisted on the return of the deposed Dalai Lama to Lhasa.[35] The rebels had toppled the Chinese superstructure in Lhasa, and their troops were driven across Nathu La by 1913. The new Republican Chinese government construed that a British Dalai Lama alliance had been nurtured in Darjeeling during 1910–1912[36] for a pro-Lamist aspiration in Lhasa. The republican government under Yuan Shikai, who had managed to head

---

[33] Maxwell, *India's China War*, 44.

[34] The territorial integrity of dynastic China was undermined in the north as well as the west, supported by the imperialist ambition of Russia, which encouraged Mongolia and Sinkiang to question the political sovereignty of Peking.

[35] Bhardwaj, *1914*.

[36] *Ibid.* The British had transported the fleeing Chinese to Calcutta, and then to Shanghai; Guruswamy and Singh, *India China Relations*, 25–26.

the government, however, adopted a proactive conciliatory attitude towards Lama and his followers, allowing the Lama to return to Lhasa with all the privileges he enjoyed earlier. The Chinese government agent in Lhasa, who had perpetrated atrocities against the Tibetans, was dismissed and a new government was appointed in Tibet.

Britain Stands for Tibet's Autonomy

In the political environment that emerged with the fall of the Ching dynasty and a reciprocal Yuan Shikai on the throne, Whitehall felt the need for active intervention in favour of Tibetan autonomy and also to secure the Indian borders. On 13 January 1912, the Foreign Office in London sought the opinion of its officials in India about a possible British involvement in Tibet, without harming the interest of the English settlements in China, but which would serve their aspirations in Tibet. The officials of British India were enthused about opposing inclusion of Tibet in China proper in order to better serve British interests.[37] Overwhelmed at the proposal, the political officer in Sikkim, C. A. Bell, went a step further and proposed that the Chinese would not be allowed to go to Tibet via India and join hands with Bhutan, Nepal and Sikkim to deny rice to Chinese soldiers stationed in Tibet. An excited Henry McMahon proposed 'active assistance to Tibet' by providing money and arms, in addition to temporarily deputing British officers for the organization of their forces.[38] Excited officials in British India considered an immediate bilateral talk between Tibet and China under the supervision of the British home government. But Sir J. Jordon, the British minister in Peking, opposed the idea of a Sino-Tibetan bilateral dialogue and insisted on a tripartite agreement.[39] After obtaining consent for the tripartite dialogue, on 17 August 1912, Jordan submitted a memorandum to the Chinese government placing conditions on which the negotiations should progress. This memorandum

---

[37] Bhardwaj, *1914*.

[38] Ibid.

[39] The Tripartite agreement was opposed by the government because Britain did not want to get entangled in the process of its implementation. But India's viceroy was able to convince London on a tripartite conference.

had restrained Peking's right to intervene in the internal administration of Tibet and also suggested a reduction in the number of the Chinese troops maintained at Lhasa.

But Yuan Shikai refused the demands on the basis of Article II of the 1906 Anglo-Chinese Convention, yet maintained that Britain would have the right to trade with Tibet as per the 1906 agreement. The British thereby reassured Yuan on the autonomous status of Tibet. They neither wanted to establish a protectorate nor annex that—their intention was to protect the British Indian borders and, as a friendly government, would not interfere with their frontier and trade interests. They also maintained that the Chinese would enjoy suzerainty rights over Tibet, but without jeopardizing the British interest in the territory and its borderlines. A military option, however, was not considered among other reasons. But McMahon opposed the idea of reinstallation of China in Tibet, as he feared that it would lead Russia to sign an agreement with Tibet along the lines of the Mongolian agreement. McMahon had cunningly put forth another condition before Yuan that, if his cooperation was ensured, the British acknowledgement of the legitimacy of the new Republic under him would be offered.[40] However, even before going to the discussion table, there were still several points on which China and Britain disagreed with each other.

Finally, a tripartite convention among China, Tibet and British India was decided upon, and in January 1913 the Chinese agreed to resume negotiations on the basis of the memorandum of 17 August 1912.[41] On 13 June 1913, Yuan Shikai, eager to protect his 'monarchical aspiration', revoked his earlier (21 April 1912) presidential order, which reiterated that Tibet was an administered province of China and emphasized on the tripartite nature of the Simla Conference.[42] On 7 August 1913,

---

[40] This was originally a suggestion put forth by Major W. F. T. O'Connor on 21 April 1912.

[41] In a memorandum addressed to China on 17 August 1912, they did not recognize China's sovereignty over Tibet and declared that China was no more than a suzerain. R. P. Anand, *Studies in International Law and History: An Asian Perspective* (Boston, MA: Springer, 2004), 116.

[42] R. S. Kalha, *The McMahon Line: A Hundred Years On* (New Delhi: The Institute for Defence Studies and Analyses, 2014). Available at https://idsa.in/idsacomments/TheMcMahonLine_rskalha_030714 (accessed on 20 October 2020).

the Chinese Foreign Minister wrote to the British government that the Chinese plenipotentiary would proceed to India to 'open negotiations for a treaty jointly with the Tibetan and British plenipotentiaries'.[43] On behalf of Tibet, the Dalai Lama requested the British to send a delegate to discuss the terms of peace with General Chung in India in March 1913.[44] Accordingly, it was all set for a tripartite convention to begin soon at the British Indian summer capital of Simla.

On 28 July 1913, in the House of Lords, Morley presented the objective of Britain in convening the Simla Conference as an attempt to mend relations between China and Tibet, with Britain being the 'honest broker'.[45] So the British government's primary objective in convening the convention was not to draw a borderline between India and Tibet, as is generally assumed, but to formalize the independent status of Tibet and to ensure the stability of this Himalayan territory during the complex political turmoil that prevailed thereafter. At the same time, the British Indian authorities had already visualized a plan by taking cue from the successful Russian division of Mongolia, for a similar division of Tibet into 'outer' and 'inner' with 'outer Tibet' as a buffer zone between China and India. Although it was not the professed aim of British Indian officials to demarcate an Indo-Tibetan border in the conference, it seems, as later developments attest, that such an idea was part of their planned scheme and that they had ulterior motives behind it.

Tripartite Simla Accord in Stalemate (1913–1914)

On 13 October 1913, Sir Arthur Henry McMahon choreographed 'an intricate exercise in diplomacy, power politics and espionage'[46] in Simla. The members present were Henry McMahon, the foreign secretary to the Government of India, who presided over the sessions,

---

[43] Ibid.

[44] The department of foreign and political affairs in India was pushing London on the grounds that they were receiving repeated requests from the Dalai Lama to help him make Tibet independent.

[45] Lamb, *The McMahon Line*, 468.

[46] Maxwell, *India's China War*, 47.

C. A. Bell and Rose (British),[47] Lonchen Shatra, Techi Kusho, Depon Taradeba and Kusho Nyendron (Tibet) and Ivan Chen, an experienced diplomat at the Chinese embassy in London, accompanied by subordinates Shah and Wang (China). While an overwhelmingly enthusiastic Tibetan team had reached Simla quite early, on 24 September 1913 itself, as their spiritual and political head Lama had been repeatedly requesting the British for such a meeting, a reluctant Chinese team had reached the venue as late as 3 October 1913, after a month-long sea voyage via Singapore. It is reported that in Simla, while Ivan Chen was desperately trying to convince the British that Tibet was part of China,[48] the British were treating the Chinese and the Tibetan delegates on equal footing so as to convey the message of an independent status to Tibet. On the other side, it is also reported that, as a reciprocal gesture to ensure the cooperation of Peking, McMahon assured Chen at a courtesy meeting on 7 October 1913 that Great Britain would recognize the Chinese Republic under President Yuan Shikai.[49]

The conference, which began on 13 October 1913, witnessed protracted deliberations and debates between the plenipotentiaries of China and Tibet, and lasted several months until it reached a deadlock. In the meanwhile, McMahon had drafted a resolution on 10 November 1913 in a hurry and it was forwarded to the Government of India, the authorities in London and to the British minister in Peking for their consideration. The proposal envisaged the division of Tibet into inner and outer zones. Nevertheless, Chen refused to discuss the division of Tibet but insisted that the following discussions were a priority: (a) the political status of Tibet, (b) the reinstatement of a Peking representative (Amban) in Lhasa and (c) frontier issues, in addition to a clause that (d) any finality of decision should be ratified by Peking.

---

[47] McMahon was considered to be an expert in drawing boundary lines as he had spent two years demarcating the Durand Line on the north-west frontier of India.

[48] Bhardwaj notes that Ivan Chen was making efforts to impress upon the British that the Chinese were free to move in and out of Tibet, and he had been trying to convince others on their hold on Tibet by informing the British that their 'party had brought very warm clothes for wearing in Tibet, where they expect to go immediately after the conference'. Bhardwaj, *1914*.

[49] Ibid.

The deliberations prolonged over two months until it was suspended for winter vacation, to be reconvened on 12 January 1914. In the subsequent session on 17 January 1914, McMahon again announced his proposal to divide Tibet into inner and outer regions. It is alleged that in this proposal, McMahon recognized an extended Tibetan territory covering the whole area included in Lonchen's claim and, after that, the entire area was divided into two zones, namely inner Tibet and outer Tibet.[50] According to the proposal, while the integrity of Tibet as a geographical and political entity was respected, China was allowed to exercise its historical rights to control only inner Tibet, while outer Tibet under Lhasa was granted autonomy. This proposal, however, was not acceptable to both parties (China and Tibet) and, therefore, on 7 March 1914, they communicated their reservations against the actual proposal. Ivan Chen held that China would be willing to grant limited autonomy in an area of Lhasa and a large division of Tibetan autonomous region would not be acceptable. The main objection of China was (blue line) on the boundary between the inner and outer divisions. The Tibetans also defied the proposal for an inner zone under China and maintained that the whole of Tibet, irrespective of the inner or outer areas, belonged to the direct jurisdiction of the Lhasa government. The Tibetan team justified that they had enjoyed the rights to levy and collect taxes, appoint hereditary chiefs, etc., in the whole region of Tibet. Similarly, after receiving directions and documentary clarification from Peking on 19 March, Ivan Chen presented his arguments at the convention, rejecting the zonal division as unacceptable. Since both parties were aggrieved about the nature of the proposal, the convention was heading towards failure.

Secret Bilateral Negotiation and 'Foetal Death' of the 'McMahon Line'

While the inconclusive tripartite conference focusing on the larger issue of the division of Tibet was pending in Simla, a secret bilateral meeting between British officials and Tibetans (in the absence of Ivan Chen) was also reported to be in progress in Delhi. It was

[50] Ibid.

rumoured that 'in February and March 1914 secret meetings were held in Delhi between representatives of Britain and Tibet, to discuss the Tibet-NEFA boundary, the result of which helped to arrive at the creation of the "so-called McMahon line."'[51] Accordingly, McMahon and Lonchen Shatra concluded an agreement on the division of Tibet and the boundary between north-eastern British India and Tibet as a package deal, and for this secret consensus, notes were exchanged in Delhi on 24 and 25 March 1914.[52]

It seems that, at the inception of the idea of the Simla Conference itself, the officials of British India had intended to reach an agreement with Tibet on the Indo-Tibetan border. But this was absolutely beyond the perception of their government in London. It is quite natural, at this point, to raise a question as to why the British considered keeping the terms of such a treaty secret? The British apprehension of the impact of such a direct Anglo-Tibetan agreement seems to be on account of not merely provoking Peking but fearing that (a) it would become a breach of the 1907 Anglo-Russian Convention,[53] (b) it would also be against the terms of the Anglo-Chinese Convention of 1906 but, above all, (c) McMahon was particularly concerned about the secrecy of such a deal with Lhasa, because he desired to get a more favourable alignment to the Indian border from Tibetans and in return was reportedly lenient to Tibet in their bargaining with Peking. The existing debate between the PRC and New Delhi over Tawang should be studied in this light. China was kept in the dark about such a secret discussion in Delhi during February–March 1914.[54] Accordingly, both sides agreed on a new boundary line running along the crest of the Himalayas and the British political officer in Sikkim, Charles Bell, made necessary arrangements for the deal. It was acceptable to the Tibetans and was confirmed by an exchange

---

[51] Maxwell, *India's China War*, 49–50.

[52] Liu, 'Look Beyond the Sino-Indian Border Dispute'.

[53] According to the 1907 Anglo-Russian agreement, Britain and Russia were barred from negotiating directly with Tibet 'except through mediation or permission of China'.

[54] Karunakar Gupta, 'The McMahon Line 1911–45: The British Legacy', *The China Quarterly*, no. 47 (1971): 521–545. Available at http://www.jstor.org/stable/652324 (accessed on 2 August 2020).

of letters between McMahon and the Tibetan plenipotentiary on 24 and 25 March 1914.[55]

As per this understanding, Tawang was included in British India, but in order to maintain secrecy, the letters exchanged did not describe this boundary. Instead, it was shown on an attached map in a sealed cover. The letters did not include a verbal description of the new boundary and did not mention any principle upon which it had been drawn, so that the only authority on the McMahon alignment lay in the original maps, copies of which were kept with the Lhasa authorities and the British authorities.[56] So the irony about McMahon's extended red line beyond the Sino-Tibetan region, covering India's north-eastern borders, discussed at the beginning of this chapter, is revealed.

The boundary fixed on the basis of this secret agreement later came to be exclusively known as the McMahon Line.[57] Whether or not China got information of these hushed talks, ill-feeling and distrust developed among the participants of the convention leading to a possible deadlock. In this context, by 14 April, there were talks of Chinese withdrawal from the negotiations and a consequent breakdown in the convention. Despite the deadlock, Ivan continued to be present during further meetings and, on 21 April, presented the Chinese demands as received from Peking,[58] signalling to the British officials that the convention was moving in the direction of failure. However, on 22 April 1914, McMahon submitted a draft proposal of the convention with the map to be initialled, but clarified that, in the event of refusal to initial the draft, the entire proposal would be withdrawn.[59]

As discussed earlier, the attached map had demarcated two lines, red and blue—the first depicting Tibet as a geographical and political unit, and the second dividing Tibet into inner Tibet and outer

[55] Lamb, *The McMahon Line*, 618; Woodman, *Himalayan Frontiers*, 384–385.

[56] Maxwell, *India's China War*, 51.

[57] Gupta, 'The McMahon Line 1911–45'.

[58] Bhardwaj, *1914*.

[59] Bhardwaj writes that, after this, Ivan Chen was locked up in an intense 10-hour discussion at the Foreign Office. According to McMahon, this prolonged interview was of little interest because Ivan Chen did not raise any substantial issue.

Tibet. The red line in its southern extension curved round to show the boundary between Tibet and India, and it followed the alignment that McMahon had agreed upon with the Tibetans.[60] The red line, however, was not specific on the western extremity near the Bhutan border, leaving the nature of Tawang uncertain[61] as per the maps submitted to this tripartite session.[62] In order to avert a deadlock, the Chinese representatives were offered some minor concessions and, after extensive discussions with his team members, in order to avoid an impasse, Ivan Chen finally agreed on 27 April 1914 to initial the draft[63] on the condition of ratification from Peking; he also clarified that 'to initial and to sign are two different actions', and that his initials would not bind his government, whose views he would immediately seek.[64] But, on 28 April, the government of China, in a telegraph, informed Chen to explicitly notify McMahon that he 'was forced to initial the draft convention, the Chinese government cannot accept it. You should declare it invalid'.[65] Accordingly, on 29 April, Chen informed McMahon that his government had disavowed his initialling of the draft convention and declined to recognize the settlement. The British, however, intimated to the Tibetan team that China had agreed to all the clauses of the agreement except Article IX relating to the boundary.[66]

McMahon was quite eager to complete the prolonged process of the convention by formalizing the status of the treaty and, therefore, on 17 June 1914, he wrote to London expressing his desire to sign

---

[60] Maxwell, *India's China War*, 52.

[61] Liu, 'Look Beyond the Sino-Indian Border Dispute'.

[62] Government of India, *Atlas of the Northern Frontier* (New Delhi: Government of India, 1960); PRC, *The Sino-Indian Boundary Question*.

[63] Bhardwaj, *1914*.

[64] 'Ivan Chen's Notes Concerning the Simla Conference', in *A Selection of Documents and Materials Concerning the Tibet Issue* (Beijing: Xinhua News Press, 1959), 299. Quoted in Bhardwaj, *1914*.

[65] The Chinese Foreign Office's telegraph of April 28 1914 to Ivan Chen in *A Selection of Documents and Materials Concerning the Tibet Issue* (Beijing: Xinhua News Press, 1959), 301. Quoted in Bhardwaj, *1914*.

[66] Refer to note 80.

the agreement. But the telegram message from the secretary of state for India stated that, pending further instructions, he should 'not sign the convention unless the Chinese delegate also signs'.[67] Once again, on 21 June 1914, the secretary of state for India confirmed that the Foreign Office was strongly averse to a separate convention with Tibet. So, while McMahon repeatedly tried to convince the home government to formalize a bilateral treaty with Tibet, the home government insisted on a restrained course of action.

The Government of India continued its efforts to convince the home government on the one side and to pressurize China on the other. On the final date of the convention, 3 July 1914, when all three parties attended the session, McMahon announced the draft of the convention, but once again Ivan Chen refused to sign it and, therefore, the draft was amended to conclude the treaty on a bilateral basis between Britain and Tibet, and it was initialled on the same day only by McMahon and Lonchen Shatra.[68] 'The signing took place with the knowledge of Ivan Chen although he was sent into the next room while it took place, but he was not told what was being signed'.[69] Before McMahon proceeded to sign the bilateral agreement with the Tibetans, London had forbidden him, by clear instruction, from entering into a bilateral agreement with Tibet without Chinese consent. However, the instruction did not reach him in time, as it was delayed, and he signed the (bilateral) agreement before the communiqué reached him.[70] However, 'London gave retrospective approval to McMahon's action as *fait accompli*'.[71]

What were the reasons for the refusal on the side of Peking? Since the Indo-Tibetan (China) border demarcation was secretly concluded and was not part of the written documentation, there was no reason for a refusal regarding the so-called McMahon Line along the NEFA border. The fact is that the Chinese refusal was on the ground of the zonal division (by red line between China and Tibet) designed

---

[67] Quoted in Bhardwaj, *1914*.

[68] Liu, 'Look Beyond the Sino-Indian Border Dispute'.

[69] Maxwell, *India's China War*, 49.

[70] Woodman, *Himalayan Frontiers*, 176.

[71] Gupta, 'The McMahon Line 1911–45'.

to serve the separation of a great part of Tibet from China. Their 'opposition to the proposal was oblique...focusing not on the essence, the question of division, but on where the proposed line of division should run. This was the issue upon which the conference finally broke down'.[72] 'Thus the Simla Conference ended in diplomatic hugger-mugger with two participants in what was meant to be a tripartite conference openly signing a secret declaration'.[73] Thus, the final outcome from Simla was a fractured mandate through a secret bilateral agreement instead of a tripartite one and, therefore, the Chinese claimed that it was not bound by the terms of the agreement.

Writing in his final report to London, McMahan himself admitted, 'It is with great regret that I leave India without having secured the formal adherence of the Chinese government, to a tripartite agreement'.[74] An unwilling Yuan Shikai, prompted by inducement and hope for a better deal from the British, had sent his representative to Simla. But all that was shattered in the Anglo-Tibetan secret deal that left only mutual distrust between the participants. The Chinese expressed their help-lessness in the situation against what was expected in Simla. Hence, on 6 July 1914, a desperate Ivan Chen wrote to McMahon regarding his government's latest message that stated, 'The Government of China has no right to alienate any portion of her territory and this account for their inability to sign the Tripartite Convention'.[75]

Simla Convention: An Appraisal

As far as the principal objective of the tripartite Simla Conference was concerned, it was a total failure on account of the Chinese refusing to sign the draft. There were major and minor concerns for China in the terms of reference of the convention, as it necessitated the disowning of the sovereign right that it had once enjoyed in Tibet. The Chinese objec-tion to the proposal was mainly based on two grounds. The first was the

---

[72] Maxwell, *India's China War*, 48.

[73] Ibid., 49.

[74] Ibid.

[75] Quoted in Bhardwaj, *1914*. *Reuters* reported a failure of the convention.

proposed zonal division in Article IX on the basis of which the Chinese administration had been restricted from certain areas. Whatever the draft reiterated in stating that the treaty recognized 'Chinese suzerainty in Tibet', this article and the attached map demarcated larger tracks of territory under Tibet, and the demarcation of an extended inner Tibetan autonomous region was a larger concern, while the outer line demarcation and its specifications were minor ones for them. It is suggested that the Chinese objected only to Article IX of the Simla Convention that laid down the boundaries between inner and outer Tibet,[76] with an implication that China had not first objected to the Indo-Tibetan borderline. However, the fact of the matter is that this is the only article of the draft that refers to the borderlines and about an attached map mentioning the red and blue lines together. There were neither any separate articles regarding the red and blue lines nor even a separate sentence.[77] The Chinese were more concerned with their loss of sovereign rights in Tibet, which was embodied in the draft, specifically in Article IX. Hence, the argument that China refused to accept only the inner line and that it did not refuse or mention anything about the red outer line, or more specifically the part of the red line demarcating India and Tibet, does not stand. China had repeatedly lodged its protest and disagreements with the plan in Simla, and Ivan Chen had already communicated to McMahon that 'With the exception of Article Nine of the draft convention, we are prepared to take the main principles, embodied in the other articles, into favorable consideration'.[78] Again, immediately before the final sitting on 3 July 1914, Ivan Chen emphatically said,

---

[76] Kalha, *The McMahon Line*.

[77] Article IX of the convention states:

> For the purpose of the present Convention the borders of Tibet, and the boundary between Outer and Inner Tibet, shall be as shown in Red and Blue respectively on the map attached hereto. Nothing in the present Convention shall be held to prejudice the existing rights of the Tibetan Government in Inner Tibet, which include the power to select and appoint the high priests of monasteries and to retain full control in all matters affecting religious institutions.

Agreement signed between the PRC, Tibet and British Government in India, MEA, Government of India.

[78] Chen to McMahon, 26 April 1914, Proceedings of the 7th Meeting/Annexure 3. L/P&S/10/344. [File No. P.464/1913, Pt. 5]. Kalha, *The McMahon Line*.

'This government has several times stated that it gives its support to the majority of the articles of the Convention. The part it is unable to agree is that dealing with the question of the boundary'.[79] Here as well, the reference was to 'the boundary' without a separate mention on the inner or outer boundary.

The second issue that the Chinese protested was the alleged secret agreement reached on the Indo-Tibetan border. The basic premise on which the British convened the conference was to give an autonomous status to Tibet and to keep Chinese power away from the borders of India. As per the perception of the London authority, the delimitation of the Indo-Tibetan borders was not among the purposes of the conference. But it seems likely that McMahon and team had, from the beginning itself, set a goal for an Indo-Tibetan boundary out of the Simla Conference. No doubt, the plans and programmes of the convention were directed to that end. Accordingly, a secret agreement defined a new boundary alignment

> advancing the limits of the British territory from a line along the foot of the hills to the crest-line of the Assam Himalayas, some 60 miles to the north. Such a boundary would not only put a wide swathe of tribal, no-man's land, within India; but would also annex a salient of Tibetan territory, adjacent to Bhutan, which ran right down to the plains, the Tawang Tract.[80]

It is suggested that the military in India had been urging a rectification of the boundary in this sector since June 1912.[81] So a secret attempt to redefine the Indo-Tibetan border, favourable to British interests, was successfully completed in collusion with the Tibetans, the result of which was covertly incorporated[82] in the draft of the tripartite conference. China could not have made an official denial of the specifications

---

[79] L/P&S/10/718. [File No. P.3260/1917 Pt.6] John Jordan to British Foreign Office no. 250 dated 30 June 1914 contains memo from Wai Chiao Pu (Chinese Foreign Office) dated 29 June 1914 containing paragraph cited. Ibid.

[80] Gupta, 'The McMahon Line 1911–45'.

[81] India Office Records (IOR): L/P & S/10/181. Confidential Note by Chief of General Staff, 1 June 1912.

[82] While the draft convention was silent on the specifications of the Indo-Tibetan border, an attached map in two sheets of papers in a sealed cover provided the details.

of an Indo-Tibetan borderline then and there, as it was not formally included in the details of the tripartite meeting, and what was perceived from the rumours of a secret meeting had not been specifically disclosed to the Chinese except what was shown on the map as an extension to the red line on the area of the Indio-Tibetan borders. The nitty-gritty of the southern extension of the red line would not have perturbed China as of then (1914), as the area was exclusively in the Tibet autonomous territory (not even in the outer Tibet under Chinese control). So the Chinese rejection to sign the draft in toto was basically about the borders defined against its will. It was nothing specific to the Indo-Tibetan border which, as of then, was insignificant for the reasons explained, but the issue became a concern only later when China forcefully annexed Tibet (1950) and began to share the border with India. Gupta argues that the McMahon Line was not dealt with at the Simla Conference and that it had been called to fix the Sino-Tibetan boundary. 'The India Office records indicate that the British Cabinet as well as the Chinese government were kept in the dark about McMahon's attempts to negotiate a new boundary with Tibetans'.[83] The record suggests that no clear intimation of this intention was ever given to the Foreign Office in London, which might well have judged such an attempt as being against Britain's wider interests, and thus forbidden it. On 23 July 1914, the Viceroy, Lord Hardinge, made it clear to the home government that the proposals from McMahon regarding India's north-eastern frontier with China were purely his personal views. Forwarding a copy of the Final Memorandum of McMahon to the secretary of state, London, Hardinge wrote:

> we recognize that a consideration of the eastern or Indo-Chinese portion of the North-Eastern Frontier did not form part of the functions of the Conference; and we would therefore request that the views and proposals put forward may be regarded as personal to Sir Henry McMahon, and not at present carrying the endorsement of the Government of India. As soon as we have time to examine this enclosure we shall address Your Lordship separately with reference to various points raised therein.[84]

[83] Gupta, 'Distortions in the History of Sino-Indian Frontiers', 1265–1270.

[84] Hardinge to Crew, 23 July 1914, India Office Records: Pol. 464: Pts. 5 & 6: L/P & S/10/344. Political and Secret Memo 13, 206. No. 90 of 1914 GOI. Foreign and Political Department.

Writing to C. A. Bell on 3 September 1915, the foreign secretary to the Government of India observed, 'the negotiations conducted last year in Simla broke down simply and solely because the Government of India attempted to secure for Tibet greater advantages than the Chinese Government were prepared to concede'.[85] He also added that since 'the convention had not been signed by the Chinese government or accepted by the Russian government...it becomes invalid and does not give any advantage to China'.[86]

During the prolonged negotiations in Simla, and even after its conclusion, China was found to be eager about reconciliation. It had responded to the British on three occasions after the 1914 dispersal. Immediately after the bilateral decision of 3 July 1914, on 6 July, Chen expressed Chinese helplessness in the signing of a tripartite decision mandating them to alienate their territory. Chinese initiatives of a similar nature for reviving the Tripartite Conference of 3 July 1914 were found in 1915 and 1916.[87] But the British policy of accommodating a powerful Tibet, annihilating Chinese interest, annoyed the latter. Britain had induced China, once again, to come to the negotiation table for a tripartite discussion in 1919, under the threat that, if Peking refused, Britain would recognize Tibet as 'an autonomous state under the suzerainty of China and deal with Tibet in future on that basis'.[88] China did not fall into this but, at the same time, avoided an outright refusal on account of a totally disturbed internal political situation. However, on 30 May 1919, the Chinese foreign minister conveyed a strong objection to the British perception of the Sino-Tibetan boundary on the basis of the Simla Convention of 1914.[89] The British policy towards Tibet in the later years further testified to its anti-China attitude by extending 'military aid, arms and ammunition, and training in their use' to the Tibetan rebels.[90]

---

[85] India Office Records: Pol. 464: Pts. 5 & 6: L/P & S/10/344. No. 448 E. B. Simla, 3 September 1915. From Foreign Secretary to the Government of India to C. A. Bell.

[86] I.O.R.: Pol. 464: Pts. 5 & 6: L/P & S/10/344. No. 448 E. B. Simla, 3 September 1915. From Foreign Secretary to the Government of India to C. A. Bell, Political Officer in Sikkim.

[87] Guruswamy and Singh, *India–China Relations*, 28.

[88] H. E. Richardson, *Tibet and Its History* (London: Shambhala, 1962), 122–123.

[89] Agarwala, 'Is Arunachal Pradesh Part of China?'

[90] Richardson, *Tibet and Its History*, 124.

The Chinese Dilemma in Simla

The Chinese failure in Simla is explained from multiple aspects. First, even when the Convention reiterated Chinese suzerainty over Tibet, the Chinese dilemma in Simla was that it was constrained to accept an equal status with Tibet and that the Chinese plenipotentiary, Ivan Chen, was treated on par with the Tibetan counterpart. China was forced to negotiate the border and other issues with Lonchen Shatra on an equal footing for an independent foreign policy for Tibet. So, taking advantage of the prevailing political turmoil in the country, Britain bestowed Tibet with a higher disposition at the cost and displeasure of China. Yuan Shikai had no choice but to accept these terms as he was deeply preoccupied with internal strives and was eager to see himself as the monarch of the Peking throne.

Second, when Britain professed the idea of dividing Tibet into two zones, the Chinese acquiescence for this was partially obtained. But their strong objection was registered only against a larger extent of the autonomous area under Tibet,[91] and the specifications of the Indo-Tibetan boundary which falls under the autonomous region of inner Tibet did not much bother the Chinese then. But the Chinese awareness of an intriguing secret deal for an Indo-Tibetan border had perturbed them, and it was a major concern, even if the nitty-gritty of it was not in their immediate attention. Hence, the southward extension of the red outer line was still not further investigated. Even when the Simla Convention failed, due to the absence of a tripartite consensus, the Tibetans followed these definitions of the border which falls within their autonomous area. It was this borderline that was later falsely recreated on records by British officials in India. However, once the convention failed to reach an amicable solution, especially pertaining to Article IX, Ivan Chen and the Chinese government unsuccessfully tried to follow up on the Simla Convention for years, even after its dispersal in 1914.

Third, questions were raised on China's silence over the border map with India, drawn in Simla, for a long period of time until the

---

[91] It is a fact that the Chinese had agreed, in principle, on most of the articles of the convention except Article 9 with respect to border delimitations.

1950s. Peking's silence on the boundary is explained in terms of their indifference to the tribal country north of Assam as, by and large, they were excluded from Tibet until 1949, under the British patronage of the latter. Moreover, 'the Chinese claim to this territory had no historical validity; they were never physically present on this frontier except briefly in 1910–11, when they probed it on a few occasions'.[92] China did not pursue it any further until the Chinese Communist Party (CCP) came to power in 1949 because the Peking government had not exercised any control over inner Tibet, including the Indo-Tibetan border region, after 1912. The borderlines were under the political jurisdiction of the Lhasa government, over which the Chinese had no direct control. Later, neither during the domination of provincial warlords in major parts of the country, nor when it was preoccupied in a civil war (nationalist versus communist), the Peking government was perturbed about the status of its southernmost borderline until the Tibetan rebel uprisings called their attention to the issues. However, the Chinese republic had brought out a few communications in the 1940s expressing regret over the nature of British India's border perception in the south.

Fourth, it is suggested that China was not 'forced' to attend the Simla Conference, nor did Chen's performance suggest in any way that he was negotiating 'under duress'.[93] The fact of the matter is that China was brought to the negotiation table after several repeated efforts, and Yuan was urged to delegate his team on the implication that the new Chinese Republican government would get Britain's formal recognition. In this situation, even when a bitter prescription was put forth by McMahon, China was neither prepared to accept nor reject it outright, because 'weakness had brought an unwilling China to the conference, weakness and the coercive diplomatic method of Britain and McMahon (had) kept her there'.[94] In the words of a Chinese official, Lu-Hsing, China went to Simla because 'our country is at present in an enfeebled condition, our external relations are involved and difficult and

---

[92] Guruswamy and Singh, *India–China Relations*, 28.

[93] Ibid.

[94] Maxwell, *India's China War*, 47.

our finances embarrassed'.[95] The newly born Republican government under Yuan was desperate to get international recognition amid a totally turbulent internal polity.

Finally, in Simla, McMahon was largely generous to Lonchen Shatra, while he was found to be less negotiable to Ivan Chen's demands. The British delegation in Simla worked throughout the session 'in close cooperation not far short of collusion, with the Tibetans'.[96] It is suggested that the convention in Simla ultimately failed because the government of (British) India had been 'unduly anxious to secure the best terms they could for Tibet'.[97] This was evident even before the beginning of the conference, as it was attended by 'the Tibetans quite eagerly while the Chinese were under constraint'.[98] Since the British interests in Tibet were in tune with the aspirations of the Tibetans, they worked throughout the conference in cooperation and collusion with the British. It was under these circumstances that London reached a conclusion that the convention failed 'simply and solely because the government of India attempted to secure for Tibet greater advantage than the Chinese government were prepared to concede'. The case of Tawang is an apt example of this British complacency with respect to Tibet. The British policy of supporting Tibetan autonomy later made for strong reluctance on the part of Tibet to relinquish their rights in Tawang. The Tawang region was a major point of dispute between Tibet and India. Later it became the crux of the tussle between the PRC and independent India.[99]

[95] Quoted in Woodman, *Himalayan Frontiers*, 166.

[96] Maxwell, *India's China War*, 47.

[97] IOR.L/PS/10/344 letter no. 448 EB from the Foreign secretary to the Government of India to Bell, dated 3 September 1915, in C. A. Bell in Melvyn C. Goldstein, *A History of Modern Tibet 1913–51: The Demise of the Lamist State* (Berkeley, CA: University of California Press, 1991), 80.

[98] Gupta, 'The McMahon Line 1911–45'.

[99] There were three maps related to the Simla Conference. One attached to the 24 March notes, another to the 27 April convention and the third to 3 July, the final day of the Convention. As far as the Tawang tract was concerned, all three maps show the McMahon Line quite differently. On the first map, the McMahon Line was shown running along south of the Thagla range far north of Tawang (including in British India).

Fractured Mandate from Simla and British Ambivalence

A few pertinent questions arise here. Why was the outcome of the Simla Convention (1914) lying in a dormant state until it was resurrected in 1929? Why was the attempted demarcation of an Indo-Tibetan border forgotten over the next two decades even by its own creators? It is a fact that while the government in London had downplayed the outcome of the convention, the officials in Delhi were not that eager to disclose the actuality of the border for a long time. This attitude of ambivalence in formalizing the finality of the Simla Convention and its outcome is explained in various contexts. First, the British home government was convinced of failure on the part of McMahon and his team in Simla and, therefore, the London authority was not willing to accept the fractured mandate that the officials in India claimed to have obtained in Simla. Since the Chinese repudiated the Simla Convention, the British government concluded that McMahon's efforts were abortive and the objective of the tripartite convention had not been achieved, as it was finally signed only by Britain and Tibet. Whitehall had not recognized the validity of the bilateral agreement and McMahon was not able to convince them.[100] Naturally, the official maps published by the Survey of India over the next two decades had not shown the McMahon Line on it,[101] nor was the treaty published for several years. This makes it explicit that Whitehall was not willing to accept the fractured mandate on the Sino-Indian border.

Second, the international equations in the Asian region prompted Britain for a studied negligence of the outcome of the convention. It is suggested that the Anglo-Russian Convention of 1907 and its clause of self-denial vis-à-vis Tibet persuaded the British to maintain silence

---

On the second map, it is ambiguous and the line does not show the part of Tawang tract. On the third one, the word 'Tawang' is superimposed. Liu, 'Look Beyond the Sino-Indian Border Dispute'.

[100] Hardinge to Crew, 23 July 1914, India Office Records: Pol. 464: Pts. 5 & 6: L/P & S/10/344. Political and Secret Memo 13, 206. No. 90 of 1914 GOI, Foreign and Political Department.

[101] Liu, 'Look Beyond the Sino-Indian Border Dispute'.

over the proceedings of the Simla Conference. So the dubious risk of 'attracting Russian and later Chinese attention continued to be the principal reason for non-publication of the full texts of the Convention and its adjuncts'.[102] The British opted to play safe in China, and in 'the emergence of hostile Kuomintang regime the British sought to keep the Convention agreements under wrap'.[103]

Similarly, as far as Peking was concerned, its internal polity under warlords in the early decades, and the civil war between Kuomintang and the CCP in the decades that followed, until the mid-20th century, made them show restraint on the matter for the time being. This political turmoil in China allowed Britain not to pay immediate attention until some practical difficulty alerted the British bureaucrats. It was only in 1929, while proposing to publish the new edition of the *Aitchison's Treaties*, that the outcome of the Simla Convention had first appeared in any official record. Publishing the Simla accord would naturally bring to the fore a trade agreement that was also part of the secret Anglo-Tibetan bilateral understanding.[104] Hence, while publishing the convention, in order to avoid possible problems, any explicit reference to the Trade Regulation had been purposely omitted. They explained further why such an omission was required due to the secrecy involved in the Indo-Tibetan dealings and cautioned of possible problems if the trade regulations were included in the publication.[105] Accordingly, in the 1929 edition of the *Aitchison's Treaties*,[106] there was no reference to the Anglo-Tibetan trade regulations in 1914 and it was stated that 'a tripartite convention was drawn up and initialled in 1914 by all

---

[102] Ibid.

[103] Mehra, *Essays in Frontier History*, 236.

[104] Even though the Anglo-Russian Agreement (1907) had no significance after the fall of Tsarist Russia in 1917, Britain was bound by the Washington Treaty of 1922 not to transgress upon the territorial and administrative integrity of China.

[105] Letter from Foreign Secretary, Government of India, to Secretary, Political Department, India Office, London, Simla, 22 May 1928, I.O.R. L/PS/10/1192. No. P 2972/1928.

[106] C. U. Aitchison, *Collection of Engagements, Treaties and Sanads*, Vol. XIV (New Delhi: Foreign and Political Department, Government of India).

the Plenipotentiaries, but the Chinese government refused to permit its representative to proceed to full signature'.[107] So the *Aitchison's Treaties* of 1929, Volume XIV, brought out an accurate version of the Simla Convention (excluding secret trade and border understanding between British India and Tibet). However, in 1924, Sir Charles Bell had already published in his book the secret Indo-Tibetan negotiation details and the frontier as established between Tibet and north-eastern India, stating that they were fortunate to establish such a long frontier with Tibet.[108] This contradiction in the public domain was, no doubt, disturbing to those in the government of British India. However, it did not come up as an issue until there emerged a technical difficulty in 1935 with respect to an inadvertent entry of a British officer into the Tawang territory, the status of which was uncertain. This incident[109] called the attention of the British to an active consideration of the reversal of its earlier frontier policy in the north-east of India, and also to a reconsideration of what was published in 1929 in the public records. When the issue came to the notice of the Deputy Secretary, Foreign and Political Department, Government of India, Olaf Caroe, who was keen on seeing Tawang in British India, he tried to ascertain the position of Tawang on the basis of the 1914 Simla Convention. Before going into the details of the underhand dealings of Olaf Caroe, let us take a look at another major issue of debate.

Ambiguity on the Status of Tawang

Inconsistency in border delimitation was the general characteristic of the Simla agreement, not only due to China's refusal of the dictated terms but also in terms of an apparent indecision in arriving at any final conclusion among the British officials. The uncertainty over the status of Tawang, a major spiritual centre for the Tibetans,

---

[107] Ibid.

[108] Charles Bell, *Tibet Past and Present* (Oxford: Clarendon Press, 1924). Reprint MBP Pvt Ltd Delhi, 1992, 155.

[109] Captain Kingdon Ward, while trekking in the area, was arrested by Tibetan officials for his alleged unauthorized entry into Tawang, against which he claimed that he had obtained permission from the Tawang authorities.

a geopolitically strategic region as well as a significant trade route in the western extremity of the eastern sector, is a typical example of the failure of the convention. Tawang had emerged as a disputed territory among India, China and Tibet, and the status of this region was the crux of the matter that had dragged these neighbours to war in 1962. In October 1913, McMahon suggested that Britain would abide by the fact that Tibet was in the possession of the entire region of Tawang, and subsequently 'in November it was decided that the boundary should run through Sela-Pass', 20 miles south-east of Tawang, 'leaving the Tawang monastery itself to Tibet' (Figure 3.1). But by the February secret agreement (in Delhi) in return for the alleged favour to Tibet, 'the British advanced their demand, so that the line on McMahon's maps ran about twelve miles north of Tawang'.[110] Later, Tibet, which was party to having conspired with McMahon, itself raised the banner of dispute questioning the status of Tawang as per the Simla agreement. The available maps pertaining to the Simla agreement provide a totally inconsistent picture, as all three 'maps show the McMahon line quite differently. On one map, the McMahon line was shown far north of Tawang, running along south of the Thagla ridge; on the second, Tawang was not marked; and on the third one, it had "Tawang" superimposed on it'.[111]

McMahon's interest in Tawang was not only to ensure a strategic but also the shortest trade route to Tibet. He thought that control over the Tawang monastery was 'necessary to free that route from the undue exactions and oppressions'[112] of the Tibetan authorities. However, he was not that emphatic about this and had proposed that Tibet would continue to enjoy the right to collect taxes in Tawang, but that 'the Line would be open to modification…in the light of more detailed knowledge which may be acquired in future'.[113] In reality,

---

[110] Maxwell, *India's China War*, 50.

[111] Of these three maps, one is attached to the 24 March notes; one to the 27 April convention and the third to 3 July convention. Liu, 'Look Beyond the Sino-Indian Border Dispute'.

[112] Maxwell, *India's China War*, 50.

[113] Quoted in Lamb, *The McMahon Line*, 548.

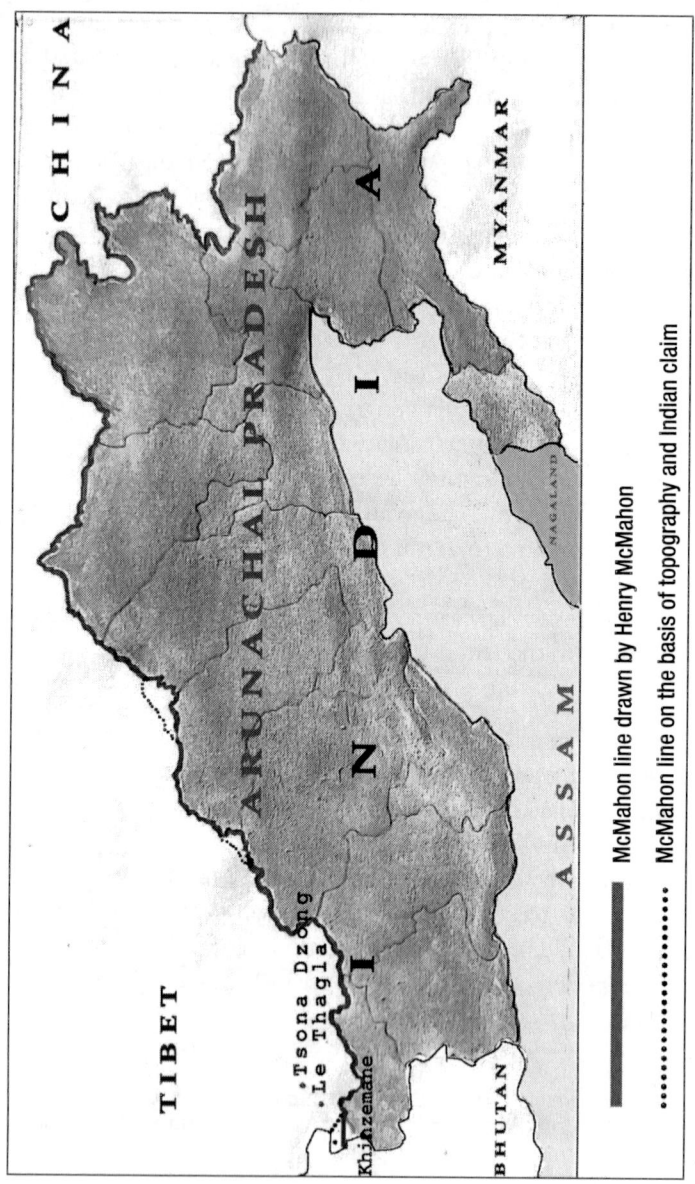

Figure 3.1 *Map of Arunachal Pradesh Showing the McMahon Line and the LAC*

Source: Author.

Disclaimer: This figure has been redrawn and is not to scale. It does not represent any authentic national or international boundaries and is used for illustrative purposes only.

━━━━ McMahon line drawn by Henry McMahon

•••••• McMahon line on the basis of topography and Indian claim

there are no records to show that the Tibetans were persuaded to cede the Tawang tract to British India. But from later events, it seems that McMahon had tactfully succeeded in creating an impression upon the Tibetans that the British would help them extract more concessions from China in return for minor adjustments in favour of the British. On account of such gestures, the Tibetans regarded the proposed boundary as compensation for the cession of some territories to the British and would bring about a great degree of independence from China. Once the British failed to produce those compensatory concessions, the Tibetans refused to abide by their agreement on the McMahon Line arrived at in Simla Convention.[114]

After the Simla Convention, for about two decades, neither party had bothered about these until the 'Olaf Caroe diplomacy' alerted the Tibetans to what had really happened in 1914 in Simla. On 13 November 1935, when the Assam government submitted a report stating the status of Tawang, more or less, as an independent territory and that it held some indirect allegiance to Tibet,[115] the British sent Basil Gould, a political officer in Sikkim, to discuss the status of Tawang and to obtain written reaffirmation of the 1914 frontiers from the Tibetan government. When Basil Gould discussed the subject with the Tibetan cabinet during his visit to Lhasa in November 1936 and raised the issues of collection of revenue and Tibetan administrative control over the territory,[116] they categorically stated that Tawang had been part of Tibet until the 1914 convention, and that at no time since then the Indian government had questioned Tibetan right or asserted British authority on Tawang.[117] Subsequently, Britain reminded Lhasa that 'the Indo-Tibetan frontier was separately agreed to by exchange of Notes on 24 and 25 March 1914'. However, seeing Tibet's persistence of their demand, Gould expressed the possible disadvantage

---

[114] Sir Robert Reid, *History of the Frontier Areas Bordering on Assam*, 296.

[115] I.O.R.: Pol. (External) Dept.: Collection 37/File 28. No. P.Z. 9019/1935).

[116] London officials had serious reservations about lodging a protest with the Chinese; hence, such an idea was dropped to avoid undesirable discussions and a possible increase in Chinese interest in the tribal territories. I.O.R.: Pol. (External) Dept.: Collection 36/File 23. No. 6153/1936.

[117] I.O.R.: Pol. (External) Dept.: Collection 36/File 29. No. P.Z. 3850/1936.

of insisting on a written reaffirmation from Lhasa. He expressed his apprehension that his action would tend to create an impression that the 1914 engagement needed further reaffirmation.

So the efforts of Gould could not find any success in the British endeavour to obtain credulity to their fraudulent actions. Without doubt, 'maps and the covert publication of documents would not outweigh an effective long-established and indeed unchallenged Tibetan administration in Tawang', and in this situation, New Delhi instructed the Assam government to 'emphasise the interest of British India in Tawang either by actual military tour or by collection of revenue'.[118] But Robert Reid, the governor of Assam, wrote back stating that Tawang 'has been controlled by Tibet, and none of the inhabitants have any idea that they are not Tibetan subjects'. Therefore, 'examine the country, get into touch with the inhabitants, and form some estimate of its revenue possibilities'.[119] To forestall a possible intrusion by China into Tawang, he proposed that a British officer with a military escort be sent to reside in Tawang every summer. The Government of India, however, reluctantly agreed only for a small expedition.[120] In the meantime, in 1938, the Survey of India published a map of Tibet showing the Tawang tract as part of its territory and, as urged by Sir Robert Reid, a force was sent to Tawang under Captain Lightfoot. This expedition invited strong protest from the Tibetan cabinet demanding immediate withdrawal of the force.[121] Having failed at this first attempt, in early 1939, Assam Governor Reid further urged Viceroy Lord Linlithgow to undertake a second expedition,[122] but the British government turned down this proposal.[123]

---

[118] Maxwell, *India's China War*, 56.

[119] Sir Robert Reid, *History of the Frontier Areas Bordering on Assam*, 295–296.

[120] Maxwell, *India's China War*, 56.

[121] Sir Robert Reid, *History of Frontier Areas Bordering on Assam*, 297. I.O.R.: Pol. (External) Dept.: Register No. P.Z. 3507/38. Telegram R. No. 899, 4 May 1938. From Gould, Yatung to Foreign, Simla.

[122] I.O.R.: Pol. (External) Dept.: Collection 36/File 29. Reid's confidential letter to Linlithgow dated 3 January 1939.

[123] However, a punitive expedition against some troublesome tribes was dispatched.

On 17 March 1939, Henry J. Twynam, acting governor of Assam,[124] wrote to Lord Linlithgow, disputing the juridical validity of the McMahon Line and questioning the logic and urgency in occupying Tawang. He challenged the proposal to annex Tawang on both practical and legal grounds and ruled out any possible danger from China in the north-east.[125] Twynam also proposed that the McMahon Line be modified to run through Se La, a few miles to the south-east of Tawang, so that the monasteries would be left to Tibet.[126] The response of Lord Linlithgow was encouraging and he underlined Twynam's argument.[127] The British home government agreed to this stand and distanced itself from the policy of any further expedition to Tawang. Later, in August 1940, a conference was held in Shillong, attended by all the important officials in charge of the affairs of the north-east frontier, and in the meeting it was decided that the Government of India not press their claims to Tawang.[128]

However, the situation in the region turned around differently in the midst of the Second World War. By the end of 1941, with the entry of Japan into the war and its active presence in China and South Asia, a perceived threat to India pressed the British into strengthening its control again on the north-east frontier. They realized that India's eastern borders were vulnerable and the government needed to fill the political and administrative vacuum that had been allowed to develop between Assam and Tibet since the establishment of British rule.[129] This not only revived their FP but also followed a deliberate attempt to make the McMahon Line the effective boundary. During this time,

---

[124] In February 1939, Henry Twynam, a moderate and experienced person on the north-east frontier who had been credited for his long tenure in the Indian Civil Service in the Assam cadre, took over as acting governor of Assam from Robert Reid.

[125] Questioning the validity of the 1914 agreement, Twynam pointed out that the letters exchanged between McMahon and the Tibetans in 1914 lacked the formalities associated with a treaty. Maxwell, *India's China War*, 58.

[126] Maxwell, *India's China War*, 58.

[127] I.O.R.: Pol. (External) Dept.: Collection 36/File 29. Lord Linlithgow's private and personal letter to Twynam.

[128] Gupta, 'The McMahon Line 1911–45'.

[129] Maxwell, *India's China War*, 59.

efforts to persuade the Tibetans to give up their claims to Tawang continued. Later J. P. Mills, a senior Indian Civil Service officer and the government's advisor on tribal affairs, was deputed for the expansion of the British administration in Tawang. Despite stiff resistance from the Tibetans,[130] by 1944, Mills was able to establish the British administration in the entire belt from Walong in the east to Dirang Dzong in the west. Several posts of the Assam Rifles were established and soon Tibetan government officials were packed off from the Tawang tract as well.[131] But the Government of India was convinced that pursuing a diplomatic effort to win over Tibetan authority or any political or military action in Tawang would not be as easy as to seek other means by incorporating existing doctoral documents as being beneficial to British interests. Hence, in October 1944, Basil Gould attempted to persuade the Tibetans to acquiesce the British encroachments in Tawang.

During this time, the Tibetans had begun pressurizing the Chinese government into entering into a tripartite agreement among Tibet, China and British India to open a new supply road from north-east India through Tibet. But the Chinese flatly refused on the grounds that Tibet was part of China. Britain became apprehensive of a possible Chinese invasion of Tibet to build its own road.[132] This newly emerging situation prompted Britain to make a last-minute effort to bring back the old Simla agreements within legal purview. The viceroy justified his stand by stating, 'Tibet is a separate country, in full enjoyment of local autonomy, entitled to exchange diplomatic representatives with other Powers'.[133] So the British, once again, tried to encourage Tibetan separatism, with the aim of excluding Chinese power from Tibet. But their attempt to win over favourable world opinion for the efforts to legalize the McMahon Line could not succeed due to the intervention of the USA.

[130] J. P. Mills, 'Problem of the Assam–Tibet Frontier', *Journal of Royal Central Asian Society* 36, no. 2 (1950): 5–7.

[131] Guruswamy, 'The Battle for the Border'.

[132] Richardson, *Tibet and Its History*, 160–164; Tieh-Tseng Li, *Tibet To-day and Yesterday* (New York, NY: Bookman Associates, 1960), 189.

[133] Office of the Historian, *Foreign Relations of the United States: 1943: China* (Washington, DC: Department of State, 1963), 626–628.

McMahon's Fractured Mandate and Olaf Caroe's Fraudulent Manoeuvring

After the Simla Convention, as discussed earlier, for the first two decades, 'McMahon's line was in effect forgotten'[134] by the British, and no effective engagement in Tibet and its southern border regions had been noticed until the 1940s, when certain new developments in China and its southern peripheries alerted them. In the 1940s, Britain felt the need for a vigorous, proactive approach to its north-eastern borders with China due to (a) a fierce Communist (CCP) versus Kuomintang (KMT) Nationalist Civil War reclaiming its spheres of influence in the southern provinces, (b) Japan's overwhelming military exploits in the Chinese territories and (c) the active presence of the USA, a power axis in the region. It was around this time in 1935 that the Kingdon Ward incident occurred,[135] which alerted British officials to the need to reaffirm what McMahon had failed to achieve at the Sino-Indian border. It was Olaf Caroe, the deputy secretary, Foreign and Political Department, who tried to reaffirm what was secretly transacted at Simla as an official, thereby ensuring that the status of Tawang remained undisputed. Caroe realized that the north-eastern frontier had a potential possible border dispute between India and China, and, therefore, the secret agreement reached between India and Tibet in 1914 had larger significance. Thereafter, Caroe showed personal interest in this border issue, which finally led to the revival of the almost forgotten Simla agreement and its suppressed and concealed terms.

Caroe's eagerness for expansion of the British territory in the north-east borders prompted him to follow a FP, at least on paper, and for this purpose he called the attention of the British authorities to the hidden aspects of the agreement and proposed that the 'Anglo-Tibetan

---

[134] Maxwell, *India's China War*, 54.

[135] Unauthorized entry by F. Kingdon Ward, a British explorer and botanist in the tribal area in Tawang, was disputed by Tibetan authorities and he was arrested, creating a diplomatic crisis. This called the attention of the British for an active consideration of the reversal of its earlier passive policy in the north-eastern frontier. K. N. Raghavan, *Dividing Lines, Contours of the India–China Discord* (Mumbai: Leadstart Publishing, 2012), 20–24.

agreement should be published without further delay'.[136] On 5 November 1935, he wrote to the British Political Officer in Sikkim, F. Williamson:

> International frontier between India and Tibet east of Bhutan...was defined by red line on map drawn by McMahon and accepted by Tibetan Government in accordance with article IX of 1914 Convention. This line lies well north of Tawang.... It is important that you should not in any way compromise with the Tibetan Government validity of international boundary agreed to in 1914.[137]

Caroe had not mentioned anything about the absence of China at the session and secret Indo-Tibetan dealings to reach a bilateral agreement between India and Tibet. Emphasizing his argument, Caroe wrote again in November 1935: 'Indeed the agreement then reached carries India's frontier right up into the heart of the Himalayas to a line at least 60 miles north (of the foot of the hills)'.[138] He justified his argument by saying, 'Tibet could not in any case put forward a claim to sovereignty over any territory in the foothills east of Bhutan'.[139] An excited Caroe wrote to J. C. Walton in India Office:

> Officers to whom the international position in the north-east frontier is known is in any case a small one and it seems to us that there is a real danger that important matters of this kind may go wrong if we refrain any longer from publishing our agreements with Tibet...the Government of India think there would be advantage in inserting in their public records copies of the 1914 Convention, ... Their absence from such a publication as *Aitchison's Treaties*, if it became known to the Chinese Government, might well be used by them in support of the argument that no ratified agreement between India and Tibet is in existence.... We therefore feel strongly that no time should be lost in inserting in *Aitchison's Treaties* the text of the 1914 Anglo-Tibetan Convention

[136] Maxwell, *India's China War*, 55.

[137] I.O.R.: Pol. (External) Dept.: Collection 36/File 29. Telegram No. 3028, 5 November 1935. From Foreign, New Delhi to Political Officer, Sikkim, Lhasa) in Gupta, 'The McMahon Line 1911–45'.

[138] I.O.R.: Pol. (External) Dept.: Collection 36/File 23. No. P.Z. 2661/1936. Quoted in Gupta, 'The McMahon Line 1911–45'.

[139] Ibid.

together with the exchange of notes regarding the boundary and the Trade Regulations. We think that steps should be taken without delay to show this boundary on the maps of the Survey of India. Omission to do this has already led to the delineation of the frontier between India and Tibet....[140]

Caroe insisted on inserting the outcome of the secret bilateral discussion between British India and Tibet into the draft convention and emphasized that the documents be published in public records as early as possible.[141] He also tried to apprise his higher authority of the fact that this was in the public domain as early as 1924 in Charles Bell's book.[142] But he could not fully convince the home government of the urgency of such a dubious action. It was after a prolonged consultation with the Government of India that finally his proposal was considered positively. Accordingly, on 16 July 1936, the secretary of state conditionally approved[143] the Government of India's proposals with certain points of precaution to be taken as noted in Walton's letter to Caroe which stated:

> When the agreements are published it will be most desirable to avoid unnecessary publicity and to refrain from drawing the attention of the press or news agencies to the publication; ...it would be desirable not to publish the text of the declaration of 3 July 1914 by the Plenipotentiaries of Great Britain and Tibet accepting the Simla Convention as binding on their two Governments, but to deal with it merely by means of a note to be inserted in Aitchison in the sense suggested at the end of para. 4 of the letter to the Foreign Office of 13 June 1936.[144]

But Caroe knew that this partial approval would not sanctify the secret deal. Therefore, to convince higher officials of the impact, in the event of failure in correcting the documents, he visited British officials in

---

[140] I.O.R. Pol. (External) Dept.: Collection 36/File 23. No. P.Z. 2788/1936. Caroe to Walton, 9 April 1936.

[141] I.O.R.: Pol. (External) Dept.: Collection 36/File 23. No. P.Z. 2905/1936. Ibid.

[142] Bell, *Tibet Past and Present*.

[143] Liu, 'Look Beyond the Sino-Indian Border Dispute'; Guruswamy, *Emerging Trends in India–China Relations*, 219.

[144] Letter from Walton to Caore, I.O.R.: Pol. (External) Dept.: Collection 36/File 23. No. P.Z. 4911/36.

London. Meeting R. A. Butler, the parliamentary undersecretary of state for India, Caroe submitted:

> Owing mainly to our failure to publish the 1914 agreement…Chinese cartographers have absorbed…a huge mass of territory…our unofficial cartographers, e.g. the Times and Bartholomew's Atlases support the Chinese claims…, and show the international frontier right down on the Brahmaputra at the foot of the Himalayas. This is a typical result of British, or British-Indian apathy…and is an instance of the lack of contact between Whitehall, Delhi and Peiping (Peking) in Far Eastern Affairs….[145]

After studying the issue in consultation with J. C. Walton, in the India Office, London and Sir Robert Reid, the Governor of Assam, Butler said:

> The Simla Convention of 1914, …were not published on account…of complication arising from the Anglo-Russian Convention of 1907, and…to avoid stimulating Chinese interest in Tibet. These reasons have now ceased to be valid, and it was decided last autumn to publish them in a revised edition of Volume XIV of *Aitchison's Treaties* to be brought out specially for the purpose.[146]

He further directed that these details be shown on maps published by the Survey of India, kept in the official records of the India Office, and that copies be sent to all the leading firms of cartographers in this country, in addition to informing the Royal Geographical Society and the War Office. Subsequently, Robert Reid responded in the affirmative to take necessary action to confirm that Tawang was in British possession, including the stationing of a European police officer with a platoon in the region. However, the insertion of the secret bilateral dealing between Tibet and Britain was yet to be sanctified as Caroe desired.

Doctored Documentation: The McMahon Line or the 'Olaf Caroe Line'

As the documentation part of the work to sanctify the status of the line in the archival records was not successful as yet, it was agreed, in principle, to confirm the status of steadfast efforts towards serving

[145] I.O.R.: Pol. (External) Dept.: Collection 36/File 23. S 4/3.
[146] I.O.R.: Pol. (External) Dept.: Collection 36 (2)/File 23.

British interests on the frontiers had not satisfied Caroe of Tawang in British India, and accordingly the 1937 Survey of India, for the first time, began to show the McMahon Line as the official boundary between India and Tibet,[147] but still left more questions than answers.[148] The narration ahead discusses the process of legitimizing a fraudulent action that took place in 1914, where the truth was suppressed and facts were distorted to reincarnate the McMahon Line in the archival records. Caroe now revised the *Aitchison's Treaties* by reprinting Volume XIV of 1929 again in August 1938. The new edition was identical to the previous edition, including the date of publication (1929), except for the details referring to the Simla Conference, which had been rewritten to insert the secret bilateral deal as part of the Simla agreement. Caroe and his team had taken enough precautionary measures against any possible detection of the truth. Seeing the danger in the existence of copies of the 1929 *Aitchison's Treaties*, all the originals of the 1929 versions were replaced[149] with the distorted version printed in 1938 but with an imprint of 1929.[150] Due care was taken by the Government of India for very minimum publicity to the new reprint, so as to avoid further complications which, according to Karunakar Gupta, was 'not far short of a diplomatic forgery'.[151] Sixty-two copies of the new volume were sent to the India Office in London, with the request that all copies of the original be destroyed. It was thus ensured that only this distorted version of the new volumes of the *Aitchison's Treaties* was available in circulation.

Moreover, the Surveyor-General of India was requested to make changes in the maps to show the McMahon Line as the alignment of the north-eastern boundary of India as described in the *Aitchison's Treaties*. But the 'Surveyor-General pointed out numerous anomalies

[147] Guruswamy, *Emerging Trends in India–China Relations*, 219.

[148] Guruswamy, 'The Battle for the Border'; Maxwell, *India's China War*, 55.

[149] But three copies of the original 1929 edition survived, one in the Harvard University Library, one in the India Office Library and one in the Peking Library.

[150] Political (External) Dept Collection no. 36 File 23 R 2222/38 quoted. In Maxwell, *India's China War*, 55.

[151] Quoted in Gupta, 'The McMahon Line 1911–45'.

and inaccuracies in the Red Line that had been sent to him for publication'.[152] However, the Survey of India maps from 1938 began to show the McMahon Line, indicating in their legend that it was a delimited but an un-demarcated boundary.[153] The British government soon sent copies of the new maps to leading firms of cartographic publishers in England, showing the McMahon Line as a border, along with a request that only the new version be included in their subsequent editions. But *the Times* was not willing to make changes in its map until 1940. However, since 1939, 'most of the officials in the External Affairs Department, New Delhi, were unaware of the authentic narrative of the Simla Conference, as the original Aitchison had been withdrawn and replaced by a spurious edition published in 1938, but falsely bearing the imprint of 1929'.[154] So a doctoral document of the *Aitchison's Treaties* of 1938, with a 1929 reprint, was the basis on which the McMahon Line was validated in the official records.

Hence, the Simla agreement was a total failure and was initially refuted by the British government on the grounds that a bilateral agreement between British India and Tibet had no relevance and no actual basis for existence as per the terms of the treaty. Many British officials had also doubtlessly reiterated that 'the McMahon Line which sought to secure the main crest of the Himalayas as the frontier does not exist and never has existed'.[155] Even McMahon had to concede to the fact that he was unsuccessful in the effort. The outcome of the treaty was not only rejected by Peking but also not fully acknowledged even by Tibet later in the 1940s. The fact is that the McMahon Line was a 'daydream' of Hendry McMahon and the forward school of British officials in India, but which never came to be realized. But the McMahon Line exists in history from the imagery of the 1914 documents as recreated by Olaf Caroe in the 1940s. Further, the Caroe group of the forward school sanctified their fraudulent actions,

[152] Ibid.

[153] Ibid.

[154] Gupta, 'Distortions in the History of Sino-Indian Frontiers', 1265–1270.

[155] Twynam in *The Times*, 2 September 1959.

made the mystery surrounding their actions a part of history, inserted fraudulent and falsified documents into the archives which, in due course, largely influenced the historical narrative of the nature of the Sino-Indian border. Since the Simla Convention had given a fractured mandate, the McMahon Line had a foetal death at its inception itself. What remains in the archives is the presence of Olaf Caroe's distorted version and, therefore, the borderline could better be called the 'Olaf Caroe Line'.

Issues beyond Border

Evolving of Dispute in the Early Phase (1950–1956)

The 1950s ushered in new hopes and aspirations for both nations. At the stroke of midnight on 15 August 1947, when India awoke to a new dawn of independence from almost two centuries of colonial rule, China was prepared to emerge from a prolonged civil war that lasted two decades and to relieve itself from the shackles of imperialist treaties to a Communist Socialist state with the October Revolution of 1949. Neither party, therefore, in the initial days was interested in going into the nitty-gritty of the 'colonial mischief' and harming their age-old friendship. Even when both sides realized they had to come to an understanding on the nature of the frontiers, neither party was immediately interested in investing time on this. The actual disputes came to the fore only after the mid-1950s, once both nations were politically consolidated from within and began to play a larger role in the external arena and on the borderline. While Mao and the CCP were preoccupied in the consolidation of a greater China, all inclusive of the Middle Kingdom, the Nehru government was preoccupied with the internal consolidation and national integration of the states in the Union of India, while it was itself obsessed with building an Afro-Asian unity for a new international order.

However, the colonial vestiges had left behind enough reasons for a mutual contest and confrontation. The areas of confrontations were mainly on two aspects. First, during the British inroads to Tibet, they enjoyed certain privileges in that territory maintained in Lhasa even after independence by the British India. With Peking's 'liberation' of Tibet in 1950, these colonial privileges were to be revoked. But there was an effort from a section of Indian political parties to hold onto those imperialist privileges for independent India as well. This had created much resentment in Peking, as they were under the impression that independent India was interested in holding on to the British colonial legacy and liked to be a bourgeoisie partner of Western imperialism. Even when official India had a different outlook in this regard, clamour in the Indian press was a concern.

Second, the nature of the border dispute left behind by the British at their departure remained dormant between the two nations. The official documents of the government of British India in the years preceding their departure show a vivid picture of such a dispute that had been lying latent in both sectors. Records reveal that the nationalist government in China had served several protest notes to British India, because border posts in the north-east frontier region were pushed from the foothills of Assam towards the vicinity of the McMahon Line.[1] The republican government had sent protest notes to the British Embassy in China and, in April 1947, during the Asian Relations Conference in New Delhi, Chinese delegates protested against a map of Asia showing Tibet outside the boundaries of China, and subsequently the map was withdrawn.[2] This shows that the disputes were present even before the departure of the British and that it did not originate between the PRC and independent India. However, in the early half of the 1950s, Peking and New Delhi adopted cordiality in relations and did not immediately speak their minds on the border issue. But a silent phase of frontier consolidation was in progress on both sides, without leading to clashes.

In 1951, India peacefully annexed Tawang and started implementing the reports of Himmatsinhji Committee in the period 1951–1954 by mobilizing frontier posts. At the same time, India extended several friendly gestures, including recognition of the Chinese occupation of Tibet, and relinquished all its privileges in that territory.[3] But during

---

[1] Gupta, *Hidden History of the Sino-Indian Frontier*, 765–767, 769–772.

[2] Ibid.

[3] India officially recognized the PRC on 1 April 1950 as the first non-communist nation and firmly stood for Chinese entry into the UN when most nations opposed the idea. India vigorously fought against the idea of taking action against China in the Korean crisis and recognized the Chinese occupation of Tibet and relinquished its privileges in that territory.

this period, the PRC made an impression that it was by and large silent on the border issue. However, Peking was also actively working on a secret construction of a road connecting Sinkiang and Tibet through Aksai Chin. China strongly believed that independent India's perception about the frontiers with China was basically based on the outcome of British imperialist devices. But the issues were slowly entering a phase of complication by 1954–1955 with the publication of a new map by India in 1954 specifying the Sino-Indian borderlines as per its claim. So the divergence between the two nations in the perception of the border started getting stark as early as the *bhai bhai* days (1954–1955). In the meantime, the news of Aksai Chin road also began to get attention by 1957. When the issue of the road was brought to the attention of Peking, they pointed out that New Delhi's occupation of the NEFA was on the basis of an imperialistically devised McMahon Line that was illegal. Despite all these grey areas, bilateral relations were cordial and not complicated, and any serious divergence in perception of the border began to get aggravated only at a later point.[4] It was with the Tibetan Uprising in 1956 and New Delhi's expression of empathy with the rebellion. The present chapter will look into the developments in colonial legacy that evolved into a potential spoiler of post-colonial bilateral relations, influenced by issues beyond territorial dispute and swayed by certain internal influences. In the following pages, we will address the early stages (1950–1956) of Sino-India border relations and the factors that determined the major course of events during this period.

Post-colonial Perception of the Border Issue

After taking over the political mantle from the British, New Delhi was not keen on negotiating its territorial relations with its neighbours; instead, whatever the colonial interventions had left behind was inherited as a legacy. When the Mountbatten plan was reluctantly accepted for internal political dispensations, New Delhi was also willing to acknowledge the existing border specifications as a British heritage even without any negotiations with its neighbours. Despite the PRC

---

[4] Nayyar, *Between the Lines*, 139.

holding the view that the Sino-Indian borders had to be formally delimited immediately after the October Revolution (1949), they too did not raise any such issue with New Delhi. India took everything from the British past as final and unchallenged, neglecting the territories on which it later staked claim, on the basis of customs and traditions. India's immediate attention was turned to the annexation of the north-eastern region, which was accomplished in 1951. Even the official maps published by New Delhi between 1948 and 1950 showed that all borders from the Afghan–India–China tri-junction in the west to the India–China–Nepal tri-junction in the east as undefined.[5] However, the least attention was paid to exploring the status of the frontiers in the records, and no serious homework was carried out to ascertain their proper definition. The western sector was virtually left unattended to, thanks to the nature of the terrain. However, there was greater interest in taking possession of the frontiers in the north-east, and the Government of India tried to bring the tribal people under the control of the NEFA which was set up in 1950 under the Constitution of the Indian Republic.[6] Disputes were not notified to each other at an early stage (1947–1956) despite the fact that they were apparent in the western sector and that the NEFA had not emerged as a major area of contest, other than in certain pockets in that region. The area of debate in this part of the border before 1959 was limited to the status of Tawang and a few smaller pockets near the Chumbi Valley. Even the legality of the McMahon Line, a colonial dispensation, was quite late.

So the dispute began to emerge quite late in 1958 and soon began to strengthen, intertwined with other factors. The Sino-Indian border dispute was considered to be 'one of the biggest land disputes in Asia'.[7] The significance of the dispute involves the size of the area as well as the potential strength of the disputants. As per the latest official data presented in the Lok Sabha, China is 'illegally' occupying 38,000 km^2 in the north-east of Ladakh, besides the 5,180 km^2 ceded by Pakistan to China[8] in the western sector, and 2,100 km^2 in various pockets in

---

[5] Noorani, 'The Truth about 1962', 17–30.

[6] Gupta, *Hidden History of the Sino-Indian Frontier*.

[7] Scott, 'Sino-Indian Territorial Issues', 4.

[8] This territory includes Kaurik, Shipkila, Pulam, Sumdo, Jadhang and Barahoti.

the central sector, bringing the total to 45,280 km², while Peking holds that India is 'illegally' occupying about 90,000 km² of its territory in Arunachal Pradesh.[9]

The Crux of the Matter

The crux of the issues between India and China can be summarized in the following text. First, as we have already found, the early discord apparent between the two nations, not necessarily at the official level, but as reflected in the press and the Parliament by the political parties, was about the status of Tibet in the PRC and the nature of the privileges of independent India (residual colonial) in Lhasa. Despite maintaining an active diplomatic hotline at the official level, dissension and distrust continued to be a stumbling block towards good bilateral relations, and discord began sweeping areas beyond Lhasa.

Second, it was over the issue of territorial dispute, which can be divided into three sectors, such as the western, eastern and central sectors. In the early stage, any territorial dispute revolved around Aksai Chin in the western sector, where there was something substantial to be disputed. However, the dispute in this region was also not immediately notified to each other. But, since 1952, Peking had been slowly and steadily, taking control of a larger part of the western region, building a 160-km road through Aksai Chin.[10] Even when news about such a huge infrastructural development was known, it was either neglected or denied by New Delhi. Until its opening was publicly announced in 1957, India was not willing to acknowledge such a major appropriation. The western sector includes another complicated disputed area, the Shaksgam Valley,[11] over which India maintains its Kashmir-derived claims. Since it was under the control of POK, the 'right' over that was relinquished by Pakistan in favour of the

---

[9] Digvijaya Singh, Minister of State for External Affairs in Lok Sabha, New Delhi (30 July 2003), quoted in Verma, 'Sino-Indian Border Dispute at Aksai Chin'. Some records provide a more accurate extent of the territory at Aksai Chin 37,250 km² (14,380 sq. miles) and the NEFA 83,740 km² (32,330 sq. miles).

[10] Scott, 'Sino-Indian Territorial Issues', 2.

[11] It has an area of around 5,180 km² (1,930 square miles) in the north-western part of Kashmir. Scott, 'Sino-Indian Territorial Issues'.

PRC in a treaty signed in 1963. This inexplicable delay (till late 1958) in any official response against Peking's encroachment and also against Islamabad's 'overbearing benevolence' to Peking is explained in the context of the pending nature of the Kashmir dispute in international fora.

The second major area of dispute, which emerged a little later, was in the NEFA, south of the McMahon Line in the eastern sector. The basic premise of the origin of the dispute on this sector (as discussed in Chapter 3) derives from the validity of the Simla Agreement. The disputed territory in this sector is inhabited by over 1 million Indian citizens and is under the exclusive control of India since its annexation in 1951. The nature of China's claim over this territory is weak. In fact, the MEA officials brought the gravity of the McMahon Line to the notice of the concerned personnel in 1952 itself.[12] Nehru was equally aware of it, and he believed that it was in his capacity to convince Peeking through candid negotiations with Chou and Chinese officials. The PRC was later willing to negotiate on the eastern sector on the condition that New Delhi recognized Peking's right over Aksai Chin. It was on this basis that the PRC had time and again agreed to relinquish claim on this area on a mutual agreement.[13] This area includes Tawang, an important Indian-controlled Buddhist centre which has been under dispute between India and Tibet since the British period (for details, see Chapter 3).

Other than these two major sectors, there are other areas of disputed territories in smaller pockets of the 'central sector' at the borders of Himachal Pradesh and Uttarakhand. Although small in size, the Sino-Indian border dispute begins from this sector. Similarly, India's incorporation of Sikkim in 1975, the uncertainty over China's recognition of this move and a continuing armed occupation of the finger-pointed Chumbi Valley area in the east of Sikkim add to the existing problem.[14] Although China has reached a settlement with Bhutan on the borderline, an unsettled portion of the tri-junction around the

---

[12] K. S. Bajpai, 'Weightlifting', *Outlook*, 16 November 2009.

[13] The latest such readiness was expressed on 14 February 1979, in Beijing, when Deng Xiaoping offered External Affairs Minister A. B. Vajpayee 'the package deal' de jure recognizing the *status quo* by both sides.

[14] Scott, 'Sino-Indian Territorial Issues', 3.

Chumbi Valley, on account of a pending settlement with India, adds further concern to New Delhi.[15] The frequent military face-off in the Doklam area in recent times adds to the urgency of reaching a lasting solution to avoid any tension in the frontier regions.

Looking at the response of both New Delhi and Peking towards the disputes, it was apparent that Peking was more enthusiastic to reach a negotiated settlement and stood for demarcating of the borders,[16] whereas New Delhi maintained that borders were sufficiently settled by traditions and geography. Actually Nehru, despite knowing the gravity of the existing issues, was not in a position to respond positively to Chou's suggestions due to a hard-line approach that also existed in New Delhi. India, therefore, missed out the opportunity to come to a diplomatic solution due to internal political pressure. It is suggested that Peking had a three-stage approach towards settlement of the border. In the first stage (1950–1954), it adopted a policy of temporary maintenance of the status quo, in the second stage, (1954–1960) Chou actively tried for a negotiated settlement and even for the swapping of the sectors, while in the final stage (1960–1962), it opted for a military response.[17]

Neither Party Has Valid Merits in the Debate

In the prolonged debate over territorial claims, both sides call on historical evidence for their respective claims.[18] However, inconsistency and logical flaws are apparent on both sides. 'Neither China, nor indeed India, has a case of any undisputed merit in the cartographic

[15] The location of Chumbi Valley is vitally significant for the security of the northeastern states of India as the area projects down onto India's sensitive Siliguri corridor which is the only link between mainland India and the north-eastern states. Scott, 'Sino-Indian Territorial Issues', 3.

[16] In the 1955 Bandung Conference of Afro-Asian nations, Chou declared his country's willingness to settle the border alignment. Maxwell, 'Sino-Indian Border Dispute Reconsidered', 905–918.

[17] Dai Chaowu, 'China's Strategy for Sin-Indian Boundary Disputes, 1950–1962', *Asian Perspective* 43, no. 3 (2019). Available at http//doi.org/10.1353/apr.2019.0022 (accessed on 2 September 2020).

[18] Woodman, *Himalayan Frontiers*; Lamb, *The McMahon Line*; Lamb, *The Sino-Indian Border in Ladakh*.

border claims'.[19] However, both sides argue in the name of traditional rights as well as natural and geographical alignment. New Delhi holds, 'The India–China boundary is not a complicated question left over from history, but one definitely settled by history'.[20] Since both parties had acknowledged that these inaccuracies existed, they could have averted this colonial legacy from becoming a contentious issue. The matter was allowed to persist and get entangled with internal and external pressures of an emotional nature. Why did this happen? What were the factors that made it impossible to arrive at a solution? To answer these questions, we have to understand the nature of the newborn republics on both sides of the border and the factors influencing these republics. Independent India was in the midst of post-partition political turmoil, and the de jure government was swayed and restricted to various internal political influences. Similarly, the newly created Communist Republic under Mao Zedong was struggling to parry the onslaught of the attacks from the capitalist world. Naturally, these factors weighed high on decision-making if they did not altogether fully influence it. Not only internal political consolidation but also the imminent need for internal reconstruction and rehabilitation of a shattered economy and a turbulent social order were the immediate concerns of both governments. It seems that these factors might have prompted both nations to pay the least attention to the realities on the frontier.

Sardar Patel for Armed Preparedness on the Border

The tension in the Sino-Indian border region, as already noted, began to erupt not on account of any territorial issue, but rather from apprehension prevailing in India about a possible Chinese offensive against India in the background of its military intervention in Tibet. The presence of communist revolutionaries in the southern provinces of China bordering India and the CCP's occupation of Sinkiang in September 1949 had already created uneasiness within the political circle in

---

[19] Subramanian, 'Looking beyond the Border Issue'.
[20] Gopalachari, 'The India–China Boundary Question', 33.

New Delhi. Soon after assumption of power by the PRC in October 1949, the storming of the PLA into Lhasa in 1950 made the entire Sino-Indian borders militarily alive. This created worry about a possible Chinese border intrusion further south, awakening a section of Indian politicians and bureaucrats pressing for a precautionary Indian military move into the border. There were strong demands emerging from within the country to protect border regions against external forces. In the context of the Tibetan rebels' movement on the frontiers, the Intelligence Bureau (IB) advised the government to impose restrictions on the entry of Tibetans into the country.[21] In August 1950, the IB sent additional proposals for the establishment of 21 checkpoints on the Indo-Tibetan frontier passes, covering Ladakh in the northwest and the Lohit division in the north-east. On the basis of these proposals for an 'effective protection' of the border region, IB–army joint checkpoints were set up at Shyok (Panamik). Intelligence posts were opened at Leh in Ladakh and summer patrols were sent to areas up to the Karakoram Pass to check trespassers.[22]

The intelligence input from the IB about the developments on the frontiers and a possible security threat to India from the other side of the border prompted the home minister to warn the prime minister about an offensive from the PRC. On 3 November 1950, IB Chief B. N. Mullik sent a detailed note to Sardar Vallabhbhai Patel, apprising him on a possible threat to the internal security of the nation. On the basis of this report, Patel suggested to Nehru on the need to take immediate measures to address the military threat from Communist China. On 7 November 1950, a few weeks before his death,[23] the home minister wrote a strongly worded letter to the prime minister explaining the situation on the basis of IB inputs.[24] In response, on 18 November 1950, Nehru replied, 'it is exceedingly unlikely that

---

[21] Mullik, *My Years with Nehru*, 120–124.

[22] Sinha and Athale, *History of the Conflict with China 1962*, 36.

[23] Sardar Patel died on 15 December 1950.

[24] Letter of Deputy Prime Minister Sardar Vallabhbhai Patel to the Prime Minister Jawaharlal Nehru on 7 November 1950. Published by Nayyar, *Between the Lines* (Appendix).

we may face military invasion from Chinese side, in peace or war, in foreseeable future'.[25] In the new world scenario, with many countries having hostile relationship with the new Communist China, Nehru held that they would not divert their forces across the inhospitable terrain of Tibet and undertake a wild venture across the Himalayas. He believed that any such course would weaken China, and there was therefore no possibility of a Chinese attack on India. His mind was ruled largely by the thought of a military response on a big scale, not only impractical from a strategic point of view but also unwarranted on several grounds. However, he could not completely discard the suggestion because he too suspected that China might create trouble for India by military infiltration and by occupying territory along the border in the event of Tibetan rebels taking refuge on Indian soil. Therefore, the Government of India, on the basis of the advice from the home minister, the defence establishments and the IB, formally sanctioned the Indo-Tibet checkpoints and other logistics for the purpose.[26] Thus, from the beginning of 1951, border posts were established along the proposed area.[27]

As the home minister, Patel had intelligence input on a possible volatile situation on the frontiers, and he believed that if a large number of Tibetan rebels flooded the frontiers, the PLA might follow them to the frontiers to defeat them which, in turn, could create tension along the border. Here, the proposal of Sardar Patel was based on the intelligence input from the IB, the veracity of which was doubtful, because Mullik's proposals were criticized by many in the defence establishments. Mullik himself admits that, on several occasions, fingers were pointed against him for misleading the army[28] either on wrong or falsified intelligence inputs. Moreover, Patel was already of the opinion

---

[25] Prime Minister's note forwarded to Vallabhbhai Patel on 18 November 1950. Extracts in R. K. Jain, ed., *China South Asian Relations*, 1947–1980, vol. I. (Atlantic Highlands, NJ: Humanities Press, 1981), 43.

[26] Mullik, *My Years with Nehru*, 122.

[27] Border posts were established as proposed in Ladakh (1), Himachal Pradesh (3) including one in Punjab (later the areas came to Himachal Pradesh), Uttar Pradesh (6) North Bengal (5) Sikkim (3) and the NEFA (3).

[28] Mullik, *My Years with Nehru*, 243–244.

that communist governments were not reliable neighbours.[29] Patel's warning to Nehru was influenced by the Red phobia that was strong in post-partition India.

Even though Nehru believed that the best means to safeguarding the border would be to strengthen relations with neighbours, the necessary military preparedness and other security measures were introduced as per intelligence and military advice. Accordingly, on 28 March 1951, the Deputy Minister for External Affairs, B. V. Keskar, presented the government's stand on the issue in the Parliament stating:

> The government is not unmindful of the protection of our frontiers adjoining Tibet…. It is obvious that such a complicated and big frontier cannot be well-protected if we have a border country which becomes hostile to us. Therefore, a friendly China and Tibet is the best guarantee for defence of the country.[30]

But the situation in the Indian political circle was already volatile. The Indian media had already succeeded in creating fear psychosis among the public about an imminent threat from the PLA, and this strongly echoed in the Parliament as well. Keskar's presentation could not calm the uproar in the Parliament, demanding for military intervention in Tibet, and this was widely publicized in Indian print media. Naturally, despite official clarifications to Peking about the nature of the democratic debate in the press and the Parliament, bilateral relations began to be adversely affected, and China began to view these developments in India as a bourgeoisie culture in collusion with Western imperialism.

There were differences of opinion between Nehru and members of his own cabinet on the nature of frontier preparations. Deputy Prime Minister Patel, especially, was of the view that Communist China would not be a reliable and friendly nation, and that the move must be made with caution. Here, Nehru differed from Patel about any possibility of immediate action from Peking, especially taking into account

[29] Sardar Patel to the Prime Minister Jawaharlal Nehru on 7 November 1950. Published by Nayyar, *Between the Lines* (Appendix).

[30] *The Parliamentary Debates*, part 2, vol. IX, Second Part Col 5320 (1951); Sinha and Athale, *History of the Conflict with China 1962*, 49.

the international situation. However, in this premise of an emerging demand for precaution, soon after the Chinese troops entered Lhasa in October 1951, a meeting was convened by the foreign secretary, which was attended by India's ambassador to China, the director of the IB and the Chief of the Army Staff (COAS) to discuss a possible eventuality in the case that India needed to intervene in Tibet. After deliberations on the question of sending troops to Tibet to stop the Chinese, the proposal was rejected. General Kariappa categorically stated during a high-level meeting that he could not spare any troops or spare no more than a battalion for Tibet due to various commitments.[31] It seems that the volatile nature of the western border with Pakistan was a major concern for Kariappa. This also reveals that there were differences of opinion within the defence establishment itself on the need of military mobilization on the China border. The differences in decision-making among the various governmental establishments had naturally influenced official actions. Despite these, necessary precautionary measures were taken at the borders.

Himmatsinhji Committee and Other Reports

But the Nehru government responded to this volatile situation in a proactive manner. In the course of this emerging turbulence on the frontiers as well as within political circles, due to the armed presence of a militarily-superior neighbour in the northern frontiers, the Government of India proposed to constitute a committee to analyse the situation in the whole northern border. In 1950, the government constituted a committee,[32] and the immediate implementation of all major border preparedness thereafter was based on the recommendations of this committee. It was constituted of experts from the military and IB teams and had been entrusted with the task of studying and reporting the situation in the NEFA. However, considering the reported gravity of the prevailing situation in the northern border in general, taking note of the recommendations of the IB in particular, and also

---

[31] Mullik, *My Years with Nehru*, 80.

[32] The North and North East Border Committee under Major General Himmatsinhji was constituted in 1950.

with due respect to the home minister's earlier letter to the prime minister, the committee was expanded with extended jurisdiction.[33] Represented by members from the army, the air force, the IB, the MEA and the Ministry of Communications and Home Affairs, the mandate of the newly reconstructed body was to study and report on the whole Sino-Indian frontier areas in the background of Chinese military intervention in Tibet.[34] The committee submitted its reports in two separate volumes, first for the eastern sector (the NEFA in 1951), including Sikkim, Bhutan and Myanmar, and the second on the Ladakh region of Jammu and Kashmir, and on the areas of the central sector, including Nepal.[35] Some of the major recommendations of the committee[36] were (a) reorganization and redeployment of the military in the Himalayan frontier (Ladakh and the NEFA); (b) abolition of the Military Intelligence Organization (MIO) and merger of the MIO with the IB; (c) setting up of intelligence corps; (d) establishment of maximum posts along the border passes, etc.[37] For the Ladakh region, the committee had suggested administrative improvements, strengthening of militia, troop deployment at the frontiers, strengthening of the intelligence network as well as the road and communicative infrastructure.

These recommendations were, no doubt, accepted in principle by the cabinet, but there was much laxity and negligence on the part of their implementation. The comprehensive report actually included several administrative improvements in the various sectors.[38] However, at the implementation level, other than civil administrative improvements, the Government of India paid attention only to immediate military preparedness by establishing border checkpoints. Accordingly, nearly

---

[33] Sangeeta Thapliyal, *Mutual Security: The Case of India Nepal* (New Delhi: Lancer Publishers, 1998), 50.

[34] Sinha and Athale, *History of the Conflict with China 1962*, 38.

[35] Ibid., 36.

[36] The Government of India kept this report classified for decades on the grounds of national security interest.

[37] Thapliyal, *Mutual Security*, 50.

[38] The committee had suggested certain comprehensive steps to be taken by the government in defence and security including in the army, air force and civil armed forces like the Assam Rifles.

30 frontier posts were set up in 1952 (7 in Ladakh, 4 in Himachal Pradesh, 6 in Uttar Pradesh, 5 in Sikkim and 8 in the NEFA). Border checkpoints were increased from 6 to 14 in Uttar Pradesh by 1954 and 10 in Himachal Pradesh by September 1958, drawing staff mainly from the state police. Although inadequate, for Ladakh and the NEFA, the central government provided the required staff from the IB, and an Indo-Tibetan Border Police (ITBP) was raised for this purpose. The 7th Jammu and Kashmir Militia under the army was deployed to provide assistance at the Indo-Tibetan border posts.[39] Hence, within a decade, by gradual increase in the number of border posts, the Sino-Indian frontiers were provided with border posts at almost all regions. In Lingzi Tang, Aksai Chin, Soda plains, Depsang Plains, etc., where the terrain was hazardous, a gap existed. However, these border posts were far behind the actual boundary line, as per the claims of the Indian maps of 1954, and also nowhere near Aksai Chin, through which a Chinese road construction had been in progress. This shows the absence of a proper understanding of border alignments at an early stage.

Analysing the actual situation in relation to Tibet and other neighbouring states, in addition to the Himmatsinhji Committee, as early as 1950–1953, a few more committees submitted reports to the government suggesting the required remedial measures. In August 1951, Major General S. P. Thorat submitted the findings of his investigation about the political situation in Nepal and its borders.[40] Thorat suggested that the Government of India consider providing adequate security requirements to Nepal to safeguard Indian interests and security in the border region.[41] Moreover, under the supervision of K. Zachariah, Director of the Historical Division, MEA, a comprehensive paper based on archival documents was prepared.[42] These reports, including a few others, are still lying in cold storage with the Government of India.

---

[39] Sinha and Athale, *History of the Conflict with China 1962*, 38–51.

[40] S. P. Thorat, *Thorat Committee Report* (New Delhi: Government of India), 1951. This report is yet another report in the declassified category of the Government of India.

[41] Thapliyal, *Mutual Security*, 50.

[42] The paper called 'Studies on the Northern Frontier' discussed the history and circumstances under which the different frontier lines were suggested. The content of this paper is still kept secret from the public. Thapliyal, *Mutual Security*, 50.

It is highly pertinent here to explore the recommendations of these expert committees, the actual situations prevailing in border regions and to explore the forces behind these exaggerated apprehensions created on both sides. The uncertainty regarding the findings of the study and the reasons behind the report being shelved put a pause on the credibility of the Indian claim and the validity of their arguments.

The outcome of the earlier discussion in the context of strained Sino-Indian relations is that it was not because enough precaution-ary arrangements had not been undertaken, nor was there any total negligence from the Indian official side; rather, it was affected by the failure of a coordinated and cohesive move from the Indian side, incorporating all sections of the defence establishments. There were very strong political and personal interests influenced by the ideol-ogy that disallowed the government to move in unison at the time of such a national defence crisis. One major alleged failure of the Nehru government was that it did not take Home Minister Patel's recom-mendations into account. But as we have already seen, there was no merit to the argument, as in 1950 itself more than a couple of border commissions had been appointed as per his direction, largely based on the IB recommendation, the nature of which was further questioned.

Silent but Active Phase of Expansion on the Frontiers (1950–1956)

Along with these programmes to strengthen the security of the fron-tiers and despite grey areas in the perception of the border, a phase of validating territorial claims was also in progress on both sides. In the absence of any officially notified dispute apparent in this early stage, and also having a perception of colonial cartographic distortions and deformities as existing in the documents, it was a very studied and cau-tious move on the frontiers. In this direction, both nations had made considerable progress in their territorial possession, in accordance with the early understanding of their 'rights'. However, there was no immediate major territorial dispute at this stage, nor was there any area of confrontation in these territorial annexations. In the early days when Indian attention was largely locked in the eastern sector alone, China showed the least interest in staking any immediate claim on this frontier, but it was noticed, quite late, that it had been active in the western sector during the same period. The 1950–1954 period, therefore, even when marked for its active stage of cooperation and friendly relations, was also a period of silent but vigorous phase of reaffirmation of each side's border perception through the activities of annexation and consolidation. While China was preoccupied with road construction activity in Aksai Chin, New Delhi had already stormed into Tawang and extended its eastern claims as per their colonial heritage.

New Delhi Validates the McMahon Line

As early as 1950, India reiterated its right over the NEFA and established a strong ground for the existence of a valid McMahon Line as a well-defined border as per the Simla Convention (1914). Soon after the official recognition of the Government of PRC on 30 December 1949, 'The government of India made it open that New Delhi considered the McMahon Line as the legally valid boundary'.[43] Tawang, during this time, was under Tibetan occupation, as they had not abided by the Simla Agreement with respect to this region. On 17 March 1950, a Congress leader from Assam had complained that Tibetan officials were forcibly collecting dues from hill tribes in the NEFA, and the Assam government had been paying an annual fee of 5,000 to the Tawang monastery. The amount was finally remitted to the Drepung Monastery in Lhasa.[44] Studying the political and military situation in the region, New Delhi soon decided to bring all these far north-eastern regions under control and, in 1950, by the provision of the Indian Constitution, all these tribal regions were brought under the control of the NEFA. Areas south of the McMahon Line, including Tawang, became part of the Indian Union. But Gupta, who has delved into the archival documents, says that the Indian claim to the 'McMahon Line in the East has a basis in geography and usage but no basis in a valid international treaty'.[45]

It was on 20 November 1950 in the Lok Sabha that the first Indian official reference to this part of the boundary came up for discussion

---

[43] Gupta, *Hidden History of the Sino-Indian Frontier*, 53.

[44] Ibid.

[45] Ibid.

when Prime Minister Nehru emphatically declared, 'Our maps show that the McMahon line is our boundary and that is our boundary, map or no map. That fact remains and we stand by that boundary, and we will not allow anybody to come across that boundary'.[46] The emphatic nature of such a statement in the Parliament was warranted not on account of any immediate reaction from Peking, but in response to the persistent demand in the Parliament by the opposition for taking possession of the NEFA in the wake of the Chinese storming in Tibet. The awareness of an existing historical controversy inherited from the British since 1914 and an ongoing demand for protection of the Indo-Tibetan border forced Nehru to make this emphatic statement. Accordingly, on 12 February 1951, Major Ralengnao Khathing evicted the Tibetan administration from Tawang and established a subdivisional headquarters there.[47] China's response to this was a studied silence, without any protest. So when, 'India forcibly, but rightly, took over Tawang on February 22, 1951, China did not protest despite its reservations on McMahon Line'.[48] Even when Peking contested the validity of the McMahon Line, it did not protest at the status of the NEFA and did not propose any claim to it until as late as 1958.

It is opined that

> the movement of some Indian forces into the NEFA and the establishment of a few scattered check posts on the McMahon line after 1951 was not bothered by the Chinese apparently because they hoped to maintain a smooth Sino-Indian relationship and because the number of Indian personnel involved was militarily insignificant.[49]

---

[46] The parliamentary debate part I, Question and Answer, vol. V, no 1, 3rd session of Parliament of India, Monday, 20 Nov 1950, Col. 156; Sinha and Athale, *History of the Conflict with China* 1962, 23.

[47] Ralengnao (Bob) Khathing was an army officer from Manipur who joined the administrative services and went on to become India's first ambassador to Myanmar. He had played an important role in bringing Tawang under New Delhi's control. Khathing is the first Indian officer to have hoisted the Tricolour there in 1951. Sunil Oinam, 'The Man Who Won Tawang', *the Times of India*, 17 November 2012. Available at https://timesofindia.indiatimes.com/city/guwahati/The-man-who-won-Tawang/articleshow/17249796.cms (accessed on 2 September 2020).

[48] Noorani, 'The Truth about 1962', 17–30.

[49] CIA, *The Sino-Indian Border Dispute Staff Study* (Polo XVI. Section I, 1950–1959; Langley, VA: CIA RSS, 1963), 2.

The PRC stated that Indian action was allowed to go unchallenged because 'New China had no time to attend to the Sino-Indian border'.[50] Moreover, since China was largely involved in the serious Korean crisis against the USA, and India had been extending a very cordial supportive hand to the new China on the issue against the Western bloc, the latter did not want to preclude India on this action, though it had some difference on the nature of the McMahon Line. It is generally suggested that India took advantage of the Korean situation for its 'military move in "forcibly pushing" the boundary up to McMahon line'.[51] But the fact was that it was a strong and right action taken at a 'wrong time' so as to create suspicion in the mind of the neighbour. Moreover, the territory claimed by this action was perfectly correct, but the fraudulent British cartographical dispensation was the issue. Officials of the PRC, however, differ. 'The Indian army took advantage of our (Chinese) peaceful liberation of Tibet' to occupy the NEFA.[52] India was aware of the Chinese border perception in the eastern sector as a challenge to its claim. In 1952, the secretary general of the MEA, Girija Shankar Bajpai, expressed the need to raise the question of the McMahon Line with China. It is said that he warned Prime Minister Nehru about the potential for a Chinese invasion[53] and said that the McMahon Line might be one of those 'scars left by Britain in the course of her aggression against China, who may seek to heal or erase this scar on the basis of frontier rectifications that may not be either to our liking or our interest'.[54] However, after a detailed discussion with the Ambassador to China, K. M. Panikkar, the prime minister decided that it was not in India's interest to raise the question of the McMahon Line, and he was of the opinion that if China raised the issue 'we can plainly refuse to reopen the question and take our stand that…the

---

[50] *People's Daily*, 27 October 1962 in CIA, *The Sino-Indian Border Dispute Staff Study*, 2.

[51] CIA, *The Sino-Indian Border Dispute Staff Study*, 2.

[52] *People's Daily*, 25 October 1962, quoted in CIA, *The Sino-Indian Border Dispute Staff Study*, 2.

[53] Bajpai, 'Weightlifting'. G. S. Bajpai was the Secretary General in the MEA and headed the team which, by a technical error, had filed India's appeal to the UN on Pakistan's invasion in Kashmir, which led to the issue being considered a dispute rather than an act of aggression by Pakistan.

[54] Maxwell, *India's China War*, 76–77.

territory on this side of the McMahon Line is ours, and there is nothing to discuss about it'.[55] Actually, the legality of the Indian possession of the territory has no question, and even Peking had not raised this as an issue until as late as 1959, but the nomenclature of the British legacy was the only thing that mattered.[56] All this while, Peking was silently engaged in Aksai Chin (western sector), as New Delhi paid the least attention to these distant borders, as their border posts were far south of Aksai Chin, and the Tibetan rebels' presence was not found in this most inaccessible terrain.

Peking Appropriates Aksai Chin

It is a fact that while India was engaged in the NEFA, the western sector was largely neglected for a long time. As far as New Delhi is concerned, the right answer to a question on why New Delhi neglected the western sector would address much of the enigma in the nature of the dispute in this sector. It is suggested that 'the Indian claim to Aksai Chin in the west has no basis in treaty, usage or geography'.[57] It could be due to this awareness that even in 1954 the most advanced Indian post in this sector 'was at Chushul, south of present LAC. Except a couple of patrols to Lanak La, well south of Aksai Chin, no attempt was made to stake claim or take possession of these territories, and therefore India was conspicuous by its absence in western sector'.[58] But as early as 1952, the PRC had, by and large, occupied almost all of these 'later disputed areas'. There are contesting reports about the early occupation of the Aksai Chin region by China. Hugh Richardson says that the Chinese armies had marched from Sinkiang to western Tibet in the fall of 1950 through the Aksai Chin route.[59] Although Indian Intelligence Chief B. N. Mullik contested this claim of the Chinese troops reaching Tibet via Aksai Chin in 1950,[60] he acknowledged their

[55] Ibid.

[56] This will be further discussed in the coming chapters.

[57] Gupta, *Hidden History of the Sino-Indian Frontier*, 53.

[58] Guruswamy, 'The Battle for the Border'.

[59] Richardson, *Tibet and Its History*, 229.

[60] Mullik, *My Years with Nehru*, 196.

presence as early as the 1950s and even reported that 'a major Chinese road construction project was in progress since October 1951'.[61] *The Statesman* had reported on 15 November 1950 on the 'presence of the Chinese troops in Western Tibet and their advances from Sinkiang province' as 'contained in an official dispatch from the Government of India's trade Agent at Gartok, Mr Garpon Marlampa'.[62] S. S. Khera also writes about 'the activities of the Chinese on the Indo-Tibetan border, particularly on the Aksai Chin region' around 1952 or even earlier, and suggests that this 'activity was connected with the opening up of the road through the Aksai Chin region of Ladakh'.[63]

However, India did not pay much attention to these reports of early Chinese movements in this region. 'By about 1952, and in any case well before the 1954 Agreement, the developments had become too obvious to be ignored' for New Delhi.[64] However, despite these reports of active Chinese presence in the region, except publishing a new map in 1954, including Aksai Chin, until August 1958, India had not lodged any protest.[65] And by 1957, China had completed the massive road construction project across Aksai Chin without any 'serious' objection from India. Even when China announced its completion, India did not make it a matter of much concern, and it was only on 21 August 1958 that the Government of India, for the first time, sent a note to the Chinese Embassy protesting against the map published in the China Pictorial,[66] in which India regretted that 'the border as depicted in the map includes as Chinese territory' and stated that 'large areas in eastern Ladakh'[67] were wrongly depicted as Chinese territories.

Studying archival documents available since the pre-British times, A. G. Noorani made certain emphatic assertions about the status of

[61] Ibid., 195–199.

[62] *The Statesman*, 15 November 1950.

[63] Khera, *India's Defence Problem*, 157.

[64] Ibid.

[65] Gupta, 'Distortions in the History of Sino-Indian Frontiers'.

[66] Note dated 21 August 1958, *Notes, Memoranda and letters exchanged and agreements signed between the governments of India and China* (1954–1959), 46–54.

[67] *Notes, Memoranda and letter exchanged and agreements signed between the governments of India and PRC* (White Paper, vol. I, 1954–1959), 46.

Aksai Chin. His argument is that the 1842 Ladakh–Tibet Treaty had not defined the boundary between the two, and since the boundary in this sector was lying undefined, there was a stretch of territory between Ladakh and Tibet that was no-man's land.[68] Neither China nor India were certain of their boundary limits. The Chinese map published in *China Handbook, 1937–1943*[69] compiled by the Ministry of Foreign Affairs (MFA), showed Karakoram as the border. However, they took time to disclose this. In the meantime, the Government of India did not stake any emphatic claim to the area until much later.

So in the early 1950s, there was de facto possession of the later disputed territories between both the nations, the western sector with China and the eastern sector with India. China might have been willing to settle at that time on an 'as it is' basis at that time, even when it reiterated later that the Sino-Indian borders were not delimited. India, however, held that the Sino-Indian borders were sufficiently delimited by tradition and natural geographical features. Why did the Government of India not make any serious efforts, by diplomatic or military means, to emphatically assert its claim to bring those areas under its control? Guruswamy suggests that 'legally, there was not a very good case' for India, and the military price this barren, uninhabited desolate land would demand would not make it a worthwhile cause. 'Each side argues from history, in reality the evidence from history is rather ambiguous and inconclusive for both sides' territorial claims'.[70] Therefore, both 'governments decided to keep the lid on the problems while jockeying around for local advantages'.[71]

Nehru's Self-denial in Tibet Provokes the Rightists' Red Phobia

The military intervention of the PRC in Tibet and India's reaction to the action had already caused divisions in bilateral relations. The Sino-phobic clamour in the Indian press and the Parliament got louder,

[68] Noorani, *India–China Boundary Problem 1846–1947*, 213–218.

[69] Chinese Ministry of Foreign Affairs, *China Handbook 1937–1943* (New York, NY: Macmillan Company, 1947).

[70] Guruswamy, 'The Battle for the Border'.

[71] Ibid.

inviting Peking's displeasure against India, and reflected in their approach to Indian traders and officials in Tibet. The persistence of a section of Indian politicians for continuation of the much-debated Indian colonial privileges in Tibet was the crux of the new problem. However, since China was preoccupied with the Korean crisis and New Delhi had adopted a constructive approach towards the issue of Communist China, an open rift did not happen. Even when there was strong pressure on the Nehru government to act against Communist China, the proactive role of Jawaharlal Nehru in the Korean crisis had been highly appreciated in China, like elsewhere. But in 1953, once peace was finally declared in Korea, the Chinese began to move troops into Tibet, creating uneasiness about further strain in Sino-Indian relations. However, the government's approach towards Peking was very cautious and cordial, and it did not come under the influence of internal or external pressure.

In the meanwhile, India had invited the displeasure of the USA, in the Korean issue, for extending support to Peking. This brought the USA closer to Pakistan by a military alliance in September 1952. In this newly emerged political scenario in Asia, and especially due to the active presence of the USA in the region, Nehru adopted a friendly gesture in India's relations with China. Once the USA began to play a larger role in Asian affairs and a consequent apprehension of American expansionism in the region, the Government of India was prompted to mend fences with China. It was in the aforementioned context of larger interest that, even when the Chinese military forces stormed Tibet, inviting the displeasure of the Indian public, New Delhi adopted a proactive approach. In September 1953, India and China sat down to negotiate the outstanding questions. Chinese suzerainty was recognized in Tibet and as regards India's privileges in Tibet as 'forward rights' inherited from British India a policy of self-denial was adopted.

Critics of Nehru's Tibet policy argued that at a time when Communist China was striving for international acceptance, Tibet was the best opportunity for India to use as a trump card. They proposed that 'a robust Indian intervention might have maintained Tibet as an effective buffer between India and China, or at least enabled concessions to be won by India on the Himalayas Karakoram borders'.[72]

---

[72] Scott, 'Sino-Indian Territorial Issues', 4–8.

But Nehru, a statesman who wanted to play a larger role on the international stage and as an emerging leader of Afro-Asian nations, moved with caution. He viewed that the colonial 'extraterritorial rights' had no relevance in the new modern states' systems and, therefore, believed firmly that all the colonial privileges that the British India enjoyed in Tibet must be relinquished by independent India. But this policy of 'self-denial' was much criticized by Right-wing nationalists, by the opposition and even by some cabinet members, and the press and the Parliament gave a larger space for its discussion. But these criticisms did not bother Nehru in the pursuance of his endeavours for a larger Asian interest. Nehru and Chou Enlai pursued friendship and mutual coexistence, which finally culminated in the 1954 Panchsheel Agreement. 'One of the Five Principles of Peaceful Co-existence was "mutual respect for each other's territorial integrity and sovereignty". Had China believed that there was a substantial territorial dispute pending, then that was the time to raise the question'. But it did not.[73] This means that the real character of the territorial dispute had originated much later. Meanwhile, both sides had comfortably settled in their respective regions of claim. The eastern sector was in New Delhi's possession, and China had not shown much objection to it except in the case of certain isolated areas like Tawang. Since the Indian Union had already integrated the territory by constitutional provisions and had established administrative jurisdiction, China did not want to provoke New Delhi, except quite late (1959) as a matter of bargain. Peking comfortably occupied Aksai Chin, having their own road infrastructure.

Similarly, New Delhi had already conceived the idea that even when some historical antecedents can be referred to, to make its claim to the difficult terrain of the Aksai Chin territory beyond Karakoram, taking hold of such a strip of barren land in the eastern most part of Ladakh, at the cost of antagonizing Peking, would be unwise. Since China had shown interest in this strip of territory and had invested sufficiently by venturing out to carve out a road, New Delhi was aware of the strategic significance of this plain for Peking, and also that Peking would definitely defend the case at any cost. Most significantly, except for a claim based on customs and tradition, New Delhi was aware of its

---

[73] Subramanian, 'Looking beyond the Border Issue'.

limitations for a judicious and legal claim to this south-western part of Aksai Chin, which had been candidly revealed by Nehru in the early years of his discussions on this issue. Therefore, in the Cold War era, sacrificing the larger Asian interest, India did not want to stake claim to this strip of barren and distant terrain, which was found to be militarily unsound. It was in this context that India gave up all its extraterritorial rights that the British government in India had exercised in Tibet by virtue of the secret Anglo-Tibetan Regulations of 3 July 1914. Nehru did not want to use the 'Tibet card' for New Delhi's advantage, which he despised as a 'tag of imperialism'. However, the story in later years became much more complicated and an unending dispute. This had largely originated on account of various factors.

New Maps and Renewed Interests after 1954

A major Sino-Indian bilateral negotiation for a friendly and permanent settlement of all outstanding issues, including the border dispute, was initiated in Delhi in December 1953. On 29 April 1954, in Peking, the deputy foreign minister of China, Chan-Han-Fu, and the Indian Ambassador, N. Raghavan, signed the final agreement of the five principles (Panchsheel) for trade and intercourse between the Tibet region of China and India. The agreement also pledged to respect each other's territorial integrity and sovereignty. However, the final result of the agreement was not as conclusive as Nehru envisaged. According to Khera, former cabinet secretary and principal defence secretary to the Government of India:

> Nehru, with his sense of history and of the need for long-term stability of friendly relations between the two great and ancient nations, had hoped for a 25-year agreement in the first instance. But the Indian negotiators succeeded in achieving only a comparatively short-term agreement for 8 years.[74]

The conference, which began on 31 December 1953 in Peking, was attended by an official Indian delegation that wanted a discussion with the Chinese Premier Chou Enlai on all existing issues for larger under-standing. But B. N. Mullik claims that, even as the Indian delegates

---

[74] Khera, *India's Defence Problem*, 155.

had insisted on all 'the pending questions to be discussed', it was Chou who was of the view that only 'such questions as were ripe for discussion should be taken up leaving the rest for future settlement'.[75] It is argued that there were debates in the Indian camp on whether or not to raise the border dispute at the conference. K. M. Panikker had advised Nehru not to raise the issue, but the secretary general of MEA, Girija Shankar Bajpai, insisted on settling the matter before the agreement.[76] The border question, however, was not raised by Indian delegates in Peking, and they held that unless and until China took up the issue, India would not raise it. In the absence of availability of proper documents on the deliberations, the veracity of the claim is to be verified. It is also highly unlikely that Peking, which had so far been insisting on a border settlement, was against that, while New Delhi, which had maintained that borders are sufficiently settled by tradition and customs, had now differed from that stance. Moreover, when Nehru wanted a 25-year agreement, as it was presumed that within this period all issues could be peacefully settled through friendly negotiations, the settlement was signed for a term of eight years. Naturally, Nehru was disappointed with these developments.

Whatever transpired in the diplomatic debate, Nehru finally defended the agreement but, at the same time, he also gave instructions to set up border posts to safeguard the country's northern frontiers.[77] So after the Panchsheel Agreement was signed, when there was an enhanced scope for mutual cooperation, New Delhi made efforts to strengthen its border and to give clarity to its perception on the border by publishing maps. Subsequently, in July 1954, the Government of India published a new Survey of India map that showed Aksai Chin as belonging to India.[78] It is alleged that, immediately after the 1954 friendly agreement, Nehru's 'secret' instruction for establishing border posts to formulate a new extended line for the boundary had led to strained relations with the PRC. But his action was justified in the

---

[75] Mullik, *My Years with Nehru*, 151.

[76] S. Gopal, *Selected Works of Jawaharlal Nehru* (New Delhi: Orient Longman, 1992), 16–19.

[77] Khera, *India's Defence Problem*, 155.

[78] Gupta, 'Distortions in the History of Sino-Indian Frontiers', 1265–1270.

interests of the nation, taken as a precautionary measure for which he had his reasons, as reflected in his words in the note. On 18 June 1954, he wrote to the secretary-general, foreign secretary:

> No country can ultimately rely upon the permanent goodwill or *bona fides* of another country, even though they might be in close friendship with each other. Certainly it is conceivable that our relations with China might worsen, although there is no immediate likelihood of that. Therefore, we have always to keep in mind the possibility of a change and not be taken unawares. Adequate precautions have to be taken.[79]

It was in this vein that he issued a detailed directive on 1 July 1954 stating

> All our old maps dealing with this frontier should be carefully examined and, where necessary, withdrawn. New maps should be printed showing our Northern and North Eastern frontier without any reference to any 'line'. The new maps should be sent to our embassies abroad and should be introduced to the public generally and be used in our schools, colleges, etc...[80]

The note further clarified that as

> our policy and as consequence of our Agreement with China, this frontier should be considered a firm and definite one which is not open to discussion with anybody. There may be very minor points of discussion. Even these should not be raised by us. It is necessary that the system of check-posts should be spread along this entire frontier. More especially, we should have check-posts in such places as might be considered disputed areas.[81]

This decision was part of a larger policy setting decision to publish official maps showing an unambiguous delimited boundary between India and China.[82] It was based on the recommendation of the Himmantsinhji Committee Report, submitted by leading officers from the army and air force as well as members from all major ministries

---

[79] Note from Nehru dated 18 June 1954, to the Secretary-General, Foreign Secretary and Joint Secretary in *Selected Works of Jawaharlal Nehru*, vol. 26, 477.

[80] Note to Foreign Secretary dated 1 July 1954 Para 7 *Selected Works of Jawaharlal Nehru*, 482–483.

[81] Ibid., Para 8.

[82] Hoffmann, *India and the China Crisis*, 25.

on 24 March 1953, that the decision to formulate a new line for the boundary was taken. But it was only after the Panchsheel Agreement concluded in April 1954 and buoyed by strengthened friendly relations with Peking that on 1 July 1954 Nehru gave the necessary direction for strengthening the border.[83]

The context of New Delhi's awakening in 1954 regarding publishing a new map and ordering for border preparedness immediately after a friendly treaty is explained for different reasons. First, in the post-Panchsheel *bhai-bhai* days, Nehru was confident about strengthening friendly relations and conveying the truth about the false border perception of Peking without any fear of conflict or enmity. Second, even when China was suggesting a border delimitation, which New Delhi had declined on the grounds that it believed that the borders were sufficiently delimited, when the opportunity came (April 1954) for a discussion of the nature of the existing disagreement, it was declined by China. This led to suspicion and apprehension in Nehru of the pending nature and gravity of the dispute from the point of view of Peking. Nehru, therefore, believed that publishing a map from an Indian perspective would bring clarity, and the Chinese rhetoric of a 'yet to be delimited borders' would come to a finality. Third, in the context of continued Chinese military mobilization at the border in the name of checking Tibetan rebel infiltration into the border region and the apprehension of possible border encroachment from the PRC, Nehru wanted to send a message to Peking that New Delhi was interested in settling existing issues on the border, if any, in order to bring transparency to its border limits. A more significant fourth reason occurs in the context of New Delhi's self-denial of the colonial privileges in Tibet. This brought not only strong criticism from many quarters of national politics but also invited a scathing attack from the anti-communist faction, which demanded military intervention in Tibet. By publication of the new map immediately after the Panchsheel and further strengthening new border posts, Nehru was able to send a strong message that his China policy was firm and, at the same time, proactive, so that his critics would be silenced. The fifth and major reason for this 'awaited move' by Nehru until 1954 is explained in the

[83] Noorani, 'The Truth about 1962', 17–30.

context of the Kashmir issue. The future of Kashmir was still uncertain on account of the Indian commitment to the verdict of an internationally supervised plebiscite in Kashmir, subject to the prior withdrawal of Pakistani-armed personnel from its territory.[84] Moreover, in June 1952, the 'Head Lama of Ladakh, Kui-shak Bakola, had warned that Ladakh might seek political union with Tibet as a last course left to us'[85] due to persisting uncertainty. These multiple factors seem to be the real reasons why the Government of India maintained silence over several years, even though it knew about Chinese presence in the Aksai Chin region.

This map, which was brought out in July 1954, was contradictory to what had been shown in the earlier 1950 political map of India, in which the northern frontier extending from the north-western end of Kashmir to Nepal was shown as 'undefined' and the McMahon Line as 'un-demarcated'.[86] According to Gupta, in the

> new map of India issued in July 1954, the words 'Boundary Un-defined' were erased, and by this simple process the Survey of India maps laid claim to a boundary alignment of Kashmir east of the Karakoram Pass akin to the John Ardagh Line, including the whole of Aksai Chin and reaching the Kunlun Mountain in the north-east.[87]

In the central sector, the ITBP set up new checkpoints in the previously disputed areas. The Chinese, on the other hand, were actively involved in a survey of the border region in this sector for the first time.

These territorial advancements and the 1954 *map-manship*[88] did not form part of the conversations between Prime Minister Nehru and Chinese Premier Chou Enlai during the latter's visit to India in the winter of 1956. Nehru was anxious to know the response of Chou on the McMahon Line, and he had tried to indirectly bring in a discus-

---

[84] Gupta, 'Hidden History of the Sino-Indian Frontier', 765, 767, 769.

[85] Josef Korbel, *The Danger in Kashmir* (Princeton, NJ: Princeton University Press), 230–233.

[86] Gupta, *Hidden History of the Sino-Indian Frontier*.

[87] Ibid., 765, 767, 769.

[88] Mankekar, *The Guilty Men of 1962*, 16–26.

sion by way of reference to the Burmese border with China. Chou, in the discussion, tried to create an impression that, while he did not approve of this border being called the McMahon Line, he was willing to accept this line as had been approved in the case of the Burmese border. Chou, therefore, proposed to accept this border with India as well, after due consultation with the authorities of the Tibet region 'in consideration of the friendly relations between India and China'. Nehru, however, did not raise the issue of the Kashmir border in the discussion.[89] So the 1954 Sino-Indian agreement brought with it an environment of peace between people on both sides of the border and put a halt on the tussle that had originated with the Tibet issue, and this, by and large, extended up to 1956, until the second wave of the Tibetan uprising and Peking's crushing of it. In short, the border issue came to exist in the perception of both nations as a distant mirage and did not come up as a destabilizing factor in their closer interactions until 1956 when Tibet became a 'spoiler' of this cordiality.

---

[89] Gupta, *Hidden History of the Sino-Indian Frontier*.

Tibet Factor in the Border Dispute

One of the strongest underlying factors that contributed to the Sino-Indian border conflict, no doubt, was the Tibetan issue. When China failed to internally resolve the issue with the authority at Lhasa, New Delhi extended its 'moral support' to Lhasa in its struggle for autonomy against the PRC. Quite naturally, they suspected India of secretly plotting with the Tibetan rebels, in collusion with the imperialist West. In the early 1950s, when the Indian Parliament vociferously debated the Tibetan issue, and a section of its members and media clamoured for Indian military action in Tibet, in addition to insisting on continuing with the British Indian 'imperialist privileges' in Tibet, China suspected of a legacy of British imperialism[1] inherited by India. Instead of looking at India as a friend beyond its southern borders, China was suspicious and saw India as a foe. Even when there were several occasions to share warmth and camaraderie, something or the other continued to come in the way of genuine friendship between the two nations. This became all the more apparent by 1956, when New Delhi expressed 'sympathy' with the rebels of the Tibetan uprising, which further intensified by 1959 with the third wave of the rebellion. New Delhi's enthusiasm to accommodate the Dalai Lama and his followers in 1959 confirmed Peking's suspicion of the alleged role of an outside force in Tibet. Not only was the Dalai Lama and his followers given a warm welcome in India, but even the prime minister himself showed interest in the case with his April 1959 visit to Mussoorie, where the young Lama was residing. When the Dalai Lama took shelter in Mussoorie, China alleged that it was due to Nehru's support that the Tibetan cause got the

---

[1] CIA, *The Sino-Indian Border Dispute Staff*, Section I (1950–1959), iii.

attention of the world and that anti-China propaganda had begun. In a statement on 16 May 1959, the Chinese government very strongly protested against the widespread expression of sympathy that the Indian public, the press and the Parliament showed for the Tibetan cause.[2] Naturally, the Tibetan refugee issue and Dalai Lama's political asylum intensified rivalry in the context of an already existing border issue.[3]

It is a fact beyond doubt that 'the status of Tibet' in relation to China 'and India's perception of it, has been one of the destabilizing factors in Sino-Indian relations'.[4] New Delhi had a laid-back approach to this sensitive issue, which turned out to have a considerable impact on the future of Sino-Indian bilateral relations. Intense emotional intervention by the opposition further complicated matters, and these continue to be unresolved even now. 'Publicly, the Indian government regards Tibet as an integral part of China. But in popular parlance and in many of its actions, it does not behave as if Tibet is a part of China'.[5] At the peak of the crisis, when India gave asylum to the Dalai Lama and opened its borders for thousands of Tibetan refugees to cross over and to settle on Indian land, China strengthened its argument on India playing the role of 'an imperialist'. Despite recognizing Tibet as an integral part of China, at the behest of the political opposition, India permitted the Dalai Lama and the rebel refugees to establish their headquarters in Dharamshala, where they continued to pursue anti-China propaganda. China was not pleased about this, irrespective of justifications on the basis of human rights, moral responsibility and international norms. While the Dalai Lama and the Tibetan rebels were 'allowed' to pursue anti-China propaganda on Indian soil, the situation was not well received in Peking.[6] Hence, New Delhi's Tibetan

[2] *Statement by Ambassador of China to the Foreign Secretary of India 16 May 1959* (White Paper I), 73–76.

[3] Sen, *The Sino-Indian Border Question*, 173–193.

[4] Swami Subramanian, 'Sino-Indian Relations through the Tibet Prism', *Frontline* 17, no. 18 (2000): 1–14.

[5] Ibid.

[6] Tsering Topgyal, 'Carting the Tibet Issue in the Sino-Indian Border Dispute', *China Report* 47, no. 2 (2011): 115–131,

policy was a failed diplomacy as it alienated its immediate neighbour to appease internal politics and win over applause from the Western powers. The consequence of this was that there were two major border clashes in August and October 1959.

Even when the Indian military occupied the Buddhist spiritual centre of Tawang in 1951, a territory that China considers part of its Tibetan province (and over which there existed a dispute between India and Tibet as well), Peking was silent as it had locked horns with the USA in the Korean crisis. The issue of Tawang came up in the dispute quite late, when the Tibet factor ended up being a disturbing aspect. The gestures that Nehru and the nation had carried out in due course, such as (a) the early diplomatic recognition of the new Communist China; (b) making earnest efforts to win a berth for the PRC in the United Nations (UN);[7] (c) successfully dissuading any UN action against the PRC's military storming of Tibet; (d) extending support in the Korean crisis, etc., could not convince Mao and the CCP. 'Integrating PRC into the international community by conceding its right to the Chinese seat at the Security Council'[8] was the central pillar of Nehru's foreign policy based on larger Asian unity. However, all this cordiality with Chinese Premier Chou Enlai and other officials could not change Mao's opinion, who could find nothing less than a democratic bourgeoisie in Nehru and in his nation India. Mao personally oversaw the Sino-Indian relations and dictated tough terms. He tried to attribute the Tibetan uprising to the instigation from India and its Western collaborators. Therefore, in the Chinese perception, there was a strong link between the Tibetan uprising and the Indian interest in Tibet and its eagerness to reach the most favourable border solution.[9]

[7] Anton Harder, *Not At the Coast of China: India and the United Nations Security Council, 1950* (Cold War International History Project; Washington, DC: Wilson Center, 2015). Available at https://www.wilsoncenter.org/sites/default/files/media/documents/publication/cwihp_working_paper_76_not_at_the_cost_of_china.pdf (accessed on 4 September 2020).

[8] Ibid.

[9] Dawa Norbu, 'Tibet in Sino-Indian Relations, The Centrality of Marginality', *Asian Survey* 37, no. 2 (1997). Available at https://online.ucpress.edu/as/article/37/11/1078/23410/ (accessed on 4 September 2020).

The newly formed Communist China's growing suspicion of India's intentions in Tibet was noticed way back in 1950, and China believed that India would 'maintain the privileges' it had enjoyed in Tibet since the British period. Suspicion of an attributed 'bourgeoisie' in Nehru and his government in New Delhi was so intense in Mao and the cadre of the CCP that this outlook foiled Nehru's efforts for Asian unity. An internal Chinese diplomatic note in November 1950 reported on this suspicion regarding India's interest in Tibet.[10] However, Nehru continued to be on friendly terms with China, but without deviating even slightly from support to the suppressed human rights of the Tibetans. In the first wave of the Tibetan uprising in 1949–1950, when the PLA used armed force against the uprising, India unequivocally protested against it as a human rights issue. However, in 1954, Nehru softened India's stand by recognizing the Tibet Autonomous Region as part of the PRC. By the trade agreement of 1954, India recognized the Chinese authority in Tibet and did not raise the validity of an earlier independent status of Tibet. It was the days of the 'Hindi–Chini bhai bhai' slogan, and Nehru was overwhelmed with its success, which he hoped would lead to the Third-World unity. When, as a gesture of goodwill and friendship, India relinquished all its extraterritorial rights (which were in existence since the 1906 British period) in Tibet, Nehru rightly hoped for a likely improvement in the bilateral ties. But the PRC continued to attribute a link between the Dalai Lama and the bourgeoisie West in which India, according to Mao, was a partner with the intention of destabilizing Communist China through Tibetan uprisings.[11] Late in November 1956, tensions in Tibet rose with the Dalai Lama travelling to India, ostensibly to attend a Buddhist conference,[12] but intending to seek political asylum. And the fissures in the Sino-Indian relations widened.

[10] Ananth Krishnan, 'Behind the War, A Genesis in Tibet', *The Hindu*, 20 October 2012.

[11] The Tibetan uprising occurred in three major waves. The first was in 1950, the second in 1956 and the final in 1959, and on all three occasions the Dalai Lama left Lhasa to take shelter in India.

[12] The visit of the Dalai Lama and the Panchen Lama to India in November 1956 was on an invitation issued by the Government of India in connection with the celebration of the 2,500th birth anniversary of Buddha. Chen Jian, 'The Tibetan Rebellion of 1959 and China's Changing Relations with India and the Soviet Union', *Journal of Cold War History* 8, no. 3 (2006): 54–101.

Although Nehru had persuaded the Dalai Lama to return to Tibet, he had strong internal political pressure not to do so. A meeting had also been arranged between the Dalai Lama and Chinese Premier Chou Enlai[13] in India, with the hope that it would improve the situation, but that too was, unfortunately, in vain. Chou later said that this 1956 meeting of the Dalai Lama in India was a turning point in Sino-Indian relations. Chou said that this 'exposed their desire to collude with the Dalai Lama and attempt to maintain Tibetan serfdom'. 'At that time, I found Nehru inherited British Imperialist thoughts and deeds on the border issue and the Tibet issue'.[14] Referring to the 1958 Tibet, Sichuan and Qinghai rebellions, Chou later said, 'Nehru could not wait and took advantage of the border issue to interfere with China's internal affairs. The Dalai Lama rebelled in 1959 and fled to India, and this was caused by Nehru's inducement'.[15] There were, thus, ample reasons that the PRC could site for their 'inducement theory' involving India. In 1959, after an intense armed clash between the PLA and Tibetan rebels, thousands of refugees fled to India, resulting in serious security implications on the Sino-Indian border. Taking advantage of the situation of Tibetan refugees fleeing to India, armed Tibetan rebels were also suspected to have crossed the border to resume their resistance in India. Soon, China strengthened its armed forces on the Sino-Indian borders on the pretext of preventing the rebels from crossing over. India responded to this armed presence on the border with a similar measure, but largely with the intention of preventing the armed rebel's entry. This further deteriorated relations across the border, making the situation volatile. On 31 March 1959, the Dalai Lama along with his trusted followers were provided political asylum,[16] as a result of which diplomatic relations worsened again.

---

[13] Chou Enlai was also on a simultaneous visit to Delhi to discuss the border as well as Tibet issues.

[14] Conversation between Chou Enlai and the Soviet Union Ambassador in Beijing on 8 October 1962 in Wilson Center digital documents.

[15] Krishnan, 'Behind the War'.

[16] The Dalai Lama was given asylum on the condition that he would not engage in any political activity in India. But soon the Dalai Lama revived political activity in India, establishing headquarters at Dharamshala.

While the Dalai Lama was given a ceremonial welcome in India, with Nehru himself receiving and felicitating him,[17] the Chinese found a friend of the Western bourgeoisie in New Delhi. Archival records testify that Nehru was under pressure to play a dual role during this period. A persisting demand from within the country and even from some of his own party members for militarily intervention in Tibet against the PRC, along with having to take the role of an apostle of international peace in Tibet without alienating China, was a difficult balancing act. Actually, when the Dalai Lama requested asylum in India, Nehru 'moved with care to support Tibetan rebels'. His immediate concern was the possibility of the Chinese troops entering India in the pursuance of the rebels, leading to serious clashes. He directed that permission be denied to the rebels at checkpoints on the frontiers, but they were later admitted disarmed. It was due to the persistent demand from the leaders in India that he had given assurance to provide 'asylum for Dalai Lama and his staff'.[18] But India rejected the Chinese accusation of having played the role of instigator in the Tibetan issue. The Indian response was that 'criticism is part of democracy and therefore issues come up in Parliament and the government of India is often criticized and opposed by some section of the Indian people'.[19] The expression of sympathy for the Tibetan cause and the opening of the doors to the refugees by the Government of India had, no doubt, acted as a catalyst for a rapid deterioration of Sino-Indian relations,[20] which had already started to show strain on the border issue. China, in such a context, adopted an open hostile approach in its relations with India. What was more annoying to Nehru was the fact that soon after, China was found to be moving closer to Pakistan in most issues in an attitude of 'an enemy's enemy is a friend' and that its media had adopted an apparently hostile approach on Indian issues. Trans-border traders and foreign officials began to feel the

---

[17] In April 1959, Prime Minister Nehru paid a visit to Mussoorie, where the young Lama was residing, and had discussions with him on the Tibetan issue.

[18] CIA, *The Sino-Indian Border Dispute Staff*, Section I (1950–1959), 13.

[19] Statement of the Foreign Secretary to the Chinese Ambassador, 23 May 1959 in Ibid., 77–78.

[20] Sinha and Athale, *History of the Conflict with China 1962*, 31.

repercussions in their Chinese transactions, especially in Tibet, and a mutual trust deficit developed in all future dealings. Even when the Nehru–Enlai friendship endeavoured for better relations to reach a final negotiated settlement, an increasing military mobilization on both sides of the border was also in progress. While contextualizing Tibet as a prominent factor in Sino-Indian relations, it is imperative to understand the historical relation between Tibet and Peking, and the circumstances under which a crisis evolved between the two due to the impact of colonial intervention.

Lhasa–Middle Kingdom Historical Relations

To establish a link between provincial Tibet and the Middle Kingdom is not the intention of this study. It is a wider debate, and it is argued that the province of Tibet as part of China was a new narrative that emerged from 1950.[21] The Western media, in general, and the USA, in particular, are behind such a campaign. But a strong counter-narrative prevails—there are grounds to prove that Lhasa was historically under Peking's political suzerainty.[22] However, even when cultural diversity persisted between the two, a historical relation conjoining these two territorial units under a single political organization was long apparent, even when there were intermittent intervals to this continuity. A prolonged period of Tibetan subjugation was evident under the Ching (Manchu) dynastic government in Peking. Hence, the history behind this link is more than just a day or two of modern political developments under Communist China. Tibet had for long been under the political influence of the Middle Kingdom. The earliest available information in this regard dates back to the 7th century during the Tang dynasty. Later, under the Yuan dynasty, during the 13th and 14th centuries, Tibet came under their domination. However, it

---

[21] Elliot Sperling, 'Tibet and China: The Interpretations of History since 1950', *Open Edition Journals* (2009). Available at https://journals.openedition.org/chinaperspectives/4839 (accessed on 4 September 2020); Warren Smith Jr., *China's Tibet Autonomy or Assimilation* (Washington, DC: Rowman & Littlefield, 2009).

[22] Andrew Wei-Min-Lee, 'Tibet and the Media: Perspective from Beijing'. Available at https://core.ac.uk/download/pdf/148695839.pdf (accessed on 4 September 2020); Sperling, 'Tibet and China'.

was under the Ching dynasty (1644–1911) that the actual political control of Peking over Tibet was effectively felt. During this period, as a symbol of recognition of its political sovereignty, a Chinese representative (*Amban*), with a strong garrison was stationed in Lhasa. It was only during the second half of the 19th century, when Western imperialist intervention destabilized China, that the authority of the *Amban* in Lhasa gradually waned, and Tibet increasingly became autonomous, while Chinese hegemony over Tibet remained only symbolic.[23] However, the idea of an independent status for Tibet was actually hatched in the mind of Lord Curzon, the imperial viceroy of India (the colonial game in this Himalayan territory and its buffer zone strategy to protect the British Indian possessions have been discussed at length in Chapters 2 and 3).

Curzon did not give much significance to the suzerain rights of China to the land called the 'roof of the world' wherein he had an interest. Curzon 'regarded the idea of "suzerainty" as a "constitutional fiction"'.[24] Under his direction, Francis Younghusband undertook military expeditions to Tibet (1903–1904) and an Anglo-Tibetan convention was signed in Lhasa in September 1904. One of the high points of this convention was that 'Tibet would deal directly with (British) India instead of through China'.[25] This opened the doors to the beginning of a British imperialist 'game' in the Himalayan territory. Although the Curzon–Younghusband actions were later reversed on the home government's direction under Minto–Morley, the systematic imperialist game in Tibet began with the Simla Conference in 1914 (see Chapter 3).

At the fall of the Ching Imperial dynasty in 1911, Tibet cut off its relations with the Peking authority, like a few other provinces, and the Chinese political unity was under question for a while. It was only after the fall of the Manchu dynasty in 1911 that the 13th Dalai Lama

---

[23] Melvyn C. Goldstein, *The Snow Lion and the Dragon: China, Tibet and the Dalai Lama* (Berkeley, CA: University of California Press, 1997), Chapter 1.

[24] Subramanian, 'Sino-Indian Relations through the Tibet Prism', 2–15.

[25] According to the Convention, Chumbi Valley was transferred to British India for 75 years. Subramanian, 'Sino-Indian Relations through the Tibet Prism'.

declared Tibet an independent country. It was a time when provincial warlords had taken political control of large parts of China. China was almost destabilized due to a lack of political unity. Mongolia declared independence under Russian influence. Sinkiang and Manchuria were raising the banner of dissent. The tripartite Simla Convention (1913–1914) held under British Officer Henry McMahon bestowed a separate entity to Tibet,[26] even when under Chinese suzerainty for namesake. The republican government after Ching (1912) and the successive political organization under Kuomintang nationalist were not powerful enough to maintain the political integration of these regions. Tibet during this period virtually enjoyed its de facto independent status for about four decades. Despite this, neither Peking nor the international community ever formally recognized it as an independent state. Similarly, no definite effort from the side of the Lhasa authority had been noticed to formally turn Tibet from its de facto status to a de jure one that would have been recognized by the international community.[27] Even during this period, the 13th Dalai Lama 'in 1929 had again begun to accept Chinese suzerainty'.[28]

After a prolonged civil war, when the Communist forces under Mao defeated the Nationalists and formed the PRC in October 1949, their immediate priority was to achieve the objective of creating a greater China. With this professed aim, the PRC embarked on the task of 'liberating' provinces that were once part of Ching-China. This so-called liberation of the 'Land of Snows' and its integration into the PRC got priority in Mao's strategy, especially due to its geopolitical strategic significance to China. Being located in the south-west border area, neighbouring India, Nepal and Bhutan, the province of Tibet served as China's strategic access point towards the south-west direction. Since the Russo-British imperialist game had already done much damage to its southern provinces of Sinkiang and Tibet, the Chinese were very particular about the status of Tibet. They believed that 'both the British and the US imperialists have long cast greedy eyes

---

[26] Refer to Chapter 3 for details.

[27] Goldstein, *A History of Modern Tibet*.

[28] Subramanian, 'Sino-Indian Relations through the Tibet Prism'.

on Tibet, so Tibet's position in (China's) national defence is extremely important'.[29] However, the ideological motivation of liberating the Tibetans from theocratic feudal exploitation was no less an objective of Communist China.

People's Republic of China 'Liberates' Tibet (1950)

The storming of Tibet began on 7 October 1950 by a military attack on Qamdo (Changtu) in which the PLA routed the weak Tibetan force quickly. According to Peking, it was after several rounds of repeated but failed negotiations between the PRC and Lhasa that the extreme step was taken. In this context, in March 1950, a Tibetan delegation had even met with the representatives of the PRC in Kalimpong to secure the new Peking government's promise that it would respect Tibetan territorial integrity. In the meantime, Communist China was desperately trying to convince the world community that only peaceful integration was its intention in Tibet. But the words of Communist China were not taken at face value by the Western world, which dominated the international forums. In the eventual deliberations at various levels, Britain and India, which had so far had a close link with Tibet, played a mediatory role in deciding on Sino-Tibet relations. On 16 September 1950, Tibetan representative Tsepon W. D. Shakabpa met with Chinese Ambassador Yuan Zhongxian in Delhi. The deliberation led to a deadlock when China insisted on a three-point proposal wherein Tibet would be part of China and its defence, foreign relations and foreign trade would be under Chinese control. When negotiations failed in October 1950,[30] the PLA moved to the border town of Qamdo, crushed the Tibetan Army and brought it under Chinese control.[31] Mao soon arranged for negotiations with the Dalai Lama

---

[29] The CCP Committee of the PLA's 18th Army, 'Instructions on Marching into Tibet', in Jian, 'The Tibetan Rebellion of 1959 and China's Changing Relations with India and the Soviet Union', 59–60.

[30] Goldstein, *A History of Modern Tibet*, 46.

[31] The Dalai Lama left Lhasa on 19 December 1950 and then stayed at Yadong, a small town close to the Tibetan-Indian border. Jian, 'The Tibetan Rebellion of 1959 and China's Changing Relations with India and the Soviet Union'.

and the Kashag (the Tibetan local government) in Lhasa. The CCP suggested that the prerequisite for any peaceful final solution would be Lhasa's acceptance of Tibet as an integral part of the PRC. Having no military power to defend themselves and also failing to elicit any response for outside help from the international community, including the UN, the USA, India and Britain,[32] the Tibetans had no choice but to send a delegation to Beijing in the spring of 1951. On 21 December 1950, the Dalai Lama left Lhasa to escape from the Chinese attack, settled at Yadong near the Indian border and sought political asylum in India. The Tibetan delegation in New Delhi this time had been engaged in preliminary conversations with China's ambassador.[33] They later proceeded to Peking, where negotiations between the representatives of the Dalai Lama and the Communist government started in April 1951, by which an agreement was reached on 23 May 1951. Tibet was assured of local autonomy, but provided for the gradual incorporation of the Tibetan Army into the PLA of China and the exclusive handling of foreign affairs by the Central People's Government of China.[34] The 'Seventeen Point Agreement' began with the statement that 'The Tibetan people shall unite and drive imperialist forces from Tibet and shall return to the big family of the Motherland—the People's Republic of China'. The Chinese government, for its part, agreed that it would maintain

> the established status, functions, and powers of the Dalai Lama, refrain from altering Tibet's feudal and theocratic political, economic, and social systems, and adopt 'various reforms' in Tibet only if the Tibetan people so demanded and only after consultation with 'the leading personnel of Tibet.[35]

The Dalai Lama, who had been in Yadong, a border town near India, since late 1950, approved the agreement and returned to Lhasa on

---

[32] See Goldstein, *A History of Modern Tibet*, Chapter 19–20; and Qiang Zhai, *The Dragon, the Lion, and the Eagle: Chinese-British-American Relations, 1949–1958* (Kent, OH: Kent State University Press, 1994), Chapter 3.

[33] CIA, 'The Liberation of Tibet' (CIA Intelligence Memorandum; CIA-RDP91T01172R0003002900; McLean, VA: 1951; Declassified 2006), 2.

[34] Ibid., 3.

[35] Tsering Shakya, *The Dragon in the Land of Snows: A History of Modern Tibet since 1947* (New York, NY: 1999), 449–452.

17 August 1951. The PLA units moved into Lhasa and many other parts of Tibet without encountering resistance. But tensions soon developed between the Chinese Communists and the Tibetans, almost immediately after the PLA entered Tibet. The presence of several thousand Chinese Communist soldiers in Lhasa and its surrounding areas imposed a great burden on limited local resources, especially in food supplies and a consequent surge of inflation in Lhasa. The conservatives among Tibet's political and monastic elites, who had never been happy with the 'Seventeen Point Agreement', tried to exploit this popular discontent. At the end of March and the beginning of April 1952, the newly formed People's Representatives organized a series of demonstrations and protests against the Chinese Communist presence in Tibet.[36] In these political developments in Tibet, the role of external forces was reasonably suspected by Peking.

Beginning of the Cleavage in Sino-Indian Relations

The Sino-Indian relations in the 1950s, as already seen, were cordial but, having said that, they were not completely devoid of issues, mainly because the Tibet factor loomed over both parties. As the British had already vacated the scene, leaving their imperial privileges in Tibet to independent India, the latter was keen on determining the status of its future relations with Tibet, and the fate of Tibet to be decided by Communist China. Therefore, between 1949 and 1950, despite the existence of possible mutual diplomatic cooperation between Peking and New Delhi, the suspicious approach of Peking regarding India's views on Tibet was a major issue. Hence, when the CCP leaders made plans to 'liberate' Tibet in 1949–1950, India was a major factor in their deliberations. New Delhi sent a number of official memoranda and notes to Peking expressing regret and resentment on the latter's plan of armed intervention in Tibet even before the actual storming of Qamdo. India persistently tried to follow a very cordial relationship even when it dared to say what it believed to be a 'bitter truth'.

Since August 1950, there were several communications between Indian Ambassador K. M. Panikkar and Chinese Prime Minister

---

[36] Ibid., 102–111.

Chou Enlai and other officials in the Chinese Foreign Ministry. In a note sent to the Chinese government on 12 August 1950, the stated position of the Government of India vis-à-vis Tibet made it clear that 'the Government of India never had nor do they have now any political or territorial ambitions in Tibet'.[37] Not only did it urge the PRC to stabilize Sino-Tibetan relations through peaceful negotiations, it also expressed concern over the unsettled conditions across the Sino-Indian border in the newly emerging situation. China responded on 21 August 1950 on a very cordial note, saying that it is 'happy to hear the desire of the Government of India to stabilise the Chinese-Indian border'. Peking further promised that their occupation of Tibet would be 'peaceful' and that their forces would remain in Qamdo and not march to Lhasa. On 22 August, Chou Enlai invited Ambassador Panikkar to a general discussion in which Chou told him that 'while the liberation of Tibet was a "sacred duty", his Government were anxious to secure their ends by negotiations and not by military action'.[38] He also stated that 'the recognized boundary between India and Tibet should remain inviolate'.[39] It was in this context that the Indian delegation to the UN, acting on the basis of a 'no use force' assurance, blocked the consideration of Chinese censorship in the UN. Nehru 'publicly supported the Chinese position on the ground that Tibet should be handled only by Beijing and Lhasa'.[40] However, the Chinese government viewed Indian intervention in the Tibet issue as an attempt to 'influence and obstruct the Chinese government's exercise of its sovereign rights in Tibet' and also as an attempt to make the internal problem of the Chinese government into an international dispute to increase the present deplorable tension in the world.[41]

---

[37] Note sent to government of China by the Government of India on 12 August 1950, quoted in Gupta, 'Hidden History of the Sino-Indian Frontier', 721–726.

[38] K. M. Panikkar, *In Two Chinas* (London: George Allen & Unwin, 1955), 105.

[39] Gupta, 'Hidden History of the Sino-Indian Frontier', 721–726.

[40] CIA, *The Sino-Indian Border Dispute Staff*, Section I (1950–1959), 1.

[41] Note of the PRC Government Delivered by Vice Foreign Minister Zhang Hanfu to Ambassador Panikkar, 16 November 1950, 102-00051-01, in CFMA. See also Song Enli et al., *Important Events in the Diplomacy of the People's Republic of China, 1949–1956* (Beijing: Shijie Zhishi, 1997), 60.

But the Chinese military incursion into Qamdo on 7 October 1950 prompted Indian leaders to express serious concern.[42] On 21 October, New Delhi suggested that Chinese military operations in Tibet would worsen the already tense international situation, especially in South Asia. But the response of Peking was intense and inimical. When K. P. S. Menon, India's deputy foreign minister in charge of relations with China and Tibet, expressed his concern over the Chinese military action in Tibet, on behalf of the Chinese Foreign Ministry, Mao Zedong personally drafted the response stating that 'Tibet is Chinese territory, and the Tibet issue is exclusively part of China's internal affairs. The People's Liberation Army must enter Tibet, but in the first place hope to enter Tibet without fighting a war'.[43] Similarly, when the Indian Ambassador to China, K. M. Panikkar mentioned that the newborn Communist China's military action in Tibet might hinder its efforts to be accepted by world nations and provide an opportunity for countries opposing the PRC to deny or postpone admission to the UN,[44] Mao instructed his Foreign Ministry to 'reply that Tibet is China's internal issue, and no foreign country has the right to interfere'.[45] On 30 October, Peking blasted back, saying, 'New Delhi was affected by foreign influence hostile to China and Tibet'.[46] Mao adopted a tough stand vis-à-vis India and personally oversaw his Foreign Ministry's dealings with the Government of India. Later, when K. P. S. Menon expressed 'regret' over the Chinese armed attack on Tibet, Mao instructed Chou Enlai and his Foreign Ministry to respond: 'Our attitude (toward India) should be even tougher. We should say that the Chinese troops must enter any part of Tibet they may enter, irrespective of whether the Tibetan local government is willing to negotiate and what the results

---

[42] Jian, 'The Tibetan Rebellion of 1959 and China's Changing Relations with India and the Soviet Union'.

[43] *Mao Wengao*, vol. 1, 108, quoted in Jian, 'The Tibetan Rebellion of 1959 and China's Changing Relations with India and the Soviet Union'.

[44] CIA, *The Sino-Indian Border Dispute Staff*, Section I (1950–1959), 1; Margaret Carlyle, ed., *Documents on International Affairs, 1949–1950* (London: Royal Institute of International Affairs, 1953), 550–556.

[45] Quoted in Jian, 'The Tibetan Rebellion of 1959 and China's Changing Relations with India and the Soviet Union'.

[46] CIA, *The Sino-Indian Border Dispute Staff*, Section I (1950–1959), 1.

of the negotiation will be'.[47] In an official response dated 16 November 1950, as per the direction of Mao, the Chinese Foreign Ministry averred that the Chinese government 'has repeatedly made clear that Tibet is an integral part of Chinese territory' and that 'the Tibet issue is exclusively an internal matter of China'.[48]

Factually, the Government of India's concern in this Himalayan region was not intended to influence Tibet against China or to intervene in the internal affairs of China to disrupt and obstruct its political stability, but it was more concerned about two things in Tibet. First, India was eager to see that the autonomy of Tibet was being protected so that it would stand as a buffer between India and China. This had been seen as a solace for a tension-free region along the border between the two Asian giants. As China had neither disclosed the nature of its 'recognized boundary' nor specified any principle of delimitation, New Delhi was awaiting an apt opportunity to initiate a discussion on this issue. Since it was a sufficiently documented fact that there was enough scope for a border dispute as a result of the inaccuracies and divergence in the border perception left behind by the British rule in India, it was found easier to maintain a peaceful borderline once an autonomous Tibet was ensured in the northern border. Second, it was not only a matter of continuing unrestricted trade, cultural and religious relations with Tibet but also of maintaining the special provisions and privileges that India had been enjoying since the British days. When Nehru and his close aides believed that there was no scope for maintaining such extraterritorial privileges right in the modern democratic world, there was a strong section within his party and in opposition leaders who wished in continuing with these privileges in Tibet. This was the result of the colonial legacy that a section of Indian politicians and bureaucrats wished to continue. This was the actual turning point in the post-colonial Sino-Indian relations. But the issue was approached in an emotional and passionate manner among the Indian public and the Parliament. Moreover, the government's actions were swayed by bureaucratic influences that aggravated

---

[47] Quoted in Jian, 'The Tibetan Rebellion of 1959 and China's Changing Relations with India and the Soviet Union'.

[48] Ibid.

bilateral relations with China and, at the same time, the response from the CCP and Mao was no less aggressive.

Nehru's Aspiration for International Peace and Tibet Issue

The approach of Nehru and his government towards the new Communist China was one of friendship and cordiality. After the establishment of the PRC on 1 October 1949, under the leadership of Mao Zedong, India was the first (besides Burma) non-Communist nation to recognize and establish diplomatic relations with the new Peking government.[49] It was followed by a mutual exchange of diplomatic and cultural missions. Further, when the Korean crisis of 1950 invited wrath of Western nations against Communist China, Nehru stood firm for the cause of China and strongly opposed UN intervention in North Korea.[50] Again, it was Nehru and his nation that was instrumental in getting Communist China's membership to the UN, even at the cost of displeasure of the USA. At the same time, Nehru and his government were upright in expressing displeasure through diplomatic channels wherever it was warranted. India sent a protest note on 26 October 1950 against Chinese armed intervention in Tibet. On 30 October 1950, when the Tibetan government pleaded for diplomatic assistance from India in the dispute with China, New Delhi immediately sent another strong protest note to China on 31 October 1950.[51] But, irrespective of these issues that persisted, Nehru and the Indian officials maintained a pleasant relation with the Chinese authorities during those days. Having gone through records of the interactions between Nehru and Chou Enlai, one can notice a highly informal and

---

[49] The Indian government recognized the PRC on 30 December 1949 and the two countries established diplomatic relations on 1 April 1950. Jian, 'The Tibetan Rebellion of 1959 and China's Changing Relations with India and the Soviet Union'.

[50] With the US influence, the UN Assembly passed a resolution on 7 October 1950 and under US Commander MacArthur, the UN force entered the North Korean capital of Pyongyang. It was not coincidental that the PLA stormed Tibet on the same day when the UN Army crossed the 38th Parallel and invaded North Korea. India even declined to attend the San Francisco Treaty of 1951 on the grounds that China was not invited.

[51] Gupta, 'Hidden History of the Sino-Indian Frontier', 721–726.

warm personal intimacy in all dealings. In these interactions, there was no scope for doubt or suspicion on each other's intentions.

Once the Korean War began in November 1950, China turned its attention to Korea. After the fall of Qamdo, the Chinese Army paused its march to Tibet, and the Indo-Tibetan border issue and the Tibet invasion had been relegated to the background for some time. Nehru watched the emergence of China as a formidable power to challenge American efforts to establish its hegemony in Asia. In the Korean crisis, Nehru played the role of an honest broker between China and the USA to avert a war that he thought would be disastrous for Asia. Reflecting on India's attitude towards Communist China in the context of a potentially dangerous war in Korea, Vijay Lakshmi Pandit said, 'A war is a greater threat to us than Communism in Asia'.[52] This statement is also to be viewed as a response, in the context of an emerging Communist phobia existing among certain political leaders and the media in the nation, against the idea of Nehru's Asian unity. But Nehru expected close cooperation and support from China to strengthen his Non-Aligned Movement in the newly emerging Third World. Hence, he was busy negotiating with the support of other Asian nations in the UN to reach a formula for peace in the Far East. In such a context, he wanted to avoid any dispute with China on the issue of Tibet. Nehru found enough reason for China to take the risk of challenging the USA. Instead of attacking China in the name of the brief Tibetan assault, he viewed things from a wider perspective. He said:

> China, in her new-found strength, has acted sometimes in a manner which I deeply regret. But we have to remember the background of China, as of other Asian countries the long period of struggle and frustration, the insolent treatment that they received from imperialistic powers and the latter's refusal to deal with them in terms of equality. It is neither right nor practical to ignore the feelings of hundreds of millions of people. It is no longer safe to do so.[53]

---

[52] *New York Times*, 1 January 1951, quoted in Gupta, 'Hidden History of the Sino-Indian Frontier'. The political debate in India this time was largely around whether communism was more dangerous than imperialism or not.

[53] Nehru's BBC broadcast on 13 January 1951, quoted in Gupta, 'Hidden History of the Sino-Indian Frontier'.

Hence, as regards the Tibet issue, India adopted a proactive approach considering the nation's relation with China and also the prevailing situation in the world. A decision of non-intervention was taken in the Tibet case at the advice of K. M. Panikkar, Ambassador to China, who knew better the nuances of Chinese priorities and perceptions.

Convergence in Divergence: From Tibet to Panchsheel

Even when the Tibet issue soured relations between India and China from 1950, it did not impede Nehru's and his colleagues' efforts in exploring peace and tranquillity in bilateral relations. As a result, in 1954, independent India and the PRC were once again determined to rid their relationship of differences that had crept in. Neither ideological differences nor territorial ambitions came in the way of searching for avenues of cooperation and coexistence for a better future. The signing of the Panchsheel Agreement in 1954 was the culmination of these efforts towards an emerging Asian unity. Hence, even when strong divergence persisted on various issues and policies, both nations tried to identify areas of convergence in their thoughts and actions. In February 1951, India annexed Tawang to its territory. But India extended a positive gesture to the PRC by strongly opposing the US-sponsored resolution in the UN General Assembly. This gesture had an impact in the relations between the two nations in the immediate future. Confident of the new environment, on 12 February 1951, Nehru told the Parliament that the House would remember that

> we were aggrieved at a certain turn of events in Tibet, but we did not allow that to affect our policy or our desire to maintain friendly relations with the People's Government of China. I am glad to say that our relations with the New China are friendly at present.[54]

Further on 28 March 1951, the members of Parliament were apprised of the government's Indo-Tibetan frontier policy by B. V. Keskar, the

---

[54] Nehru in the Parliament 12 February 1951, Parliamentary Debates, vol. 8 (New Delhi, 1951, Collection 2701).

Deputy Minister for External Affairs in the Lok Sabha. He said that the best way to protect our frontier with Tibet

> is to have a friendly Tibet and a friendly China. It is obvious that such a complicated and big frontier cannot be well-protected if we have a border country which becomes hostile to us. Therefore, we feel that…a friendly China and a friendly Tibet are the best guarantee of the defence of our country.[55]

On 27 September 1951, in an informal conversation with the Indian Ambassador, Premier Chou Enlai also reaffirmed Peking's official stand. He said, 'The question of stabilization of the Tibetan frontier was a matter of common interest to India, Nepal and China and could best be done by discussions between the three countries'. He said, expressing his concern at safeguarding Indian interests in Tibet in every respect, 'there was no territorial dispute or controversy between India and China'.[56]

As a reciprocal gesture, the Indian Ambassador in Peking informed the Chinese premier, on 4 October 1951, that the Government of India would welcome the negotiations on the subjects mentioned by Premier Chou Enlai. In this emerging environment for healthy dialogue, in October 1951, K. M. Panikkar presented New Delhi's stand as far as Tibet was concerned. He argued that 'extraterritorial rights had no place in the relationship between two independent countries in modern times and India would put herself entirely in the wrong by insisting on the continuance of the rights which the British had forcibly extorted from Tibet'.[57] For him, this was a means of removing Chinese apprehension about the Indian stand on Tibet, especially in the context of an emerging demand within the country to preserve and hold on to the Indian privileges in Tibet. Prime Minister Nehru also endorsed this view. He held that independent India, after its long history of struggle against imperialism, had no moral right and authority to retain those extraterritorial privileges inherited from imperialist

---

[55] B. V. Keskar, Deputy Minister for External Affairs in the Lok Sabha, 28 March 1951, in Gupta, 'Hidden History of the Sino-Indian Frontier'.

[56] Gupta, 'Hidden History of the Sino-Indian Frontier'.

[57] Mullik, *My Years with Nehru*, 147.

Britain during independence. Panikkar further clarified why such a position was imperative. He was sure that

> China would not agree to their continuance and there was no way by which India could enforce them except by force of arms which India was not in a position to employ. So the best policy would be to give up gracefully all that was untenable and insist on economic and cultural rights which were of a more fundamental nature and were not necessarily based on treaties.[58]

These reasonable arguments of the Ambassador were endorsed by the prime minister and his government. Therefore, in February 1952, Panikkar gave a report to Chinese officials about the existing conditions of Indian privileges in Tibet, but he did not insist on the preservation of privileges. Sharing his view about these extraterritorial privileges, Chou Enlai said that the situation was a scar left by Britain, 'For all of this, the new Government of India was not at all responsible'.[59] In subsequent discussions, Panikkar agreed that the 'existing conditions' need not be preserved and they mutually agreed to settle the question of the Sino-Indian relationship in Tibet. 'The Chinese Government proposed that the Indian mission, previously stationed in Lhasa, be changed into an Indian Consulate General' and the Government of India agreed to a Chinese Consulate in Bombay.[60] But this was not welcomed by many in the Indian bureaucracy. Claude Arpi states that the Indian Head of the Mission in Lhasa, S. Sinha, was deeply upset by this change.[61] The Chinese premier expressed his pleasure at India's willingness to arrive at a mutually satisfactory settlement and further clarified that there was 'no difficulty in safeguarding the economic and cultural interests of India in Tibet'.[62] On 15 September 1952, India officially announced in a press communiqué that certain changes in India's relations with Tibet had been proposed as a result

---

[58] Ibid.

[59] Claude Arpi, 'McMahon Line, More Than Just a Border Issue' (4 June 2015). Available at https://www.dailypioneer.com/2015/columnists/mcmahon-line-more-than-just-a-border-issue.html (accessed on 4 September 2020).

[60] Ibid.

[61] Ibid.

[62] Ibid.

of consultations with the PRC. Accordingly, the Indian Mission in Lhasa was designated Consulate General and the three trade agencies at Gyantse, Gartok and Yatung were to be under the general supervision of the Consulate in Lhasa.

However, the general response in India was that it was highly critical of the government's stand on its forsaken privileges in Tibet and, especially, because there was no discussion on the border question per se. This invited severe criticism in the Indian press and the Parliament and was described as weak action, reflecting India's inability to stand up against China. However, the continuing demands and queries within and outside the Parliament regarding the position of the border with China and the nature of the dispute, if any, did not waver Nehru's commitment to mutual coexistence. This prompted him to postpone the imminent border issue to a further date. In his search for peace and tranquillity in Asia, he sacrificed the aspirations of some Indians. In 1954, Jawaharlal Nehru softened India's stand by recognizing that the Tibet Autonomous Region was a part of the PRC and gave up privileges in the hope that the ties would improve.[63] But 'it was not yet clear that by these warm friendly gestures China might have been open to a compromise on the border issue in return for India's major concession on Tibet'.[64]

However, it did not prevent Nehru from exploring further avenues for peace and tranquillity in the subcontinent, and the Indian prime minister and the PRC premier jointly introduced the Panchsheel. On 29 April 1954, the 'Five Principles of Peaceful Coexistence' enhancing relations between Peking and New Delhi was inked.[65] The agreement was committed to trade and intercourse between the Tibet region of China and India for mutual cooperation and peaceful coexistence. The terms of the treaty doubtlessly reiterated both the nations' adherence to mutual respect for each other's territorial integrity and sovereignty, and mutual non-aggression and non-interference in each other's internal

---

[63] Krishnan, 'Behind the War'.

[64] Ibid.

[65] Jian, 'The Tibetan Rebellion of 1959 and China's Changing Relations with India and the Soviet Union'.

affairs, in addition to other clauses. The treaty therefore recognized Tibet as a Chinese territory and relinquished all the extraterritorial privileges existing since the British days (1904) as a gesture of goodwill and friendship. After the Panchsheel Agreement, for the next two years, the mood was, on the whole, very cordial and warm. This made India think that China was more concerned about Tibet than any minor frontier issue. New Delhi resumed efforts for border strengthening in this conducive atmosphere, while China was preoccupied with the consolidation of Tibet and border regions.

Bhai Bhai Days, but Short-lived

The Panchsheel Agreement was a milestone in Sino-Indian relations. However, even when it had given great hope to Asian unity, the *bhai bhai* days were short-lived. China, during this period of peace, was engaged in the Aksai Chin road construction project. New Delhi, in the meantime, had resumed its border strengthening efforts. On the basis of the recommendations of the Himmatsinhji Committee and various other reports, further strengthening of border posts was initiated in 1954. Confident of the conducive environment that had emerged from the relinquishing of British imperial privileges in Tibet and the recognition of Tibet as part of China, New Delhi published maps of India's northern and north-eastern borders. This action did not attract any immediate counteraction from Peking, as it had been preoccupied with the consolidation of Tibet. Even the unauthorized road construction in Aksai Chin, which was secretly in progress, was part of this preparedness in Tibet. But the map alerted China to a possible conflict against their border interests. China was of the opinion that the border perception of India was basically derived from the British Indian period. For them, the Simla Conference of 1913–1914 under the British imperialist was construed as a false pretext on the basis of which independent India claimed border regions which were shared with China. Hence, even when friendship and cooperation were reaffirmed, the 1954–1955 period was moving towards a phase of contradictions on the border issue. The construction of a road by the Chinese in Aksai Chin and its publication of a new map specifying the Sino-Indian border continued.

Kuldeep Nayyar later reported that even in 1954, Indira Gandhi had found some faint sign of Chinese aggression over the border issue, 'but Nehru did not believe that China would attack soon, but he was definite that it would come someday'.[66] It was not immediately apparent if this was true or not.

By the mid-1950s, relieved of any imminent threat, especially when the Korean crisis was averted by 1954, and confidence was assured in the Indian attitude, Peking turned its attention to quelling the Tibetan uprising and border expansion. With the construction of a new road in Aksai Chin for easy access to its military apparatus to the Tibetan terrain nearing completion, China moved ahead, forgetting the *bhai bhai* days. The map published by India, immediately after signing the 1954 agreement, can be considered as an excuse for the Chinese reversal of all terms of cooperation. But that alone does not suffice as reason to explain the China offensive that followed. The 1956 Tibet uprising and the suspected role of India in this, especially the Dalai Lama's visit to India during this turbulent time, further explain the situation. When the Dalai Lama was provided the opportunity to meet with the Chinese premier in Delhi, to bargain for the cause of Tibet, and to criticize Chinese policies in Delhi, Chinese perception was negatively affected.[67] Chou Enlai soon drew Nehru's attention to Tibetan activities in India and said that 'separatists were active across the border in Kalimpong in India'.[68]

The Sino-Indian tussle resumed in 1956 with the second wave of Tibet uprising. Even when friendship and cooperation were further reaffirmed, isolated incidents of bitterness and resentment were reported leading to strained relations due to untactful interventions by officials at both ends.[69] Hence, the centrality of the Tibetan issue

---

[66] Nayyar, *Between the Lines*, 139.

[67] Chou Enlai later disclosed that this 1956 encounter with the Dalai Lama in India, arranged by Nehru, had given him hints that India liked to play an imperialist role in Tibet.

[68] Krishnan, 'Behind the War'.

[69] After the departure of K. M. Panikkar, who stood firm for a friendly China, from Peking, there were some bickering between the officials of India and China on trivial issues. Mullik, *My Years with Nehru*, 149–150.

in Sino-Indian relations was evident by 1956. When armed revolts broke out across Tibetan territories, they had repercussions in border regions as well. Intensive armed preparedness by China in the regions bordering India alerted New Delhi to a counter-defensive measure. When the PLA began to quell the rebels in Lhasa, to prevent them from fleeing Lhasa, the Chinese forces occupied the border regions and this further intensified the heat of frontier relations. Internal Chinese documents show that India was to blame for its own failures in Tibet and that the 'resolution of the Tibetan problem was inextricably linked to the boundary dispute, a conviction that would have fateful consequences'.[70] Through the 1950s, even during the heydays of Sino-Indian friendship, Peking and New Delhi were never able to escape the shadow of the Tibet issue looming over them. The relationship began to get complicated as a result of the emergence of the Tibet issue, which later transformed into a bitter dispute on the border. But a section of Indian politicians and the public did not like China's policy of friendship and cooperation. Therefore, they severely criticized the government and the Indian media clamoured for sending a force to Tibet and reconsidering Indian privileges in Tibet.

Clamour for Intervention in Tibet and the 'Rightist' Propaganda

Since the birth of the PRC, Nehru had faced strong criticism from his own colleagues and some of the leading figures in the cabinet, including the deputy prime minister and the president, for his 'China policy'. There was a strong opinion in the opposition that Nehru's pro-socialist view had influenced his Sino-Tibet policies.[71] There was an active group of anti-communist propagandists present in the country within and outside the government, largely drawn from the Rightist political affiliation.[72] They had much influence on the opposition, in general, and on the media with a large international

---

[70] Krishnan, 'Behind the War'.

[71] His alleged leaning towards Communist Russia was highly criticized largely by the extreme rightists in the country.

[72] Subramanian, 'Sino-Indian Relations through the Tibet Prism', 2–15.

network among the American diaspora. It was a time when a strong anti-secular and Hindu-nationalist element was gaining support in the country due to the after-partition impact. These pro-Right loyalists in the opposition also maintained an anti-communist political ideology. It was a time when, through anti-Pakistan and anti-China sentiments, even in the government and the ruling party, a momentum for their ideological support base was easily mobilized. In anti-communist Tibet, they tried to notice a traditional, cultural and spiritual link for the nation.[73] During the PLA storming in Tibet, pro-Rightists elements, including higher officials and politicians, demanded armed intervention in Tibet against the Chinese invasion. According to Subramanian Swami, 'Some Indians are sentimental about the status of Tibet in China. There is the undercurrent of pan-Hinduism that is responsible for this sentiment'.[74] At the entry of the PLA to the border town of Qamdo in October 1950, there were strong demands from this section to support the Tibetan cause in maintaining its de facto independence.[75] This clamour in the Parliament and in the media created resentment in Peking and invited criticism from the CCP and its government. China began to view Indian interest in Tibet with suspicion and interference in its internal affairs. This was the real beginning of China's growing suspicion of India's intentions towards Tibet. The anti-China debate in the Indian Parliament on the Tibet issue demanded India's military intervention there. These discussions on retaining Indian privileges, which had been part of a secret agreement between Britain and Tibet (1913–1914) against Chinese interests, led to China's suspicion of New Delhi's intention in Tibet. In a diplomatic note exchanged among Chinese officials on 24 November 1950, Peking expressed concern over the long-term design of the Government of India on the status of Tibet. The note reported on the talks between India and China, which discussed the continuation of Indian privileges in Tibet.[76] The note details that 'it was exposed that India has interfered in China's internal affairs and has hindered China

---

[73] Ibid.

[74] Ibid.

[75] Gupta, 'Hidden History of the Sino-Indian Frontier'.

[76] Krishnan, 'Behind the War'.

from liberating Tibet…. India pretends not to have any ambition on Tibetan politics or land…but desires to maintain the privileges that were written in the treaties signed since 1906'.[77] These words testify to a clear division that had developed in Sino-Indian relations over a short period of time.

On 7 November 1950, some leading Indian officials and politicians, who had witnessed the emergence of a communist neighbour with much discontent to their ideological base, encouraged Tibet to submit a complaint of invasion and aggression against Communist China to the UN.[78] At the same time, however, the delegate representing the Government of India to the UN presented the issue for a peaceful settlement, strongly supported China and assured the UN members that Tibet's autonomy could be safeguarded, and that the best way to ensure this was to abandon the idea of discussing the matter in the General Assembly. Consequent to India's strong presentation on 15 November 1950, when the matter was raised in the General Assembly, the decision was that the Tibetan question should not be included on the agenda of the General Assembly.[79] India rose to the occasion to protect the interests of its neighbour by seeing better prospects for Asian unity. The opposition, on the contrary, looked at it as a missed opportunity to attack China on its Tibet policy.

The strongest criticism of Nehru's China policy came from Deputy Prime Minister Sardar Vallabhbhai Patel, who 'demanded even military intervention in Tibet and he had support from some members of the Cabinet and the Foreign Office'.[80] But the Army Chief, General Cariappa, stood strongly opposing this dangerous step of military intervention in Tibet.[81] Home Minister Patel was highly suspicious of the Chinese, and his heart beat for the Tibetan cause. Giving vent to his feelings, he urged Nehru to take action against China. His assertion of China's policy prompted him to

[77] Ibid.

[78] Gupta, 'Hidden History of the Sino-Indian Frontier'.

[79] Ibid.

[80] Ibid.

[81] Mullik, *My Years with Nehru*, 80–81.

write a strongly worded confidential letter to Nehru on 7 November 1950. He said:

> The undefined state of frontier and the existence on our side of a popula-
> tion with its affinities to Tibetans or Chinese have all the elements of
> potential trouble between China and ourselves. Recent and bitter history
> also tells us that Communism is no shield against imperialism and that
> Communists are as good or as bad imperialists as any other. Chinese
> ambitions in this respect not only cover the Himalayan slopes on our side
> but also important parts of Assam.[82]

On 9 November 1950, Sardar Patel blurted out in a public speech that there might be a world war on the issue of Tibet.[83] He warned Nehru of an imminent threat to India from China. Patel wanted India to intervene in Tibet to protect and preserve its independent status and cultural identity.

The response of the prime minister to this assertion was both prac-tical and realistic. On 18 November 1950, Prime Minister Jawaharlal Nehru replied to Patel, stating:

> We cannot save Tibet, as we should have liked to do, and our very attempt
> to save it might well bring greater trouble to it. It would be unfair to Tibet
> for us to bring this trouble upon her without having the capacity to help
> her effectively. It may be possible, however, that we might be able to help
> Tibet to retain a large measure of her autonomy.[84]

Nehru apprised Patel of the international environment and the possible danger Tibet may face. Nehru further added, 'It must be remembered that neither the UK, nor the USA, nor indeed any other power is particularly interested in Tibet or in the future of that country. What they are interested in is, embarrassing China'.[85] However, continued criticism of a soft attitude towards Communist China and persistent attacks from within the government and his own party members made

---

[82] Letter of Sardar V. Patel, 7 November 1950. For full content of the letter, see Nayyar, *Between the Lines*, 216–222.

[83] Gupta, 'Hidden History of the Sino-Indian Frontier'.

[84] Letter of Prime Minister to the Home Minister 18 November 1950, MEA Govt of India.

[85] Subramanian, 'Sino-Indian Relations through the Tibet Prism'.

Nehru really weary. The press and the Parliament insisted on clarity on the frontier question with Tibet. The attack by the opposition and the press on the policies of Nehru and his government compelled him to make certain statements against Peking's interests, which naturally led to further deterioration in relations.

In response to continued enquiries in the Parliament, and as a policy of appeasement of the opposition and his own colleagues in the Lok Sabha on 20 November 1950, the prime minister emphatically stated that the McMahon Line is India's boundary, and there is no doubt about that. He further added, 'The frontier from Ladakh to Nepal is defined chiefly by long usage and custom'.[86] Further, on 6 December 1950, Nehru reiterated in the Parliament that the Himalayas formed India's traditional northern frontier and that, since Nepal was on this side of the Himalayas, any threat to the security of Nepal would be considered a threat to the security of India. Even when Nepal was an inalienable friend of New Delhi, it was dearer to the Rightists in India. This statement by Nehru on Nepal was naturally to bring down the high tide of Rightist propaganda against him. With the assassination of Mahatma Gandhi, the Right-wing extremist had already made an assertion in Indian politics that it was a formidable 'unneglectable' element, and Home Minister Patel was finding it difficult to tackle these forces. Even when he had to sign the order banning the RSS, the mother organization of Right-wing politics in India, he had also shown gestures of softness to the Rightists, lifting the ban soon and participating in their sessions. Patel's anti-China assertions should be seen from this angle. When his assertive warning letter unfailingly pressurized Nehru, the continuing pandemonium in the Parliament and the press might have factored such an emphatic statement by Nehru on Nepal as well. It was at a time when there was neither any major border question to be debated in the eastern sector, nor was there any dissent from the other side of the border, other than the storming of Tibet. It seems that Peking realized that there was internal political pressure on Nehru and therefore did not take it seriously immediately. But in reply to a question on the status of the Indo-Tibetan boundary,

---

[86] The parliamentary debate part I, Question and Answer, vol. V, no. 1, 3rd session of Parliament of India, Monday 20 Nov 1950, Col. 156.

Nehru admitted, outside the Parliament, to the fact that parts of the Indo-Tibetan boundary had not been recognized.

Soon, in the wake of a Chinese invasion of Tibet and on account of internal political pressure, New Delhi began to intensify its border preparedness. So as to be sufficiently ready, the Government of India appointed 'The North and North-Eastern Border Defence Committee' under Major General Himmatsinhji, Deputy Minister of Defence, with representatives from the Ministries of Defence, Communication, Home and External Affairs. Nehru's immediate further action in Tawang can be seen in the light of a strong internal demand from within the country, testifying to the pressure on him to act against China as part of national politics. To settle an old border issue pertaining to Tawang, which had been in existence between British India and Tibet (China) since 1914,[87] the Government of India sent forces to the Indian union on 2 February 1951 and annexed Tawang, an important centre of the Tibetan administration. Although China was silent and did not lodge a protest for the time being, the Tibetans staged a demonstration before the Indian Mission in Lhasa. Strangely enough, even when India risked its friendly ties with China for the sake of Tibet, Lhasa did not reciprocate any leniency towards India for the territory of Tawang, which was a matter of dispute between India and China. Subramanian Swami says, 'Lhasa had even laid claims to Tawang when India was weak'.[88]

Since the validity of the Simla Agreement and thereby the existence of the McMahon Line in itself had been challenged by China, it was feared that it might attempt to claim even the NEFA. But the silence of Peking on India's taking over of Tawang convinced the latter that it would be possible to establish its control over the whole of NEFA without any opposition from Peking. And it was construed in Delhi that the acquiescence of Peking indicated that they were psychologically prepared to accept the McMahon Line as the de facto boundary. Later developments, however, prove that the silence of the PRC over the Tawang issue could have been due to absence of clarity over the border alignment at this early stage or on account of the immense

---

[87] For details, see Chapter 3.

[88] Subramanian, 'Sino-Indian Relations through the Tibet Prism', 2–15.

pressure exerted on the Korean issue, but action was awaited at a convenient point later. Girija Shankar Bajpai, secretary general of MEA, had already expressed the need to raise the question of the McMahon Line with China. It is said that he warned Prime Minister Nehru about the potential for a Chinese invasion more than a decade before it happened.[89] But Nehru was not ready to bring this dormant issue immediately to the attention of the Chinese until the case was taken up by Peking, if at all it was an issue from their perspective.

Waves of Rebellion in Tibet Intensify Border Tussle

Emerging waves of rebellion in Tibet in the late 1950s pointed to the active involvement of outside forces and, with this, Peking's suspicions over New Delhi grew as well. Those revolts had provided enough grounds for Peking's argument that the USA and its allies were interested in the Tibetan issue to destabilize China.[90] China was annoyed at the Western media and their support over the Tibet issue. The US 'sympathy' for the cause of the Tibetan rebels was proved through their supply of logistics, in addition to the moral and material support extended by the Indian and other forces.[91] This prompted China to adopt a vigorous and aggressive stance in Tibet. While the CCP pushed for 'democratic reforms' in Tibet, the Tibetans responded with rebellion. The CCP's efforts were responded to by armed resistance and revolts in Lhasa and other areas of Tibet.

The second wave of armed rebellions that erupted in Qamdo quickly spread to other areas in late July 1956. The PLA tried to crush these uprisings ruthlessly, but due to worldwide sympathy for the rebels and anti-China propaganda by the West, the rebellion

---

[89] Bajpai, 'Weightlifting'.

[90] Kenneth J. Conboy and James Morrison, The CIA's Secret War in Tibet (Lawrence, KS: University Press of Kansas, 2002); M. S. Kohli, *Spies in the Himalayas: Secret Missions and Perilous Climbs* (Lawrence, KS: University Press of Kansas, 2003); Joe Bageant, *CIA's Secret War in Tibet* (Lawrence, KS: University Press of Kansas, 2002).

[91] John D. Smith, *I Was a CIA Agent in India* (New Delhi: Createspace Independent Pub, 1967); L. Natarajan, *American Shadow over India* (Bombay: People's Publishing House, 1952); Pauly V. Parakal, *CIA Dagger against India* (New Delhi: Communist Party Publication, 1973).

only gained further momentum. The visit of the Dalai Lama and the Panchen Lama to India in November 1956 was generally believed to be for seeking asylum in India, and therefore the CCP leadership tried to turn him back to Lhasa. It was a meeting that Delhi had arranged between the Dalai Lama and Chou, reaffirming Chou's suspicions on India. Chou and Nehru were able to persuade the Dalai Lama to return to Lhasa and he reached Lhasa on 1 April 1957. After a short spell of calm, again in 1958 and early 1959, many other parts of Tibet, including Lhasa, became volatile.

On 10 March 1959, thousands of Tibetans gathered around Norbulingka, the Dalai Lama's summer residence, in response to a rumour that the CCP was planning to arrest their spiritual leader. An invitation to the Dalai Lama to attend a function in Peking was the cause for turmoil. This magnified into a popular revolt. The insurgents shouted slogans like 'independence for Tibet' and 'Chinese go away'. The situation in Lhasa worsened, especially due to international support for the rebel cause. Peking intensified its attempts to hold on to Tibet. Soon after the uprising, the 14th Dalai Lama once again fled Lhasa to avoid Chinese crackdown. The departure of the Dalai Lama caused the situation in Lhasa to spiral out of control. Reportedly, beginning on 19 March, the insurgents in Lhasa started attacking communist administrative and military targets, giving rise to a larger and more violent rebellion. The PLA ruthlessly crushed the uprising, resulting in heavy human casualties. So the 10 March 1959 uprising was mainly characterized as an anti-Chinese anti-Communist popular revolt that erupted in Lhasa. On 20 March 1959, the PLA settled the issue by using brutal armed intervention. On 28 March, the formal dissolution of the Tibetan local government, Kashag, was announced putting political power in Tibet into the hands of the 'Preparatory Committee of the Tibet Autonomous Region'. On 31 March, the Dalai Lama and his followers crossed the border to take refuge in northern India. By the end of May 1959, several thousands of Tibetan refugees had entered India to seek asylum, causing serious tension in Sino-Indian relations. It is rightly pointed out that it was after the March 1959 rebellion in Tibet and the Dalai Lama's and his followers' asylum in India that the gravity of the border issue deepened. So far, the dispute in the eastern sector had not been that apparent, but later developments in a couple of months changed the course altogether. Soon, border tensions and armed preparations intensified on both sides, leading to the first major Sino-Indian armed clashes in Longju and Kongka Pass in the next six months. The extent to which the Tibet factor had influenced the border dispute and the Chinese claim to the NEFA (which thus far had not been that emphatic) and the intervention of the CIA in the region would be discussed in the next chapters.

Aksai Chin versus the NEFA

Arunachal Pradesh, the north-eastern border state of the Indian Union, was formerly part of the Assam Province of British India. It was separated from Assam in 1914 to form the North-East Frontier Tract and until then British relations with the tribal population on these hill tracts were that of frequent punitive expeditions. After independence, in 1950, it was brought under the political control of New Delhi and, before attaining full statehood under the Indian Union in 1987, this former Union Territory was addressed to as the NEFA. It is presently an integral part of the Indian Union, and casting even an iota of doubt over its status would be considered an infringement of its national sovereignty and a transgression of its historical rights. Peking had not been very bothered about this, and since the NEFA was completely under the political jurisdiction of New Delhi, there had been no dispute over this territory for a long time, barring that of Tawang. However, over the last few decades, Peking has been raising strong objections to any Indian official visiting this state. They even issued paper visas for people from Arunachal Pradesh visiting China, which shows that this is not that trivial a matter to be neglected. Initially, there had not been any dispute over the LAC, and it was limited to whether or not to accept colonial legacy in principle. In this chapter, we will discuss how the differences over the NEFA began to emerge as a major debate by 1959 and what the circumstances that led to such a larger extended territorial claim by China were.

Nature of Dispute over the NEFA before 1959

The nature of the dispute over the NEFA is very different and distinct from that of the Ladakh sector. Even when New Delhi extended its political and administrative hold on this region as early as 1950, Peking did not contest these steps, other than questioning the validity of accepting the McMahon Line. Since Peking had never stepped into this territory beyond the Himalayas before 1962, except for a short span of time in 1910–1911, Chinese arguments regarding the NEFA were null and void. It seems that, in the early years, China was particularly concerned only with dismantling the colonial tag of the Simla Agreement (the McMahon Line of 1914) and was not interested in staking any claim to the territory beyond the south of the Himalayas. China was aware of the strong history and geography that New Delhi could turn to in order to make a claim to this territory and, therefore, had not proposed any arguments until the Tibet issue became strong. Hence, until the late 1950s, no vigorous phase of territorial contestation was apparent and while New Delhi's claim was largely locked up in the NEFA, Peking engaged in Aksai Chin. The counter-position of Aksai Chin with the NEFA was a late proposition by China to put forth their side of the argument, after which India became emphatic in their claim over the western sector.

As far as Aksai Chin in the western sector was concerned, as has already been seen, New Delhi had not made any unequivocal claim to this region in the early years; its claims were largely confined to maps published after 1954. This silence seems to be an acknowledgement of the fact that Noorani suggests: 'India's stand...has not a leg to stand on'.[1] However, Peking considered it to be its most prized possession and therefore called upon New Delhi for a border delimitation to rectify colonial damages and legacies. Simultaneously, throughout the early 1950s, Peking pursued a vigorous phase of validating processes to reiterate its claim to the area by secretly constructing a road. But it was only after 1958 when the report of the Chinese road in Aksai Chin came to the pubic knowledge and the opposition pressure on the Government of India became stronger that New Delhi began to protest Peking's claim to Aksai Chin. So once the conflict became apparent in this sector also, China began to propose an extended territorial claim in the eastern sector (the NEFA) which was a balancing act of sorts to win a better bargain at the negotiation table. We can thus see a connection to China's extended claim in the NEFA with the developments for and against Aksai Chin in the post-1958 period.

---

[1] Noorani, 'The Truth about 1962', 17–30.

Let us explore how the two debates over these two regions have been pitched against each other.

There is no major reference to the border dispute in the western sector in the government records prior to 1954. The mutual pro-test notes sent by both governments between July 1954, after the Panchsheel, and before July 1958 were largely on issues in smaller pockets, including the central sector,[2] regarding the new posts set up by New Delhi immediately after the Panchsheel Agreement. On the basis of new directions by the prime minister in July 1954, the Home Ministry deputed the ITBP to the disputed areas. The July 1954 letter of Nehru to the MEA, Home and the Defence ministries had laid out instructions only to tighten the northern border and no instructions were given to push the checkpoints to the forward areas in this sector. But to this, the army had stated that 'they could send an occasional patrol, but they were in no position to open and hold any posts in this area…it would be difficult to oust the Chinese from this region' because of the 'limited resources available at Leh and of the non-existence of any road communication from Leh to these parts'.[3] This shows that, despite the directive of July 1954, the Indian position in this sector was not that forward—only afterwards, some measure of border strengthening was taken. There was no major territorial expansion during the 1954–1958 period. The first major territorial dispute after Panchsheel, therefore, was with regard to a map that China had published in July 1958 in the *China Pictorial* showing a large area of Aksai Chin as part of China. Before this, most of the notes and communications exchanged were only on smaller issues, which even the Foreign Secretary of the MEA referred to as 'petty frontier disputes'.[4] It was by this time the Aksai Chin road emerged as a major point of contention in India. Let us now take a detailed look at New Delhi's response towards Peking's involvement and infrastructural works that were in progress since 1952.

---

[2] Barahoti, Damzan, Niti pass in Uttarakhand and Tehri-Garhwal and Shipki pass in central sector.

[3] Mullik, *My Years with Nehru*, 201.

[4] *Note Given by the Ambassador of India to Vice-Minister for Foreign Affairs of China, on 8 November 1958* (White Paper I, 1954–1959; New Delhi: MEA) 29.

The Aksai Chin Road Did Not Disturb New Delhi

New Delhi believed that as per traditions and customs, Aksai Chin plateau was part of Ladakh. But neither did they show much enthusiasm in bringing this barren, desolate plateau under their administrative jurisdiction, nor did they verify archival documents for the legality of the claim. New Delhi therefore showed less interest in Aksai Chin proper in the early years because it could not effectively defend this territory, and they were not that sure of the validity of such a claim. The British too decided to ignore the issue on the basis of the aforesaid factors despite the presence of the Johnson Line (1865). But, as discussed in the previous chapters, China looked at it as a passage for easier accessibility from the western side to the Tibet region, and occupied the area as early as 1952 for it was a geopolitically strategic region. Consequently, the Chinese occupation of the territory became easier and remained 'unnoticed' to New Delhi for a long period of time. No proper official notification regarding a disputed claim had also been sent to Peking for a long period of time. It seems that Peking had begun conducting surveys for the road way back in October 1951.[5] They built this 933-km road connecting Kashgar (Xinjiang) and Rudok (western Tibet), traversing 160 km across Aksai Chin, a local route used by Chinese traders in the past. However, until the completion of this large infrastructural project, the Government of India officials had neglected the region.

By the time the border issue came up in the bilateral discussions (1954), this road work was being carried out in full swing. On 2 September 1957, Peking announced its expected completion in October and published a sketch in *People's Daily* showing its alignment across the north-east corner of Ladakh. Later, on 6 October 1957, when the PRC openly declared the inauguration of the road, India was not ready to accept the report at face value. In the meantime, the Indian Embassy at Peking as well as the IB reported completion. But India did not protest, because Nehru, on the advice of the MEA, claimed that it was not certain.[6] According to B. N. Mullik, 'enough

---

[5] Indian IB had reported caravans using this route as early as April 1952. Sinha and Athale, *History of the Conflict with China 1962*, 23.

[6] CIA, *The Sino-Indian Border Dispute Staff*, Section I (1950–1959), 5.

information was available about the construction of the road right from 1951 to 1957'. 'All through these years no questions were raised by the Army Headquarters or the Ministry of External Affairs (MEA) about it. It was only after the road had been completed and heavy traffic had started plying that some attention was turned on it', even then, it was only considered to be 'of nuisance value and not one that affected our (India's) security'.[7] Even in 1958, the MEA was of the opinion that it was pointless to make an issue of it, and the same was, more or less, the suggestion of the army as well.[8] It is also a fact that the Chinese had already disclosed details about the road, such as the names of the terminals in Sinkiang and Tibet, and an intermediate location at Shahidullah Mazar, and that the Indian officials, especially the IB and the defence establishments, should not have failed to infer from these 'Chinese reference to Shahidulla Mazar that the new road would follow the traditional caravan route across the Aksai Plain through Indian claimed territory'.[9] But they were not inspired to enquire. However, its formal opening for transportation was reported by the New China News Agency (NCNA) in January 1958.[10] So as to gain strength on their claim of earlier possession of the territory, Chou Enlai, later (1960), said that the Chinese troops had entered western Tibet as early as October 1950 through the Aksai Chin road.[11] This appropriation of the terrain was slow and steady without provocations and deliberately avoided reference to this area in the early stage. However, Peking had doubts over New Delhi's perception about Aksai Chin, and they knew the political environment in India, and the pressure on Nehru would make it counterproductive. Therefore, it would be wrong to assume that the formal announcement of the road through Aksai Chin came as a shock to India, because it had not happened in a day or within a very short time frame. Rather it had been in progress since 1951, and records have shown that India was aware of these developments, even when New Delhi tried to ignore them till 1958.

[7] Mullik, *My Years with Nehru*, 199.

[8] Ibid., 205.

[9] CIA, *The Sino-Indian Border Dispute Staff*, Section I (1950–1959), 5

[10] Mullik, *My Years with Nehru*, 197–198.

[11] The director of IB, Mullik, refutes this claim as baseless and substantiates it with evidence against their entry in 1950. Mullik, *My Years with Nehru*, 196.

But New Delhi was awakened only when there emerged a dispute, and it began to entangle itself with other issues of greater magnitude. There is no doubt that India was not unaware of developments in this far-off region. Even though Nehru had informed the Parliament quite late that the road had been built 'without our knowledge',[12] B. N. Mullik, the director of IB and a close aide of the prime minister, claimed that he had reported on the road-building activity way back in November 1952.[13] Khera also reported on Chinese activities in Aksai Chin and the Indo-Tibetan border in 1952.[14] Indian trade agents had reported on the road in Gartok in July and September 1955, and again in August 1957.[15] S. S. Malik, the Indian Military attaché in Beijing, had reported this to the Indian Army headquarters and the Government of India in 1955 and 1956, and a similar report was sent by the Indian Embassy to the Foreign Ministry.[16] So the contradiction apparent in the Indian version underlines the fact that a claim on Aksai Chin was a late origin and it became emphatic only by 1959.

So it was after repeated alarms from various corners that the MEA convened a meeting in June 1958 to discuss the road issue and, even at this stage, the

> Foreign Secretary maintained that neither the Embassy report nor the Intelligence report conclusively proved that the Sinkiang-Western Tibet highway actually passed through our territory and no Indian party had actually traversed this route and so before any protest was lodged we should be sure of our ground.[17]

This calm response from New Delhi cannot be seen as a matter of indifference or negligence; it was rather the outcome of a studied move. Why did not India take it seriously? Why did it wait for the road to be completed? The fact is that New Delhi was well aware that

[12] Nehru in Rajya Sabha MEA, XP Division Press release, Section 31, August 1959.

[13] Mullik, *My Years with Nehru*, 196.

[14] Khera, *India's Defence Problem*, 157.

[15] Mullik, *My Years with Nehru*, 196–197.

[16] Sinha and Athale, *History of the Conflict with China 1962*, 43; Mankekar, *The Guilty Men of 1962*, 27.

[17] Mullik, *My Years with Nehru*, 201.

a legal claim over a distant Kunlun range could not be justified. It was from awareness about this fact that the Indian forward posts in the Ladakh region were 'far behind the location it was supposed to be' as per the later claim, and 'there were no patrolling up to the area of the traditional demarcation'.[18] So the Indian perception as regards the territory in Aksai Chin needed further elaboration. It was not due to the nature of the terrain that it was left neglected until occupation by China. Rather, it 'appears that the Government of India's decision to issue new maps with a well-defined Northern boundary incorporating a version of the John Ardagh Line (1897) in the Kashmir sector east of the Karakoram Pass was primarily meant to provide a bargaining'[19] point in the negotiations that they found easier to balance the dispute.

Aksai Chin versus the NEFA

Post 1954, border relations were mainly marked by two aspects: (a) frequent border encroachments and minor skirmishes over alleged infiltrations and (b) discrepancies in maps published by both China and India, and mutual exchange of protest notes against such anomalies. Regarding the first aspect, reports of border encroachments were not infrequent on the Sino-Indian border from 1954. Even earlier, most 'infiltrations' were reported from the central sector, where, unlike the other two sectors, borders were always alive with mutual interactions and transactions with people beyond the border. But the reported encroachments were, on occasions, mostly either inadvertent entry of the armed forces beyond the 'unspecific' or unmarked borders, or to areas that neither party had claimed or taken possession of. One such early case of infiltration involved the presence of the Indian troops in Barahoti, 3 km south of the border pass in Tunjun La (Uttarakhand) reported on 17 July 1954, within a few weeks of Chou's visit to India. Peking launched an official protest.[20] But the Government of India stated on 27 August 1954 by an official note that no violation of the

---

[18] Sinha and Athale, *History of the Conflict with China 1962*, 28.

[19] Gupta, 'Hidden History of the Sino-Indian Frontier', 765, 767, 769–772.

[20] *Notes Given by the Counsellor of China to the MEA on 17 July 1954 and 13 August 1954* (White Paper 1954–1959; New Delhi: MEA, Government of India, 1963), 1–2.

border had occurred and that the location was south of Niti pass, which was one of the passes mentioned in the Territorial Jurisdiction Agreement of 1954.[21] Yet again, in June 1955, the Chinese troops entered Barahoti and, in September 1955, moved to Damzan, 16 km south of Niti pass,[22] even threatening the Indian detachment. The entry of the Chinese troops into Indian territories south of the border-line was further reported in April 1956 on the Uttar Pradesh border (Uttarakhand) and in September 1956 on the Himachal Pradesh border. Similar intrusions were frequent in other areas in the central sector, like in the Shipki pass area in Himachal Pradesh around this time. Likewise, in Lanak La, in the Ladakh region, encroachments were also noticed in August and September 1956. However, these reports of border crossings by the armed forces on both sides were frequent, but were addressed so as to reach an amicable solution. These were not of a serious nature as, in most cases, the teams withdrew from the territory when they were reminded of the border limits. The increase in armed presence, infiltrations and withdrawals largely seems to have been on account of two reasons. First, infiltrations rose around the second wave of the Tibetan uprising in 1956, and PLA forces were stationed on the border region to safeguard the border against the movement of rebels into Indian territory. India too, therefore, strengthened its vigil on border regions against the encroachment of troops and armed rebels in its territory. Second, the men at ground zero had no specific information regarding the proper delimitation of the border on both sides. In the absence of any specific maps or any definite actual demarcating directions to the border force, such inadvertent 'encroachments' were frequent.[23] However, these had not resulted in any significant clashes across the border.

The second aspect was with respect to the discrepancy in the maps. During his visit to China in October 1954, Nehru brought up these

---

[21] Note Given to the Chinese Counsellor in India (White Paper; New Delhi: MEA, 1954), 3.

[22] Note Given to the Chinese Counsellor in India 5 Nov 1955 (White Paper; New Delhi: MEA, 10).

[23] The Dhola incident of 1962, which led to the war, basically arose from the inaccuracy in the map. See details in Government of India, 'The Henderson Brooks–Bhagat Report (NM)', 99–126.

differences in the Chinese map to the notice of Chou. Later, in the middle of the Tibet uprising, Chou Enlai visited Delhi in November 1956 and January 1957 and discussed various issues with Prime Minister Nehru. The outcome of this was that there were no serious issues existing on the border except for some petty problems that could be settled amicably by the representatives of both governments. Referring to the McMahon Line, Chou stated:

> The government of China of those days had dealt with this matter and had not accepted the line established by the British Imperialists and it was not fair game, and since it is an accomplished fact now, and in consideration with the friendly relation of China with its neighbours (India and Burma), the Chinese government is of the opinion that they should give recognition to the line for which the Tibetan authorities would be appraised.[24]

When New Delhi pointed to the existing official maps of China showing substantial areas of Aksai Chin and the NEFA as Chinese territory, Chou stated in November 1956 that these were old maps of the Kuomintang period which had yet to be revised.[25] He clarified that Peking did not assert any claims on the basis of these old maps, and that the PRC had not got enough time to revise them. It seems it was also on the basis of this assurance from China, and presuming that the Chinese maps were yet to be revised, New Delhi did not stay alert on developments in the western sector. Until the construction of the road was completed, China did not challenge the official Indian maps showing the boundary as being against their interests. But once again, in July 1958, when China published a new map in the *China Pictorial*, the Government of India pointed out the discrepancy and delay on the part of China in correcting the map due to their claim of paucity of time.[26] The Chinese, however, repeated the same version, stating the 'reprint of old map before 1949' as an excuse, but now added that consultations with the concerned parties were required

[24] Reproduced in Jawaharlal Nehru's letter to Chou Enlai 14 December 1958 (White Paper 1954–1959), 49–50.

[25] CIA, *The Sino-Indian Border Dispute Staff*, Section I (1950–1959), 6–7.

[26] *Note to the Counsellor of China in India by MEA, 21 August 1958* (White Paper, 1954–1959), 46.

to settle the issue.[27] But the 1958 Chinese map and the construction of the Aksai Chin road, together, reiterated the fact that China had staked claim to large tracts of land in the Kashmir region beyond the territory through which the road traversed. Chou's assurances turned out to be a delaying tactic. In this situation, on 21 August 1958, the Government of India sent its first protest note to the Counsellor of China in India. In this note also, the major concern expressed was that an extended territory of Ladakh was included in the new Chinese map, beyond the area traversed by the road, but the focus of the protest was not on the road per se.

The new map and the new road activated the political environment against the government. To address the situation, the Government of India decided to ascertain the actual developments and activities of China in the region. Accordingly, two military reconnaissance patrol teams were sent to the region with instructions to verify the truth and to report whether or not the road passed through Indian territory.[28] They were ordered to report on the border alignment and check the location of Chinese military posts on the Aksai Plain. Nehru's direction to the patrol team was to capture and bring the Chinese troops to Leh if they were a small number or, if they were to encounter a large force, to inform the Chinese troops that they were on Indian territory and 'ask them to leave'.[29] The first armed Indian patrol team under Lt. Iyengar sent in August 1958 for reconnaissance was taken into custody by the Chinese, and the detainees were held for about two months until their release on 22 October. On 18 October 1958, the foreign secretary sent a letter protesting the capture of the Indian team that had been patrolling the territory claimed by the Indian side. Once the teams were released and the Chinese government officially responded to this, the issue was resolved. The second ITBP under Dy. SP Karan Singh, which had been sent for the same purpose, reported that the road cut across Indian territory

---

[27] *Memorandum given by the Foreign Office of China to the Counsellor of India, 3 Nov 1958* (White Paper, 1954–1959), 47.

[28] Noorani, 'The Truth about 1962', 17–30.

[29] CIA, *The Sino-Indian Border Dispute Staff*, Section I (1950–1959), 6.

from Haji Langar in the north to Amtogar in the south.[30] Hence, an official protest note dated 18 October 1958 was handed over to the Chinese Ambassador by the foreign secretary of India, stating that the road is through indisputably Indian territory.

On 1 and 3 November 1958, Peking responded justifying their actions, both with respect to the road and the arrest of the Indian forces, on the grounds that it was Chinese territory.[31] Peking also held that the delay and timing of the Indian protest had much significance in connection with other developments. Chinese Premier Chou Enlai later implied that a road involving such massive engineering work in 1956 and 1957 would not have gone undetected by the Indians, as the Indian forces had been around the Aksai Plain then.[32] They also tried to convey that New Delhi became aware of the road only after the outbreak of the Tibetan revolt in March 1959, when India interfered in the revolt.[33]

Political Pressure in Delhi for Aksai Chin

Almost two years after the opening of the road, Nehru said, in response to the pressing demand in the Parliament on 31 August 1959:

> Our attention was drawn to a very small-scale map about two and one-quarter by three-quarters inches published in a Chinese newspaper indicating a rough alignment of the road. It was not possible to find out from this small map whether this road crossed Indian territory, although it looked as if it did so. It was decided, therefore, to send reconnaissance parties the following summer to find the location of this road.[34]

[30] *Informal note by the Foreign Secretary to the Chinese Ambassador, 18 Oct 1958* (White Paper I, 1954–1959), 26–27.

[31] *Memorandum by the Foreign Office of China to the Counsellor of India, 3 November 1958* (White Paper I, 1954–1959).

[32] Chou Enlai's letter dated 4 November 1962 to Nehru in CIA, *The Sino-Indian Border Dispute Staff*, Section I (1950–1959), 6.

[33] The Chinese Foreign Minister Chen Yi is reported to have told this to a Swiss correspondent in Geneva on 19 July 1962. CIA, *The Sino-Indian Border Dispute Staff*, Section I (1950–1959), 6.

[34] Prime Minister in Rajya Sabha New Delhi 31 Aug 1959, Govt of India Rajya Sabha records, Pol xxxvi 1960, Col. 2281.2287.

The Parliament and the press seemed satisfied with this statement. The issue of the Aksai Chin road, however, had begun to gain prominent attention in 1959. So by mid-1959, the government's rhetoric on the western sector began, especially regarding the Aksai Chin road. This change in the official Indian narrative is explained in terms of developments during late 1958 and early 1959. These include the following: (a) On 23 January 1959, Chou Enlai wrote a letter to the Indian prime minister clarifying Peking's perception that the eastern sector was Chinese territory.[35] Actually, this was an advance move made with the view of increasing the bargaining power during the negotiations, which Chou had proposed a couple of times later[36]; (b) the tremendous influence that the Tibetan sympathizers had on national politics hit Sino-Indian relations. Peking's concern over the Tibet issue and New Delhi's alleged support to Lhasa against Peking's interest had intensified pressure on the frontiers. An overwhelming sentiment in favour of Lhasa since 1956 resulted in a strong anti-PRC campaign by 1959.[37] By 1959, the PRC felt further offended by the secret presence of the CIA on Indian soil, extending all logistical support to the Tibetan rebels who, Peking suspected, had been known to the Government of India. Literature by those CIA officials involved in the Tibetan issue on Indian soil is available to authenticate this argument.[38] In this context, the Aksai Chin road and the ambivalence of the Government of India in responding to it, and the latest *China Pictorial* map, created further acrimony in the press and the Parliament.[39] In this political environment in the country, Nehru could not resist but move with

[35] Sali, *India–China Border Dispute*, 169–170.

[36] Robert L. Hardgrave and Stanley A. Kochanek, *India: Government and Politics in a Developing Nation* (Boston, MA: Wadsworth Publishing, 2008), 503–504.

[37] Jian, 'The Tibetan Rebellion of 1959 and China's Changing Relations with India and the Soviet Union', 54–101.

[38] Smith, *I Was a CIA Agent in India*; John Kenneth Knaus, *Orphans of the Cold War: America and the Tibetan Struggle for Survival* (New York, NY: PublicAffairs, 1999); Ralph McGhee, *Deadly Deceits: My 25 Years in the CIA* (Punjab: Ocean Press, 2002); Kunhanandan Nair, *Devil and His Dart: How the CIA Is Plotting in the Third World* (New Delhi: Sterling Publishers, 1986); Kohli, *Spies in the Himalayas*.

[39] Jian, 'The Tibetan Rebellion of 1959 and China's Changing Relations with India and the Soviet Union', 85.

the sentiment of the Parliament.[40] This situation changed the course of Sino-Indian relations and (c) with the Longju mishap on 25 August 1959 (see Chapter 7), armed clashes permeated bilateral relations. Subsequently, Nehru faced an acrimonious Parliament in the months of August–September 1959 over the border clash at Longju and the Aksai Chin road.[41] It was in this context that Nehru began talking emphatically in favour of the Indian claim in the western sector. However, he knew the reality of this issue, and it was under these circumstances that he said on 13 September 1959, 'We have no check posts there and practically little of access',[42] and therefore it is difficult to defend the region militarily. So India's interest in Aksai Chin was a later origin, and it was never emphatic to include it in Indian territory before 1958. Once such a move was made, the border dispute went out of Nehru's control. Under pressure from the opposition to intervene against the armed intervention of the PLA in Tibet, an active FP was compelled. Increased counter-armed mobilization and establishment of advanced border checkpoints in the western sector were initiated by mid-1959. This further worsened relations, increasing apprehensions on both sides.

Cracks in Nehru–Chou Comradeship

The beginning of 1959 was a turning point in Sino-Indian relations. The situation was drifting out of Nehru's hands, and by 1959 Nehru himself was seen being moved by the rigid and firm stance of his advisors. Nehru's letter dated 14 December 1958 categorically stated, 'There can be no question of these large parts of India being anything but India and there is no dispute about them'.[43] Peking's response was the same as earlier that the boundary had never been formally delimited, and historically no treaty or agreement had ever been concluded between the governments of China and India. But this time, Chou was

---

[40] CIA, *The Sino-Indian Border Dispute Staff*, Section I (1950–1959), 11.

[41] Gupta, 'Hidden History of the Sino-Indian Frontier', 33.

[42] Maxwell, *India's China War*, 131.

[43] *Letter from the PM of India to the PM of China dt 14 December 1958* (White Paper I, 1954–1959), 51.

specific to mention disputes in both sectors and suggested that a survey be carried out to determine the boundaries and, until then, to maintain the status quo. Peking also admitted that the issue was not raised in 1954 'because the conditions were not yet ripe for its settlement'.[44] In his detailed letter dated 23 January 1959, the Chinese premier for the first time made significant revelations regarding Peking's position. The letter elaborated on the fact that there were certain differences between the two sides over the border question.

> The Sinkiang-Tibet highway built by China…has always been under Chinese jurisdiction and patrol duties have continually been carried out in the area by the border guards of the Chinese government. Recently the government of India claimed that the area was in Indian territory. All this shows that border disputes do exist between China and India.[45]

He also referred to the McMahon Line as a product of the British policy of aggression against the Tibetan region of China. Chou admitted that the Tibetan local authorities had signed the convention but were dissatisfied with the 'unilaterally drawn' line. Nevertheless, Chou asserted that 'the Chinese government finds it necessary to take a realistic attitude towards the McMahon Line'.[46]

So until 23 January 1959, the Chinese had never raised the issue of the McMahon Line, and this was the first official communication that China had made regarding the McMahon Line.[47] Replaying to Chou's detailed letter (23 January 1959), on 22 March 1959, Nehru went further into history and antiquities, and stated that

> a treaty of 1842 between Kashmir on the one hand and the Emperor of China and the Lama Guru of Lhasa on the other mentions the India–China boundary in the Ladakh region. In 1847, the Chinese government admitted that this boundary was sufficiently and distinctly fixed. The area now claimed by China has always been depicted as part of India on official

---

[44] *Letter from the PM of China to the PM of India dt 23 January 1959* (White Paper I, 1954–1959), 52–54.

[45] Ibid.

[46] Ibid.

[47] Kalha, *The McMahon Line.*

maps, has been surveyed by Indian officials and even a Chinese map of 1893 shows it as Indian territory.[48]

So by the beginning of 1959, disputes in the western and eastern sectors were specific and clearly revealed to each other, even when the Nehru–Chou friendship tried to play it down in the hope that they would be able to reach an amicable settlement. However, the depth and magnitude of such a large-scale disparity in territorial claims and counterclaims were soon confounded with issues.

Despite all these new turns in relation, Nehru and Chou had maintained confidence in their efforts for peace. The capture of the Indian patrol on the road and their two-month confinement in Chinese custody, however, did not immediately come to the public notice. This allowed Nehru to pursue his efforts for peace with Chou. At the time, Nehru was reliably reported to be anxious to keep this and other recent border incidents out of public knowledge.[49] So in a conference held in Peking on 31 December 1958, discounting the magnitude of the new developments, the Indian Ambassador reiterated that there were only small questions pending between India and China, but he wished to see nothing big or small remaining outstanding between the two countries. But a gradual cooling of attitude from Peking had been developed. During the summer of 1959, the Chinese postponed Nehru's proposed trip to Tibet indefinitely and kept him waiting for three weeks before granting him and his party visas to cross a small portion of Tibet—where they were subsequently snubbed by the Chinese—on their way to Bhutan. Nehru, however, refrained from making public attacks on such Chinese actions, including minor border incursions, which he feared would stir up Indian opinion and damage his relationship with Chou. Premier Chou Enlai also maintained an attitude similar to that expressed in his statement made in February 1960 that 'two large countries like India and China with a long common frontier were bound to have some questions but all questions could be settled smoothly'.[50]

[48] *Letter from the PM of India to the PM of China 22 March 1959* (White Paper I, 1954–1959), 55–57.

[49] CIA, *The Sino-Indian Border Dispute Staff*, Section I (1950–1959), 6–7.

[50] *Note of the Government of India to the Chinese Government, February 12 1960* (White Paper III), 91.

Dalai Lama, Tibetan Rebels and India's Overreach

The outbreak of the Third Wave of the Tibetan uprising in early 1959 and the subsequent incidents totally upset the prolonged efforts that the premiers of both nations had been pursuing, the latest between December 1958 and March 1959, with the exchange of official letters. The Tibetan refugee issue and the Dalai Lama's political asylum intensified rivalry in the backdrop of an existing border issue.[51] After 31 March 1959, therefore, Sino-Indian relations further deteriorated, providing greater scope for suspicion and distrust. On 17 March 1959, the Dalai Lama, along with his trusted followers, escaped from Lhasa to seek asylum through the Consulate General of India in Lhasa. On 31 March 1959, the Dalai Lama and his followers were given political asylum on the condition that they would not engage in any political activity in India. But neither the Dalai Lama not his followers adhered strictly to this promise. Even when Nehru and the Government of India wanted the Dalai Lama to show restraint on Indian land, over-reaching support and hospitality to the spiritual leader and his followers in the country encouraged them to engage in anti-China rhetoric. The official version of Indian history by the defence department itself proves that these expressions of sympathy for the Tibetan cause and the opening of doors to refugees with much enthusiasm by the Government of India had, no doubt, acted as a catalyst for the rapid deterioration of Sino-Indian relations,[52] which were already strained due to suspicions on the border issue. After these developments, 'the Chinese Army captured the Potala palace'.[53] The Chinese *People's Daily* complained that Kalimpong was a 'command center of the rebellion and warned India against any interference in Chinese internal affair'.[54] It was after this that Peking started looking into the intricacies of the border issue under the British.

The Nehru government had been trying to avoid the border issue to be flared up into intense criticism by the opposition, which he feared

---

[51] Sen, *The Sino-Indian Border Question*, 173–193.

[52] Sinha and Athale, *History of the Conflict with China 1962*, 31.

[53] Gupta, 'Hidden History of the Sino-Indian Frontier'.

[54] *People's Daily*, 31 March 1959, quoted in CIA, *The Sino-Indian Border Dispute Staff*, Section I (1950–1959), 13.

had prevented the right moves from being made across diplomatic channels. But once the Tibetan revolt broke out on 10 March 1959, it became difficult to keep all aspects of the border dispute under wraps. Chinese military action against the rebels drew the attention of the Indian press, the public and the opposition of Nehru in the Parliament. The developments along the border 'made it virtually impossible for Nehru to employ the tactic of understatement in order to conceal, or minimize, the facts of the overall border dispute and the gradual cooling of Sino-Indian relations'.[55] Even Indian officials in Peking were reported to have expressed open distaste against their own government for the Chinese suppression of the rebels and also for the lack of will on the Sino-Indian border issue. They disagreed with Nehru's attitude towards the Chinese as 'saintliness, gentlemanliness, and too much reliance on ethics', hoping that the Chinese would eventually 'appreciate' such a tolerant attitude from him.[56] Nehru therefore moved with care in his support to the Tibetan rebels in public, but officially maintained a policy of non-interference in Tibet. His immediate concern was a possible armed clash in the event of the Chinese troops pursuing Tibetan rebels into Indian territory. Nehru, therefore, had instructed the army and the frontier checkpoints to stop the Tibetan rebels from entering Indian territory. But considering the overwhelming sense of empathy within the country for the rebels, he was willing to admit them once they were disarmed. In this atmosphere, he had already given assurances to the resistance leaders in India that he would provide asylum to the Dalai Lama and his staff. He had also promised the Dalai Lama's brother that he would take up the Tibetan issue with Peking. These were more gestures of empathy and compassion for the rebels than an indication of any firm intention,[57] because he was more concerned about non-alienation of Peking. This was reflected in his statement in the Parliament on 23 March 1959, when he announced a policy of non-interference. The NCNA reported on 28 March 1959 about Nehru's non-intervention policy in China's internal affairs with much significance. But the news also underlined

---

[55] CIA, *The Sino-Indian Border Dispute Staff*, Section I (1950–1959), 11.

[56] Ibid., 12.

[57] Ibid., 12–13.

that 'discussion of the Tibetan revolt in India's Parliament would be impolite and improper'.[58]

On 30 March, with his statement in the Parliament, Nehru stood firm on 'balancing his expression of sympathy' for the rebels, with reaffirmation of India's desire for friendly relations with Peking. But he dismissed Peking's view that the discussion of the Tibet issue in the Parliament would be improper, which, according to him, was part of democracy in India. However, he was cautious in his moves on Tibet and tried to absolve India from responsibility for any action that could have offended Peking. Once the Dalai Lama reached Tawang, Nehru tried to keep him away from the press and restrict his political activity in order to further avoid provoking the Chinese leaders.[59] He also asked the spiritual leader of the Tibetans to limit his activities to religion. Some Indian officials had privately stated their anxiety to see the Dalai Lama leave the country.[60] Even as Nehru and Chou avoided any offensive statements to each other, as both premiers were keen on maintaining their personal relationship,[61] the insinuating remarks made by members of the Indian Parliament and China's National People's Congress created an unpleasant situation. But Nehru refuted Peking's charges of collusion between Indian officials and the Dalai Lama and, at the same time, stated that it would have been wrong on political, humanitarian and other grounds not to give asylum to the Dalai Lama.

Anti-China sallies abounded in the Indian press and the Parliament. The Indian press published caricatures of Mao and Chou to provoke Peking. They vociferously attacked China and depicted its communist leaders in poor taste. To add fuel to the fire, on 25 March and 1 April 1959, *the Times of India* and *the Mail* printed cartoons depicting Mao and Chou as cavemen and Mao as 'abominable snowman'. Indian demographer Chandrasekhar wrote an article in January 1959 attacking Chinese communes as places where human beings were reduced to the level of inmates in a zoo. This article invited a formal protest

[58] The New China News Agency 28 March 1959 in CIA, *The Sino-Indian Border Dispute Staff*, Section I (1950–1959), 12–13.

[59] CIA, *The Sino-Indian Border Dispute Staff*, Section I (1950–1959), 13.

[60] Ibid.

[61] Ibid., 15.

from Peking.[62] Nehru rightly believed that these kinds of attacks on CCP leaders by the Indian media were detrimental to Sino-Indian relations. The Chinese leaders, however, maintained a policy of relative public restraint towards India, and they 'chose to level their attacks at Nehru's political opponents in the *Praja Socialist Party* and the *Jan Sangh Party* as well as others'.[63] These parties and their leaders were at the forefront of anti-Communist China propaganda, which was largely targeted at Nehru and his China policy. The pro-Rightist faction politics had a large base during this period in the Jan Sangh, especially in the aftermath of the partition. They sympathized with the Tibetans as members of their larger Hindu community. They were influenced for the idea of pan-Hinduism.[64] Such an influence was apparent among some members of the Indian National Congress as well, which virtually tied Nehru from his aspiration for Asian unity. The Tibetan cause was strongly supported by pro-Right politics both within the country and outside the Indian diaspora in the USA. The anti-Communist western intervention on the Tibetan issue was a well-documented fact beyond doubt.[65] According to John Kenneth Knaus, Washington made the decision to support the Tibetan resistance in the summer of 1956, and the first group of Tibetan rebels was secretly brought to Saipan for training in December 1956. The trainees were then sent back to Tibet in 1957 to help the Tibetan rebels establish contacts with the CIA and join the resistance.[66] The Tibetan troops in Lhasa posed a significant challenge to the CCP's efforts to pursue a path of gradual change in Tibet.

The Spiritual Leader's Political Statement in Tezpur

Inspired by these political activists and supporters from India and overwhelming support from Western countries, the Dalai Lama could not desist from political aspirations in Lhasa. The Government

[62] Ibid., 11–12.

[63] Ibid., 16.

[64] Subramanian, 'Sino-Indian relations through the Tibet Prism', 2–15.

[65] For a highly informative account of the CIA's involvement in supporting the Tibetan rebels, see Knaus, *Orphans of the Cold War*.

[66] Ibid., 139–149.

of India found itself in an embarrassing situation when, on 18 April 1959, the Dalai Lama released a statement to the press at Tezpur calling for Tibetan independence from China. He also stated that he was being held under duress, and that the Chinese had violated the Sino-Tibet autonomy agreement. Forgetting the conditions under which his asylum had been granted in India, this highly provocative statement was issued on Indian soil during his political asylum as a religious head despite all the reservations of the Indian MEA. India had tried its best to persuade the Dalai Lama to avoid such provocations while in India. Even though P. N. Menon, the MEA official, had toned down the sharpness of the draft statement under instruction from the prime minister, it had inflicted much harm on the Peking–New Delhi relationship. After this, China began to level attacks on Nehru himself, which they had so far avoided, as they counted on his sincerity to achieve better bilateralism. But now the Chinese reacted sharply and apparently felt that Nehru had been playing a double role. Peking hinted that the Dalai Lama's statement of 18 April was made at the behest of Nehru himself. On 21 April, the NCNA prominently reported on the arrangement for Nehru's proposed visit to meet the Dalai Lama on 24 April and specifically stated that the Dalai Lama's statement 'was drafted after several long meetings with Prime Minister Nehru's envoy Mr Menon at Bomdila'[67] and accused the Indian MEA of distributing the statement. Peking wondered why the Government of India had permitted the Dalai Lama to engage in political activities even after Nehru's assurance. It is pointed out that Nehru and his close aides were at pains to convince the Chinese authorities that they had been trying to dissuade the Dalai Lama from saying anything political and offensive against China, on the Tibet issue, from Indian territory.

It is also observed that the Government of India, in approving the statement of the Dalai Lama, wished to say, indirectly, certain things that would have been difficult to say directly.[68] At the same time, there was a larger group of Indian leaders who had sold themselves to the

---

[67] New China News Agency, quoted in CIA, *The Sino-Indian Border Dispute Staff*, Section I (1950–1959), 17.

[68] New Delhi AFP dispatch, quoted in CIA, *The Sino-Indian Border Dispute Staff*, Section I (1950–1959), 17.

Tibetan cause, pressing the government and Nehru to provide freedom to the Dalai Lama and his followers in India. Under these circumstances, on 22 April 1959, the wrath of the entire Chinese nation was directed against the statement of the Dalai Lama, and *People's Daily* commented the next day that certain influential figures in India took the view that 'China is weak'.[69] Having lost all expectations of dealing directly with New Delhi, on 26 April, Chinese Foreign Minister Chen Yi told the Indonesian Ambassador that 'neutrals might suggest to Nehru that he restrain Indian comments'.[70] In an oral statement, China's Deputy Foreign Minister Chi Pengfei gave China's official protest to the Indian ambassador, in which Chi charged that though Peking recognized that the Indian press worked differently from the press in China, it was clear that the Government of India had made no effort to control or tone it down. The Indian ambassador reported Chi's remarks to New Delhi, requesting the MEA to recognize that the Chinese Communists held the view that the outbursts in the press and various public demonstrations were encouraged by the Indian government.[71] In the meanwhile, on 27 April, *People's Daily* reprinted the cartoons originally published by *the Times of India* and *the Mail* to show the attitude of the Indian press towards China and denounced the Indians in general. On 28 April, *People's Daily* claimed that the Indian authorities' sympathy with the Tibetans was similar to British imperialist logic[72] and charged that the Indian 'reactionaries' were 'working in the footsteps of the British imperialists and have been harbouring expansionist ambitions towards Tibet'.[73] When the atmosphere deteriorated even further and the Chinese press openly challenged India's motives, Subimal Dutt, the foreign secretary to India, handed over a note to the Chinese ambassador on 26 April 1959 clarifying that (a) the granting of asylum to the Dalai Lama was on humanitarian grounds; (b) P. N. Menon's journey to Mussoorie to

---

[69] *People's Daily*, 23 April 1959, quoted in CIA, *The Sino-Indian Border Dispute Staff*, Section I (1950–1959), 18.

[70] CIA, *The Sino-Indian Border Dispute Staff*, Section I (1950–1959), 19.

[71] Ibid., 19.

[72] *People's Daily*, 28 April 1959, quoted in CIA, *The Sino-Indian Border Dispute Staff*, Section I (1950–1959), 18.

[73] Quoted in *Note of Indian Foreign Secretary to the Chinese Ambassador, 26 April 1959* (White Paper I, 1954–1959).

receive the Dalai Lama and his role in drafting the statements were absolutely to tone down its intensity, and otherwise the Tezpur statement was entirely that of the Dalai Lama and (c) the Dalai Lama's residence at Mussoorie was on his request.[74]

Meanwhile, Nehru, in his speech in the Parliament on 27 April 1959, stated that 'the basis of the Tibet revolt must have been a strong feeling of nationalism, and the Chinese had greatly simplified this facts. India has a feeling of kinship with the Tibetan people, and is greatly distressed at their hapless plight'.[75] This was, in fact, intended to calm the situation in Indian domestic politics due to pressure within the country. The result was that after this, the Chinese sharpened their criticism of Nehru, and it seems that this was the aim of his political opponents. A Chinese commentator, Ta Kung Pao, on 1 May, depicted this as interference in China's internal affairs and a misrepresentation of the situation in Tibet and stated that 'it is regrettable that Prime Minister Nehru…does not have respect to the view that Tibet is an inalienable part of China'.[76] On the same day, *People's Daily* exhorted the 'party and the populace to study Nehru's speech' to analyse the change in Nehru's attitude[77] and, on 6 May, *People's Daily* published a lengthy article 'The Revolution in Tibet and Nehru's Philosophy'. The general observation summed up in the article was that China and India were busy minding their own businesses, and neither of them should poke their nose in the other's business. The article was highly critical of 'certain bourgeois elements' in India which controlled the big propaganda machine and lined up with the imperialists on the matter of Tibet. The article also commented that Nehru was not one of these reactionaries, but that he has involuntarily pushed into 'an important role in their "sympathy with Tibet movement"'.[78] This observation was

---

[74] *Note of Indian Foreign Secretary to the Chinese Ambassador, 26 April 1959* (Notes, Memoranda and Letters Exchanged and Agreements Signed between Governments of India and China, White Paper I, 1954–1959).

[75] CIA, *The Sino-Indian Border Dispute Staff*, Section I (1950–1959), 19.

[76] Ibid., 20

[77] Ibid.

[78] 'The Revolution in Tibet and Nehru's Philosophy', *People's Daily*, 6 May 1959, People's Republic of China Office of the Charge d'affaires, 1959.

absolutely correct. It was the power of the propaganda machinery of Nehru's adversaries, including Socialist and even critics within the Congress, that led to the pro-Tibet anti-Communist China wave. The Tibet factor thus led to the first open exchange of words between China and India, even though Nehru was trying to avoid such a situation. However, he was deeply influenced by these propagandists at this stage and, probably because of this, his leadership image among the Afro-Asian countries seemed to have been tarnished.[79]

The Chinese kept a close watch on the Dalai Lama's appeals for independence and the response and involvements of Indian leaders on the issue. The 20 June press conference of the Dalai Lama once again invited China's wrath, and on 22 June a Chinese official sent a formal protest regarding this. In order to avoid further deterioration of bilateral relations, Indian officials opposed the plan to send the Dalai Lama to the UN to reopen the issue of Tibet's independence.[80] Even when he was further blamed for this, Nehru declared in his Parliament speech on 4 September that the actions of the PLA in Tibet caused pain to India.

The impact of these strained relations had immediate implications on the border dispute as both sides began to intensify their border security. After the Tibetan revolt, the Government of China made large-scale efforts to seal the Sino-Indian frontier with more troops, and now, instead of stationing a few widely scattered checkpoints, the policy was revamped to ensure that there were forces along the entire frontier. In this venture, the Chinese troops outnumbered Indians in all sectors. Armed Indian border police and regular army personnel intercepted and disarmed Tibetan rebels coming down into Indian territory. Although these efforts from both sides indicated a sharp drop in the movement of Tibetans reaching India, the large-scale increase in troop presence on the entire border further increased the tension in the region. It was in the midst of these that the Chinese troops seized the belonging of the Bhutanese infantry.[81] On the request of Bhutan

---

[79] CIA, *The Sino-Indian Border Dispute Staff*, Section I (1950–1959), 25.

[80] Ibid., 27.

[81] Ibid., 28.

in mid-August, the Government of India protested this violation of 'traditional Bhutanese rights and authority'.[82] On 25 August 1959, Nehru declared in the Parliament that this protest on behalf of Bhutan was part of its obligation as per a treaty in 1951.[83] This added further fuel to already burning issues.

Soon, the border situation started moving beyond the control of the efforts at the premiers' level. To add further complications to relations in an already strained atmosphere, creating further stumbling blocks to fruitful negotiations, two ominous incidents occurred within a couple of months in both sectors. On 25 August 1959, the Longju incident took place in the eastern sector. There was an armed clash between both forces, sparked by the possession of a small village near the McMahon Line, which left casualties on both sides. The 20 October incident inflicted casualty on the Indian force at Kongka Pass, where the Chinese ambushed an Indian patrol team to Aksai Chin.[84] With this, public opinion in India was inflamed, and all roads to peaceful and amicable settlements reached dead ends.[85] Analysis of these two border incidents at a critical and decisive juncture in Sino-Indian relations implies that certain shadow forces were controlling developments at the border because they had ulterior motives.

On 21 October 1959, during a press conference in Calcutta, the prime minister said that he did not think there was any 'major idea' behind the Chinese incursions into Indian territory.

> I am inclined to think that all these were tagged to Tibet. There were no Chinese forces on the other side of the border before the Tibetan rebellion. But after the rebellion, Chinese forces came partly to crush the rebellion

---

[82] This action of New Delhi was based on an existing treaty right obtained in 1951 to defend Bhutan and Sikkim to act on their foreign policy matters.

[83] CIA, *The Sino-Indian Border Dispute Staff*, Section I (1950–1959), 28–29.

[84] In the Kongka Pass incident, nine Indian frontier policemen were killed and seven were taken prisoner by China.

[85] Mohan Guruswamy, 'Peace with China' (2003). Available at https://www.rediff.com/news/2003/jun/23spec.htm (accessed on 7 September 2020).

and partly to stop the Tibetan people from coming over to India, or contact the people whom the Chinese imagined to be connected with the Tibetan rebellion.[86]

But what Nehru did not say was that the increasing presence of force on both sides was not a good sign. Thus, we see that the Tibet factor played an undeniable role in the border relations between India and China, and the efforts of the governments to reduce the impact were obstructed by forces from within and outside, ultimately pushing the two Asian giants to a military encounter.

[86] Quoted in Gupta, 'Distortions in the History of Sino-Indian Frontiers'.

The Road to Border War (1959–1962): I

The year 1959, marked by multiple developments that determined the future course of actions, was a turning point in the history of Sino-Indian relations. By the second half of the year, the dispute had been tightened and the situation was reaching a boiling point. The differences arising from the border issue started getting starker than what they were in previous years. Armed border clashes along Longju and Kongka Pass changed the course of interactions between nations. Minor clashes at Chushul, Pangong Lake and other areas became frequent. But the nature of the relationship between Peking and New Delhi over the decade until then had been very different, despite the political 'tremors' in their internal affairs. Despite several issues persisted since 1950, including skirmishes along the border, they were addressed in a proactive manner by the political leadership so as to avert them from becoming a major issue. Chou–Nehru diplomacy was able to rise above the instigations and impulses of the opposition in Delhi, as well as the aggressive foreign policy of Mao and the CCP.

The diplomacy carried forward by the premiers of both nations was strong enough to go past fissures that would have otherwise strained bilateral ties. In the post-Panchsheel period (1954–1956), as we have found, New Delhi's efforts to make cartographic changes in its maps in the western sector (see Chapter 6) had not invited any counteroffensive from the opposite side. Similarly, when China announced the opening of the Aksai Chin road (1958) and showed a significant portion of Ladakh and the NEFA as Chinese territory (1958), New Delhi's response was limited to a protest note.[1] These developments at the frontiers did not provoke both sides to start an offensive across the border. This restrained approach seems to have stemmed from bilateral talks at the premiers' level. New Delhi, by and large, did not emphatically stake a claim in the western sector until 1959, and Peking's anticipated move in the NEFA was also not different. But after 1959, there was a change in the dynamics between nations. It was apparent that a strong external factor had played a role since 1955.

The Shadow of the USA on Border Politics

The shadow presence of the CIA in the troubled Indo-China border regions and support to the Tibetan rebels in the form of money, materials and other logistics, in addition to arms training for the rebels, are facts that have been well documented[2] by reliable sources who had worked for the same objective. The CIA had already crept into the political and bureaucratic veins of India and had established itself as a determining factor within native politics[3] and, as it had desired, played a role in the border dispute as well. This, naturally, was a major concern for Peking, while it did not much perturb New Delhi. In this context, the border dispute has to be seen rather than a mere tussle between New Delhi and Peking. Chinese officials said, 'China can only concentrate its main attention eastward of China, but not south-westwards of China, nor is it necessary for it to do so'.[4] What does this actually mean, and what was the real context of such a statement?

It was proved beyond doubt that the tectonic changes in Sino-Indian relations in the post-1959 period emanated not absolutely from their boundaries. Such a drastic change would neither be confined to minor skirmishes on the frontiers alone. The game plan for this had been initiated immediately after evoking the slogan *Dilli-Chini Bhai Bhai*

[1] *Note to the Counsellor of China in India by MEA, 21 August 1958* (White Paper, 1954–1959), 46.

[2] Kenneth and Morrison, The CIA's Secret War in Tibet.

[3] Natarajan, *American Shadow over India*.

[4] *Statement Made by the Chinese Ambassador to the Foreign Secretary, 16 May 1959* (White Paper I; New Delhi: MEA).

in 1954. The Panchsheel Agreement, no doubt, was a milestone in Sino-Indian bonhomie, and the world looked at it with great hope and admiration, and had been considered Nehru's success in the Third World. However, in the backdrop of the Cold War, this move was not admired in the Western world. When the World War changed global power equations, Great Britain's weakness provided a space for the USA to position itself as a hegemonic power in the Asian continent.[5] While the unity of the Third-World nations brought with it hope and aspirations for the newly independent colonies of Asia and Africa, this was viewed by Washington against the US hegemonic aspirations in Asia. The continued efforts of the USA to reach out to New Delhi were still not successful due to Nehru's policy of non-alignment. In the context of an existing post-World War Red Scare in the USA called 'McCarthyism' and an intense indignation of Washington against Peking out of the Korean crisis brought the US attention to the Himalayas. The Tibet issue, a creation of imperialist Britain, was taken up by the USA as the potential 'weapon' to strike Communist China, and it was tactically placed between India and China to play a larger game in the region. Washington found an existing border dispute between India and China as the entry point to intervene in the region, and thereby the USA wished to target India and China, the two most powerful nations in Asia. After signing the Panchsheel Agreement with China, Nehru focused his attention on the Non-Aligned Movement.

The first major efforts to meet these Afro-Asian aspirations began with the 1955 Bandung Conference, in which more than half of the world's population sent their delegates.[6] Playing a leading role in the session, Nehru and Chou Enlai had planned well in advance for the conference. But behind the curtains, an alleged arm of the USA, through the CIA, in collaboration with the Taiwanese elements, was planning

[5] Atul Bharadwaj, 'The Cold War and 1962 Sino-Indian War', in *China's India War 1962, Looking Back to See the Future*, ed. Jasjit Singh (New Delhi: KW Publishers, 2013), Chapter 4.

[6] It was organized in collaboration with Burma, Sri Lanka, India, and Pakistan, and it took place over 18–24 April 1955 in Bandung, Indonesia. The existing tension between the PRC and the USA was one of the concerns of the meeting. The Indian Prime Minister's 'Five Principles' were unanimously adopted in the session (available at https://www.britannica.com/topic/Pancasila [accessed on 7 September 2020]).

a foul game. The culmination of the plan was the bombing of the Air-India flight Lockheed L-749 *Kashmir Princess*,[7] in which Chinese Premier Chou Enlai and his team were scheduled to travel via Hong Kong. Fortunately for Chou, he changed his plan in the last minute; however, the others in his team met with a sad fate. The flight started its journey from Bombay to Jakarta via Hong Kong and crashed into Indonesian waters on its last leg of travel from Hong Kong, where there was occasion to collaborate with the anti-PRC Taiwanese clique to plan on the sabotage with the active support of the CIA. This incident clearly points to the CIA's role.[8] This was an issue that needed an in-depth investigation, as Peking suspected even IB Chief B. N. Mullik's later involvement in ensuring the failure of the investigation. Mullik was accused of collaborating with Anglo-British officials in Hong Kong, helping to remove traces of the CIA's involvement in the crash,[9] and finally exonerating the main accused arrested in the case. This incident left many grey areas in the investigation, with many angles being probed. However, there were no theories against India. The Chou–Nehru comradeship remained as strong as ever. The key takeaway from this incident is that if the plan to assassinate Premier Chou Enlai,[10] that too on an Air India flight from Bombay, had gone through, the turn of events post such an incident would have been just what the perpetrators would have hoped for. This would have resulted in the failure of the Bandung Conference, nipping the aspirations of the Afro-Asians in the bud, with the ulterior motive of the CIA to intensify the Sino-Indian enmity. But things turned around differently.

---

[7] A. S. Karnik, *Kashmir Princess* (New Delhi: Jaico Publishing House, 1958).

[8] This is an issue which will be discussed in greater detail in my forthcoming volume tentatively titled *Deep State in Nehru Government: Collaboration of CIA–IB and the Indian Bureaucracy on the Road to Border War*.

[9] Mullik, *My Years with Nehru*, 165. The former CIA officer testified that the CIA and MI5(UK) maintained a declared, or overt, security liaison officer in New Delhi and enjoyed close collaborative relations with India's intelligence services. Paul McGarr, '"Quiet Americans in India": The CIA and the Politics of Intelligence in Cold War South Asia', *Diplomatic History* 38, no. 5 (2014): 1046–1082. Available at https://academic.oup.com/dh/article-abstract/38/5/1046/516951 (accessed on 7 September 2020).

[10] Of the 16 on board, all but three of the crew members of the flight died in the disaster. Karnik, *Kashmir Princess*.

In the context of the aforementioned narratives, Peking had already observed a worsening of Sino-Indian relations with the involvement of external factors. This not only included the Tibet rebellion and the role of Indian reactionaries, along with Rightist propaganda against Communist China, but also pointed to Peking's real concern of the active presence of the USA in the Tibetan issue and South Asian politics. A later official communication from Peking emphasizes that the problem was not confined to certain minor provocations within the Indian press and the Parliament, and that it had larger ramifications in Asian politics, especially against Communist China. It stated:

> The enemy of the Chinese people lies in the East, the US imperialists have many military based in Taiwan, in South Korea, Japan and in the Philippines which are all directed against China. China's main attention and policy to struggle are directed to the east, to the west Pacific region, to the vicious and aggressive US imperialism, and not to India or any other country in the southeast Asia and South Asia. Although the Philippines, Thailand and Pakistan have joined the SEATO which is designed to oppose China, we have not treated those three countries as our principal enemy; our principal enemy is US imperialism. India has not taken part in the Southeast Asia Treaty; it is not an opponent, but a friend to our country. China will not be so foolish as to antagonize India in the west. The putting down of the rebellion and the carrying out of democratic reform in Tibet will not in the least endanger India.[11]

But these sensitive messages could not gather enough appeal in partisan internal politics.

Volatile Border and Rebel Movement

The impact of Tibet on Sino-Indian relations should be read in the aforementioned context of external interventions. The Nehru government was aware of this. The borders had become volatile due to the presence of the PLA on the frontiers to check the rebel movement, which naturally made the Indian side stay alert. Therefore, in the wake of the Tibetan uprising of 1959, as part of the precautionary measures, the need for border preparedness was felt in New Delhi and

[11] *Statement Made by the Chinese Ambassador to the Foreign Secretary, 16 May 1959* (White Paper I).

subsequently a number of border posts were established and minimal necessary force was moved to the frontiers. New Delhi, however, still maintained hope of an effective and secure border with friendly Tibet (under China) in any possible offensive by the formidable military power in the neighbourhood. Hence, the overwhelming Indian support for the cause of the Lhasa government, even when it raised questions in Peking, has to be viewed from the apprehension in protecting the border region against a formidable military power in the proximity. This prompted the Government of India to further extend moral and logistic support for the cause of Tibetans.

The third wave of the Tibetan uprising in early 1959 and the increased overreach by New Delhi towards Lhasa provided ample reason for Peking to assert that Indian interests in Tibet were in collusion with the Western imperialists. The fanfare in welcoming the Dalai Lama and the privileges that he enjoyed in India, against international refugee norms, vindicated this argument of Peking. At the same time, an increasing number of PLA personnel in border regions in search of Tibetan rebels created havoc in India, which in turn justified New Delhi securing its frontiers by mobilizing the armed forces. This resulted in the establishment of extended border posts and a reinforcement of armed forces on both sides of the border, leading to repeated reports of the Chinese troops incursions by the middle of June 1959 in search of Tibetans. The military presence of both nations along the border made clashes almost inevitable.

Peking Turns Offensive by Mid-1959

Within a few weeks of the Tibetan uprising (1959), incursions and incidents of minor clashes became frequent. The presence of an armed Chinese detachment in the Indian territory of western Pangong Lake in the Ladakh area was reported in late June and early July 1959. Peking believed that Tibet had begun an armed revolt against the Government of China on India's 'instigation and support of the imperialists and foreign reactionary elements'.[12] But on 3 April 1959, the Indian foreign

---

[12] *Statement by the Vice-Minister for Foreign Affairs of China to the Indian Ambassador, 22 March 1959* (White Paper I, 1954–1959).

secretary informed the ambassador of China that the Dalai Lama had entered Indian territory with a small party on 31 March at his request and in accordance with international norms, and that his stay was arranged in Mussoorie. 'All the Tibetans crossed into Indian territory seeking refuge will be disarmed'.[13]

But tensions soon began to escalate, leading to two important incidents that occurred in Longju and Kongka Pass in August and October 1959, respectively. These two incidents not only intensified the dispute but also brought the entire border region on both sides under the control of the armed forces, which ultimately proved to be the beginning of a more intense border war. Soon the conflict began to intensify in other areas as well, and traders and other personnel involved in various activities on both sides of the border also began to face the heat.

Longju Uncertainty Leads to the First Major Armed Clash

The first major armed clash in the history of the border dispute occurred on 25 August 1959, when a Chinese troop detachment exchanged fire with an Indian picket in the south of Migyitun, capturing the Indians. The next day, a Chinese force outflanked Longju (the NEFA), opened fire and forced the Indian troops to abandon the post. The Indian Embassy in Peking accused the Chinese troops of entering the Indian border, first opening fire on the Indian troops, encircling the Indian post at Longju and even arresting 12 Indian soldiers. New Delhi's protest on 28 August characterized Chinese actions as 'deliberate aggression' and pointed out that until then New Delhi had observed a 'discreet reticence' about them, but that they constituted a matter 'which is bound to rouse popular feelings in India'.[14] On 28 August, Nehru made a statement in the Lok Sabha that a 200-member armed Chinese patrol team had entered Eastern Khenzemane (the NEFA) and indulged in a scuffle with

---

[13] Reference in the Statement made by Foreign Secretary to the Chinese Ambassador, 26 April 1959.

[14] CIA, *The Sino-Indian Border Dispute Staff*, Section I (1950–1959), 32.

the Assam rifles.[15] He cautioned the Parliament against being 'alarmistic' and indulging in shouting and strong talk. However, the members of Parliament were not subdued as they expressed anxieties over the incidents and Chinese intentions along the entire border. A senior member of the Congress Party even asked if bombs could be dropped to chase the Chinese out of the NEFA. Nehru tried to calm tempers by condemning Peking, but 'the explosive temper of Parliament and the press spread and pervaded non official Indian thinking'.[16] Another parliamentarian conjectured that if India failed to defend its own territory, what would be the fate of small Asian countries which look to India for guidance? Nehru reaffirmed that any aggression against Bhutan and Sikkim would be considered aggressions against India.

China rejected the Indian version of the narrative regarding what had happened on 25 August at Longju and alleged that the Indian troops had first opened fire at the Chinese without warning, discharging dozens of rounds of machine gun and rifle shots and that the Chinese troops, in self-defence, had to fire back. They alleged that, on 26 August, the Indian troops used several hundred rounds of shots at the Chinese troops in Migyitun and Indian aircraft many times violated China's airspace. China argued that their troops had fired entirely in 'self-defence'.[17] Peking further argued that Longju was among a series of the continuing instances of tension going on for a couple of months.

It is reliably believed that the Longju attack was started by the Chinese due to an increased Indian presence along the eastern sector of the border, where the Indians had established eight new checkpoints. Post-Tibetan uprising of March 1959, several instances of the Indian troop movements and violation of territories were reported by China as they suspected that 'India was providing support to

---

[15] PM Nehru's Statement in Lok Sabha on 28 August 1959, *Lok Sabha Debates* 33, no. 19, col. 4863–4864.

[16] CIA, *The Sino-Indian Border Dispute Staff*, Section I (1950–1959), 32.

[17] *Note Given to the Ambassador of India by the Ministry of Foreign Affairs of China, 1 September 1959* (White Paper II).

Tibetan rebels in its soil as a sanctuary'.[18] New Delhi denied these charges and stated that India was not responsible for rebel activities and that all Tibetan refugees 'were disarmed as soon as they entered Indian territory'.[19] Similar charges were reported of Indian armed personnel entering into the Kechilang pasture ground, west of Shatze, and setting up Sino-Indian boundary marks at Latze Pass and in Shatze and Khenzemane on 7 and 9 August 1959, respectively.[20] Refuting these charges of unauthorized entry, New Delhi argued that all of these mentioned places belonged to their territory as the boundary ran along Thangla Ridge north of Namkha Chu Thangmu valley.[21] From these protests and counter-protests, one fact became evident—the dispute in the borders largely emanated from an existing uncertainty about the nature of border alignments in the perceptions of both sides, which led to mutual encroachments advertently or otherwise. So the Longju mishap was a result of the absence of clarity on whether or not the line was at Khenzemane or Longju in the Migyitun area.[22] New Delhi, however, expressed its willingness to discuss the exact alignment of the McMahon Line at Khenzemane and the location of Longju and Tamaden with China, but insisted that the status quo should be maintained at all these places.[23] After the Longju incident, an atmosphere for negotiation to settle the issues prevailed before 'unknown forces' came in between.

[18] CIA, *The Sino-Indian Border Dispute Staff*, Section I (1950–1959), 32.

[19] Ibid., 29.

[20] *Note Given to the Ambassador of India by the Ministry of Foreign Affairs of China, 1 September 1959* (White Paper II, September–November 1959, New Delhi: MEA, Government of India).

[21] *Note Given to the Ambassador of India by the Ministry of Foreign Affairs of China, 1 September 1959* (White Paper II, September–November 1959; CIA, *The Sino-Indian Border Dispute Staff*, Section I (1950–1959), 32.

[22] Here, the issue was with respect to certain pockets in the McMahon Line that departed from well-recognized geographical features. The international boundary departs the watershed near Tsari in order to include the pilgrimage route of Tsari Nyingpa (which was used every year by a large number of Tibetans) in Tibet. Similarly, the village of Migyitun was included in Tibet in view of the importance that the Tibetans attach to this village.

[23] *Note Given by the Ambassador of India to the Ministry of Foreign Affairs of China 10 September 1959.*

Efforts to Ease Border Tension

Expressing readiness to talk to reduce tension on 3 September, Nehru proposed the following conditions: (a) both sides should agree to maintain the status quo; (b) neither side should use force and (c) the territory occupied by the Chinese troops should be vacated immediately so that the Indian frontier outpost at Longju can be re-established.[24] To the Parliament, which demanded military action against China, the prime minister clarified on 4 September that a 'big country could not behave as though at war and hit out all around'.[25] He was categorical in stating, 'India would not try to reoccupy the Aksai Plain by force, or bomb the Sinkiang-Tibet road, but would send another request that New Delhi's 8 November 1958 protest note regarding the illegal construction of the road be answered'.[26] As a reciprocal move to Nehru's suggestion, Chou Enlai wrote a detailed letter to the prime minister on 8 September 1959 in which he expressed his apprehension about the further worsening of the situation. He pointed out that many political figures and propaganda organs in India seized the occasion to make a great deal of anti-Chinese utterances, some even openly advocating provocative actions of an even larger scale such as bombarding Chinese territory. An anti-Chinese campaign had been launched in India in (last) six months trying 'to bring pressure on China by military, diplomatic and through public opinion'.[27] Despite being disturbed by these kinds of remarks by responsible leaders at home, in response to Chou, he rejected internal clamour as a factor and conveyed willingness for negotiations and emphasized India's desire for settlement through discussion only. The leadership in Peking was also eager to come to a solution and, in the backdrop of the Longju armed clash, Mao Zedong and Liu Shao-chi had a discussion with Ajay Ghosh, leader of the Communist Party of India (CPI), on 5 and 6 October 1959, in which Ghosh, despite expressing his displeasure

---

[24] Note Dated 3 September 1959 Given by the Counsellor of India to the Ministry of Foreign Affairs of China on 5 September 1959 (White Paper II).

[25] CIA, The Sino-Indian Border Dispute Staff, Section I (1950–1959), 34.

[26] Ibid.

[27] Letter from the PM of China to the PM of India 8 September 1959.

at Indian support to the Tibetan rebels, expressed interest in border talks with Nehru.[28] The Chinese leaders reportedly told Ghosh that they were prepared to exchange the NEFA for their claim in Aksai Chin for reaching a settlement, and that, for this purpose, the leaders of the CPI had to put pressure on India to do so. They were prepared to accept the de facto status of the McMahon Line with minor adjustments and they believed that it would be necessary to develop a 'proper atmosphere'[29] in India.

Wrong Timing of the Kongka Pass Tragedy

The political will of the leaders from both sides was so strong that they were committed to diplomatic solutions until things went beyond political control in New Delhi. A proposal was made for the visit of Indian Vice-President Radhakrishnan to Peking and, on 19 October, Chou Enlai wrote a personal letter to Nehru confirming the proposal. But before the letter was delivered in Delhi on 24 October, another border clash occurred. The Kongka Pass incident of 21 October in southern Ladakh, in which 9 Indian soldiers were killed and 10 captured, reversed the atmosphere for dialogue. Nehru and the vice-president turned down the proposal angrily.[30] As reported by the Ministry of Defence, a three-member Indian police patrol team was detained by the Chinese near Kongka Pass on 21 October, and another 20 members under the command of SP Karan Singh were attacked by the Chinese troops with advanced weapons on the next day. Nine personnel of the ITBP were killed and the remaining members, including Karan Singh, were taken into custody.[31] What had caused this sudden change in such a short time? Who was responsible? This was not an isolated or an accidental incident. While addressing the factors that opened up the roads that led to the border war, such mishaps should also be taken into due consideration.

---

[28] CIA, *The Sino-Indian Border Dispute Staff*, Section I (1950–1959), 32.

[29] Ibid., 40.

[30] CIA, *The Sino-Indian Border Dispute Staff*, Section II (1959–1961), 4.

[31] *Note Given by the MEA to the Ambassador of China in India, 23 Oct 1959* (White Paper II), 14–15; Johri, *Chinese Invasion of Ladakh*, 32–35.

As regards the Kongka Pass mishap, both sides held their ground. The Chinese alleged that on 20 October 1959, three men of the Indian armed forces intruded into their territory south of the Konkga pass and were taken into custody by the Chinese frontier guards when they refused to withdraw. The next day, when this was repeated by a larger Indian force and opened fire on the Chinese frontier guards and attempted to seize their horses, it led to mutual exchange of fire.[32] The Indian narrative stated that their police party had been subjected to sudden and aggressive firing by Chinese forces in the region of Kongka Pass, about 16 miles from Tsogtsalu in Ladakh. New Delhi stated that:

> on 20 October, two members of an Indian Police Party went out on patrol duty in the neighbourhood of Kongka Pass in Ladakh. When they failed to return another team was sent in search of them, but they also did not return. The next day (21 October) when another team of armed personal under the direction of a senior officer went out in search of these members, they were entrenched on a hill-top where they were faced heavy firing by the Chinese armed force. Though the Indian personnel fired back in self-defence, they were overwhelmed by the superior strength of the Chinese troops, and as many as 17 persons belonging to the Indian force including the officer-in-charge, had lost their lives, a few had been severely injured[33]

and seven were captured by the Chinese frontier guards.[34] India rejected the Chinese government's account and repudiated the assumption that the Indian police party, armed with only rifles and also in a totally disadvantageous location, would attack a heavily armed Chinese force which was on a hilltop above them and was equipped with mortars and hand grenades.[35]

---

[32] *Memorandum Given to the Ambassador of India by the Ministry of Foreign Affairs of China, 22 October 1959* (White Paper II).

[33] *Note Given by the Ministry of External Affairs, New Delhi, to the Ambassador of China in India, 23 October 1959* (White Paper II).

[34] *Note Given to the Ambassador of India by the Ministry of Foreign Affairs of China, 25 October 1959.*

[35] *Note Given by the Ministry of External Affairs, New Delhi to the Embassy of China in India, 4 November 1959.*

Who Directed the Forward Movement of the Armed Forces?

The most pertinent question about the Kongka Pass mishap is this: who ordered the movement of forces in the forward direction and what was the context and compulsion for such an action when there was already a proposal for immediate negotiation pending at the diplomatic level? Moreover, when it was already apparent to both sides that there was some lack of clarity about the specifications about the exact boundary and its exact whereabouts, what might have prompted the armed forces to move into such a difficult terrain leading to high casualties? Whose interest was protected in this case? Was this an Indian forward move in the western sector (Kongka Pass) in response to the Chinese move in the eastern sector (Longju)? The DMI justified the forward move as he had stated privately on 14 October that the Chinese troops had come to the Indian outpost at Khenzemane (the NEFA) between 9 and 11 October to warn the Assam Rifles for the 'last and 17th time' to vacate or be pushed out 'in a few days'. He also stated that the Chinese had sent a warning to New Delhi and threatened border posts in Bhutan and Sikkim.[36] Further, there was evidence of provocation from New Delhi as well. But when the political leadership at the higher level had already taken a decision on the vice-president's visit to Peking, and both sides had exchanged positive overtones, and the armed movement was restricted before that, how was this decision not taken care of by the DMI? Also, who had actually passed on instructions on these forward movements? It is reported that the movement of the Indian troops to the border had been indicated by Foreign Secretary Subimal Dutt, who stated on 12 October that 'although Nehru (was) afraid of and dead against military action, the Indian Army brought pressure on him and placed crack Indian troops along the NEFA-Tibet border: Jats, Gurkhas, Sikhs, and Rajputs'.[37] The Indian Army Chief at the time was General Thimayya. The CIA

---

[36] CIA, *The Sino-Indian Border Dispute Staff*, Section I (1950–1959), 41–42.

[37] The CIA document does not clarify the full truth behind this as the document here is subjected to the editing/deletion of certain words in that particular area which makes things more ambiguous. CIA, *The Sino-Indian Border Dispute Staff*, Section I (1950–1959), 41.

document has deleted references to some names which makes things more obscure. But one thing is to be noted—the Kongka Pass incident was a real game changer in border relations.

A Military Move beyond Political Decision

Looking at developments in both Longju and Kongka Pass, it can be concluded that such incidents had occurred despite ongoing efforts for peace and that the Government of India was not able to stop the clashes between the Indian and Chinese patrol teams. Once the news of the Longju mishap went public, it got massive publicity in the Indian press and the Parliament, combining their attacks on the government. The Parliament and the press insisted on military action against China. While the *Hindustan Times* called for limited reprisals in order to avoid demoralizing Indians, the *Indian Express* advised acceptance (military) of aid from non-Communist countries 'without qualms'. However, Nehru rejected these pieces of advice on the grounds that military aid from abroad would jeopardize India's freedom and undermine India's place in the world.[38] In fact, both New Delhi and Peking did not want to drag nations into a military face-off, because both feared repercussions of a large nature. During the same time, however, there were forces from within that were eager to push their forces to the border. As a result of the emerging tension at the borders after Longju, Nehru instructed all parties concerned to show restraint on the frontiers. Despite his directive (dated 13 September 1959) for restraint and the prohibition of further movement of forces in Ladakh, the ITBP under the Home Ministry clashed at Kongka Pass.[39]

It is apparent that Nehru was aware of the limitations of the Indian military in Ladakh and, therefore, would not have given a directive against what he believed. Moreover, during this particular time, he warned against any talk of a counter-attack on the Chinese. Regarding the issue of stationing more troops at Ladakh, there was a level of uncertainty in the thinking of the Indian military and the political

---

[38] Ibid., 42–43.

[39] Gupta, 'Distortions in the History of Sino-Indian Frontiers', 1265–1270.

leadership. In the Governors' Conference convened by Nehru in late October, Army Chief General Thimayya told President Rajendra Prasad and Finance Minister Morarji Desai that he had proposed taking 'necessary military steps' against the Chinese after it was discovered that they had built a road through the Aksai Plain. But Defence Minister Krishna Menon had turned down the proposals on the grounds that the 'main military danger' was on the India–Pakistan border.[40] He was also of the view that he 'could not strip the Pakistan border to man the entire border with China'.[41] It is reported that Thimayya was of the firm opinion that the strategic insignificance of the Aksai Chin plain was strengthened by the Indian military and that 'there was really no strategic reason for recapturing it (Aksai Chin) from the Chinese troops even if it were possible to do so in the face of preponderant Chinese military power'.[42] The army officials had expressed their limitations to send forces to the China border, except for occasional patrols. The army justified it as not being in a position 'to open and hold any posts in this area', and said that 'it would not be possible to oust the Chinese from this region'.[43] In the aforementioned premise, one should believe that Thimayya would not have given such a direction in Kongka Pass over and above the political decision. Here the question is, if what the Foreign Secretary Subimal Dutt on 12 October stated was correct, why was the Indian Army under pressure for such a decision, and who was behind this?

According to the statement of SP Karan Singh, the commander of the force, who moved to establish new checkpoints in the forward areas in Ladakh that led to the Kongka Pass clash, some officials of the Home Ministry and the Indian IB had directed forward patrols in the

---

[40] CIA, *The Sino-Indian Border Dispute Staff*, Section I (1950–1959), 42–43. Reference to General Thimayya is partially deleted in the declassified CIA document.

[41] Ibid., 43–44.

[42] General Thimayya's opinion was that it was not Kunlun but Karakoram range that was the only defensible frontier in the entire Ladakh area. Thimayya stated that it was 'militarily indefensible' by implication. It is interesting to observe as it arouses suspicion as to why most references to Thimayya in the CIA report have certain parts deleted.

[43] Mullik, *My Years with Nehru*, 201.

Kongka Pass region.[44] This testimony proves that, on 22 September 1959, the deputy director of the Ministry of Home Affairs had given instructions to establish new checkpoints in the forward areas in Hot Springs, Ladakh.[45] This action was highly provocative and might have invited the Chinese offensive. This narration of the incident from an officer at ground zero, who was involved in the operation, reveals that the vested ulterior interests had played a role in this mishap at a crucial time. These developments in Longju and Kongka Pass show how the involvement of the bureaucracy was contrary to the political decision.

In fact, it was the bureaucrats in the IB and the Home Ministry, with a few military officials, who pushed the forces into this unfortunate encounter. The blame game in the official meeting that was held immediately after the mishap, to discuss the fault lines, is testimony to this. In the high-level official meeting called by the prime minister and attended by the defence minister, the COAS, chief of the IB and senior officials of the External Affairs and Home Ministries, the mudslinging that ensued reveals the role that the Indian bureaucracy played in worsening the situation. The army headquarters and the MEA accused the IB of expansionism and responsible for causing provocations on the frontier. Therefore, 'the Army demanded that no further movements of armed police should take place on the frontier without their clearance'.[46] A detailed study of the developments at that time reveals that these charges against the IB chief were not without substance. After the Kongka Pass incident, New Delhi explained its version of arguments to the Chinese government on 4 November 1959.[47] But even before that, Assam Rifles was brought under the operational control of the army and the security of the Ladakh region was taken over by the army. This desperate and hasty move of the armed forces to the frontiers is suspected to have provoked enemy forces. The IB as

---

[44] *Statement of Karan Singh* (White Paper III; New Delhi: MEA), 14.

[45] Ibid.

[46] Mullik, *My Years with Nehru*, 243–244.

[47] *Memorandum Given to the Ambassador of India by the Ministry of Foreign affairs of China 22 October 1959* (White Paper II), 13 and *25 October 1959*, 16–18. Also, the *Note Given by the MEA to the Ambassador of China in India, 23 October 1959* (White Paper II), 14–15.

well as the Ministry of Home Affairs are equally responsible for such a situation. With the Kongka Pass incident, public anger in both nations reached a boiling point causing a critical turn in the Sino-Indian frontier dispute, virtually crippling premiers-level diplomacy.

The ego clash and the individual interests of higher officials in the defence had adversely affected fund allocation towards the immediate requirement of logistics of the army. The tussle at the ministerial level was more acute that the Ministry of Finance under Desai was highly non-cooperative with the Ministry of Defence under Menon. When Menon took charge of the Ministry, the armed forces were virtually starved for resources. The personal ego clash between Desai and Menon was known in public. The 'interests' and aspirations of the bureaucrats in the highest echelons of the IB and the armed forces were instrumental in decision-making that was beyond the control of the prime minister and his cabinet. Internal rifts and personal ambitions had implications in the decisions of the armed forces, leading to the presentation of facts beyond common understanding. Nehru took the advice of the IB chief and a few trusted army leaders and bureaucrats in the MEA. But official records reveal that the suggestions and recommendations of some of those at a higher hierarchical level in the bureaucracy were unreliable and that their 'loyalty' seemed demanding of a probe. The illogical movement of Indian forces in the borders with very little preparedness and logistics has been explained in various records. The Henderson Brooks report testifies to several such instances of illogical establishments of border posts and irrational force movements to borders for such dubious actions.[48]

Armed Forces Take Control of the Frontiers

The Longju and Kongka Pass incidents and the subsequent increase in the frequency of encounters and infiltrations into Indian territory forced New Delhi to intensify security along the borders. This was the real reason behind initiating the most controversial FP of New Delhi in the later years. Subsequently, on 27 August 1959, the Assam Rifles were replaced by the Indian Armed Forces on the border with Tibet

---

[48] Government of India, 'The Henderson Brooks–Bhagat Report (NM)'.

in the eastern sector and, on 24 October 1959, the western sector was brought under the army. So by the end of 1959, Sino-Indian border relations had entered a new phase with intensified armed mobilization on both sides of the frontier region.

Indian Reactionaries Put New Delhi on Defensive Mode

Around late October 1959, during a session of the External Affairs subcommittee, Nehru expressed his willingness to negotiate for an 'exchange formula' (Aksai Chin, north-east Ladakh where the road traversed) with disputes in the eastern sector and for the purpose he was preparing Indian public opinion.[49] It was a wise decision and, had it been implemented, would have benefitted both nations; (a) India would not have lost the area of Ladakh beyond the Aksai Chin that China was occupying since the border clashes of 1959; (b) the military occupation in this remote region could have been reduced drastically with a significant reduction in defence expenditure; (c) the high number of casualties of armed personnel in this difficult terrain with a hostile climate could have been averted and (d) the NEFA issue, which became a permanent dispute, could have been settled forever with a single move of the exchange decision. But unfortunately, some of the prominent cabinet members in Nehru's government adopted a harder bargaining line. Both Foreign Secretary Dutt and Vice-President Radhakrishnan complained bitterly that Nehru was on his way to sell out the Aksai Plain.[50] President Prasad disliked the letter that Nehru had drafted for the Chinese government on 29 October on the grounds that it 'lacked firmness' and insisted that the language should be modified in tone and rigour.[51] Now the Chinese leaders feared that Nehru's advisers might use these armed clashes to push him and the entire government further 'right' towards a militant anti-China policy and willingness to accept some degree of American support in this respect. The Chairman of the CPI, S. A. Dange, stated that border

---

[49] CIA, *The Sino-Indian Border Dispute Staff*, Section I (1950–1959), 44.

[50] Ibid.

[51] Ibid., 41–43.

developments were providing the 'Right wing' with the opportunity 'to pull India towards the Anglo-American camp',[52] which urged the Chinese to try for negotiations.

Thus, we see that the actual factors that contributed towards the further straining of bilateral relations were not armed clashes, but were influenced by several aspects such as ego clashes, partisan interests and winning political mileage at the expense of national interest. This deterioration of relations began immediately after March 1959. Until then, the USA had made sufficient inroads into the region, and these were reflected in the developments in the country. Several politically motivated protests were organized in the capital city and major metropolitan areas that were financially aided by outside forces. In the name of sympathy with Tibet, these demonstrations were basically anti-China propaganda. As a consequence of one of these, China lodged a serious protest on 27 April 1959 to the Indian Foreign Ministry regarding certain developments in Bombay on 20 April 1959. In this particular incident, about 80 members of the Socialist Party had allegedly insulted Mao Zedong,[53] and Peking had provided evidence in support of their allegation.[54] The Socialist party, involved in this demonstration, shouted slogans at the Chinese Consulate-General and branded China as an imperialist in Tibet, portrayed Mao Zedong in a bad light and stuck caricatures on the consulate walls and further threw tomatoes and rotten eggs at the office. All of these events took place in the presence of Indian policemen, and the public was allowed to photograph and circulate these incidents. This note detailing these activities of the protesters was one such instance among many others. They considered such actions to be a huge insult to China and insisted that if the Government of India did not take appropriate action against such instances, it would cause deep wounds in their relationship.[55]

---

[52] S. A. Dange, 'Neither Revisionism nor Dogmatiam Is Our Guide', *New Age*, supplement, 21 April 1963.

[53] *Note of the Government of China, 27 April 1959 to the Ministry of External Affairs, New Delhi.*

[54] *Note of the Government of India, 30 April 1959* (White Paper I; New Delhi: MEA).

[55] *Note no. M/129/59 Presented to the Ministry of External Affairs of the Government of India on 27 April 1959 by the Government of China* (White Paper I; New Delhi: MEA).

India responded by confirming most of the narratives of the Bombay episode with the exception of police inaction. The Government of India deeply regretted this discourtesy to Mao Zedong and deplored the actions taken. On 27 April 1959, in his statement in the Lok Sabha, the prime minister expressed his deep regret over this incident.[56]

In another instance, Peking lodged a protest against the objectionable ways and language used by India's Foreign Secretary Dutt during his conversation with the Chinese on 26 April 1959. The Chinese alleged that certain

> responsible persons of many Indian Political Parties, including the (Indian) National Congress, and a few Indian publications openly called Tibet a (separate) country and the Chinese are 'practicing banditry and imperialism' in Tibet. They demand the Tibet question to be submitted to the United Nations and political parties in India went so far as to organize support for Tibetan rebels.[57]

Peking asserted that it will not tolerate these under any pretext[58] and expressed apprehension that these words and deeds were targeted to 'sabotage the Sino-Indian friendship'.[59] Peking strongly protested that Tibetan rebels were being encouraged by Indian sympathizers and observed that relations were going from bad to worse. However, the note concluded that the Indian 'Prime Minister Nehru has expressed the wish to end this argument and called on Indian newspapers to exercise restraint and wisdom, which is worthy of welcome'.[60]

There were counteroffensives from the other side of the border as well. In mid-1959, the Chinese officials, the press, the Peking Radio as well as its National People's Congress began to unleash attacks on the Government of India. An article published in the *Peking Review*

---

[56] *Note of the Government of India, 30 April 1959* (White Paper I; New Delhi: MEA). The protest demonstration was organized by Socialist Party, a split-away group from the Praja Socialist Party, which had always indulged in highly objectionable behaviour towards the Government of India.

[57] Statement Made by the Chinese Ambassador to the Foreign Secretary, 16 May 1959.

[58] Ibid.

[59] Ibid.

[60] Ibid.

on 6 May 1959 titled 'Revolution in Tibet and Nehru's Philosophy' was the first time that Nehru had been vehemently criticized by the Chinese media. This was considered to be an impact of the reception accorded to the Dalai Lama in Mussoorie, Nehru's personal visit to the Dalai Lama and, later in April, the Dalai Lama's political statement criticizing China. After the Longju incident, the article was once again reprinted in the *People's Daily* with some data pertaining to the border history on 12 and 16 September 1959, which was an attack on Nehru's border policy.[61] China alleged that the Dalai Lama was under duress in India and that the statements made by him were imposed on him by foreigners. They addressed the protesters in India as 'Indian reactionaries' 'working in the footsteps of British imperialists, and have been harbouring expansionist ambitions towards Tibet'. New Delhi justified their actions on account of 'religious and cultural contacts with the people of Tibet' and also on the grounds that the Indian Constitution guaranteed complete freedom of expression in the Parliament and in the press.

Disputes and allegations basically stemmed from the following. First, the Chinese strongly believed the presence of an outside force in the Tibetan region and their collaboration with the Tibetan rebels to destabilize China. According to Peking, it was due to the extended Indian sympathy towards the Tibetan rebels, providing them moral as well as logistic support in their rebel activities and their fight against the Peking authorities that other forces were able to take advantage of the situation in destabilizing this Chinese region. The US factor was the most disturbing aspect as far as Peking was concerned, and the CIA had established a strong network in India and border towns like Kalimpong to indulge in anti-China activities. Both Peking and New Delhi complained about frequent airspace violations in border regions. After investigating hundreds of such cases, it was found that these were neither from India nor China. The US and Taiwan intrusions into the region with the support of Washington was reliably reported. The US involvement in the worsening of Sino-Indian relations demands a detailed study. Second, even when New Delhi reiterated the existence

[61] *Note Given by the Ministry of External Affairs, New Delhi, to the Counsellor of China in India, 24 September 1959.*

of a border as defined by tradition and geography, the actual reality of the specifications of the territory was not accurate in the high-altitude mountain regions, which made it difficult to determine each other's territory for force movement on ground zero. This uncertainty was the basic reason behind most cases of 'intrusion or encroachment'. In most of the pre-1959 cases, once such an inadvertent case was notified to the other side, the immediate withdrawal of the troops was noticed by the other party. But once the vested interest groups poised themselves in between, these intrusions became a reality. In the absence of any specific documentary proof of longitudinal and latitudinal directions, including maps with geographical specifications about the nature of the border, on many occasions advertent or inadvertent encroachments were noticed, aggravating the dispute.

A third possible factor responsible for the deteriorating border situation was the lack of coordination between the political powers in Delhi and the military command in border regions in which distance and other factors might have played negative roles. Some of the pertinent questions include whether or not any 'outside force' was present in the southern Tibetan regions or on the frontiers that aggravated the situation, and if the IB reported to New Delhi or to the concerned armed forces. However, despite such tremors and triggers on the border, to avoid any further eventualities, the conciliatory notes were exchanged with each other. Normalcy was once again brought back on the border on account of these conciliatory dealings. But things were not as envisaged by the political authority in Delhi, and amicable solutions and border negotiations eluded the higher political circle.

Peking for Sectoral Settlement, but New Delhi Reluctant

Despite the intense uneasiness on the frontiers, the negotiations were earnestly pursued. The premiers on both sides of the border were confident of convincing their counterparts. Despite political detractors of the government intensifying their callous criticism on political agenda, bilateral relations were characterized by mutual respect, with no scope for belligerence. Even the armed forces followed practices in keeping with moral principles and gentlemanly behaviour. According to Brigadier Shrikent, on the encounter with Chinese, 'The Indian troops were asked not to call the Chinese "enemy" and, while doing bayonet practice, they were not allowed to use Chinese dummies'.[62] This was also the case from the other side of the border. But when the Tibet issue dominated the scene, and Peking was disturbed by US involvement in this, the atmosphere began to change. Peking's suspicion of New Delhi's involvement in the Tibet issue, the collusion of the Indian Rightist with other anti-Nehru factions from within and outside the government changed the equilibrium between both nations. To add fuel to the fire, the Indian press and opposition parties vociferously attacked Communist China as an expression of their sentiments for the Tibetan cause. Consequently, Peking intensified its position on the dispute in all sectors, including the NEFA.

Considering this strained atmosphere, Nehru made some candid statements about the reality of the unclear nature of the Aksai Chin territory.[63] In response to a question raised by A. B. Vajpayee in the Parliament on 28 August 1959, the prime minster said:

> This was the boundary of the old Kashmir state with Tibet and Chinese Turkestan. Nobody had marked it. But after some kind of broad surveys, the then Government had laid down that border which we have been accepting...the Aksai Chin area is an area about some parts of which...it is not quite clear what the position is.[64]

On 31 August, he repeated this in the Rajya Sabha.

> The position in Ladakh is different from the position in the North-Eastern Frontier Agency. The Ladakh border was for these long years under the Jammu and Kashmir State and nobody knew exactly what was happening there although some British officers went a hundred years ago and drew a

---

[62] Interview of Brigadier S. P. S. Shrikent, MVC (Retd) held on 4 May 1988, quoted in Sinha and Athale, *History of the Conflict with China 1962*, 431.

[63] He was well aware of the tradition, history and geography of the frontiers, especially in Ladakh, and he had already openly revealed it on several occasions, but had to be diplomatically silent on such facts at times.

[64] Prime Minister in Lok Sabha on 28 August 1959, vol. 33, cols. 4793–4840.

line and the Chinese did not accept that line. The matter is clearly one for consideration and debate.[65]

Nehru said that Aksai Chin was of no value to India, 'the territory is sterile, barren and uninhabited region without a vestige of grass 17,000 feet high'.[66] Nehru spoke in the same vein on 10 and 12 September about this region in the Parliament.[67] It seemed that he was preparing Indian sentiments for a compromised formula that he was pondering over. A secret directive to his officials on 13 September 1959 also reveals his desire for a compromised settlement in the Ladakh sector.

On the other side of the border, the Chinese premier seemed to have read the thinking in New Delhi for a compromise between the two major sectors. He tactfully projected the issue of the McMahon Line and suggested a farther extended borderline to the NEFA as a bargaining point. Chou hinted for an extended dispute territory in his letter to Nehru dated 8 September 1959. He wrote, 'The Chinese government absolutely does not recognize the so called McMahon Line'.[68] But it seemed from the other clauses and later suggestions that this was not a blatant claim over the whole territory (90,000 km²) under the Indian administration south of the McMahon Line. Chou added that 'the tense situation recently arising on the Sino-Indian border was all caused by trespassing and provocations by Indian troops'.[69] However, on a conciliatory note, Chou further suggested 'an overall settlement' of the boundary question.[70] This meant that China wanted a friendly India on the border to quell the Tibetan uprising and consolidate the province under its political control, with the cooperation of India. The NEFA was definitely not on its agenda except for a case to bargain with.

[65] Prime Minister in Rajya Sabha on 31 August 1959. *Rajya Sabha Debates* 26, no. 14-24, cols. 2288–2292.

[66] Noorani, 'The Truth about 1962', 17–30.

[67] Gupta, 'Distortions in the History of Sino-Indian Frontiers'.

[68] *Letter from the PM of China to the PM of India 8 September 1959* (White Paper II), 27–33.

[69] Ibid., 32.

[70] Ibid., 27–28.

In the wake of the Tibet turmoil, a peaceful border was a necessity for China that could be ensured by a mutual settlement.

Nehru's response to Chou on 26 September 1959 declined the suggestion for an overall settlement.[71] He said:

> We recognize that the India–China frontier which extends over more than 3500 kms has not been demarcated on the ground and disputes may therefore arise at some places along the traditional frontiers as to whether these places lie on the Indian or the Tibetan side.... We agree therefore, that the border disputes which have already arisen should be amicably and peacefully settled.[72]

But after the Kongka Pass incident, Nehru's options became bleak. He had to survive the critics. Therefore, he chose a tougher stand with China. In addition to this, an extended claim of Peking in the NEFA prompted New Delhi to engage in a counteroffensive in the western sector. The MEA note sent to the Embassy of China on 4 November 1959 for the first time claimed territory eastwards from the Karakoram Pass. Nehru also sent a secret memorandum to key ambassadors abroad stating that he was 'convinced now that China in the present dispute is only after territorial gains from India and not interested in a settlement based on traditional frontiers, therefore he does not see much chance of a reasonable negotiated settlement of the dispute'.[73]

Nehru Lost in 'National Sentiment'

Gradually, Nehru, too, was drawn into the pressure tactics of the opposition, which were primarily backed by Rightist propaganda. No less was the influence from within his party members for such a change in attitude. As regards negotiation, an uncompromising official position had been reached largely as a result of cabinet, opposition and public pressure, and it was difficult for Nehru to satisfy public opinion as well as to open the door for negotiations. Before 1960, Nehru was firm on

---

[71] *Letter from the PM of India to the PM of China 26 September 1959, Annexure to the Letter* (White Paper II), 34–36, 47–52.

[72] Ibid, 32.

[73] Report in *The Hindu*, 13 November 1959.

his conviction for negotiation. So once, when chided by an opponent in the Parliament on 21 December regarding negotiations with the Chinese, Nehru angrily replied that there were only two choices, 'war or negotiation'. 'I will always negotiate, negotiate, negotiate, right to the bitter end'.[74] Similarly, refuting the idea of 'police action', he said that it was possible only against a weak adversary. 'Little wars...do not take place between two great countries and any kind of warlike development would mean "indefinite" war because neither India nor China would ever give in and neither could conquer the other'.[75] However, slowly he too came under influence. He spoke excitedly in the Parliament about the sacredness of the Indian soil, arousing patriotic fervour among the members. Once he said:

> When such conflicts occur, something happens which stirs our innermost convictions, something which hurts our pride, our national pride, our self-respect and all that. So it is something more precious than a hundred or a thousand miles, and it is that which brings up people's passions to a high level and it is that which, to some extent, is happening in India today. It is not because of a patch of territory but because they feel that they have not got a fair treatment in this matter, they have been treated rather casually by the Chinese government, and an attempt is made, if I may use the word, to bully them.[76]

On the same line of rigour, on 4 November 1959, the Government of India wrote to Peking:

> Traditional and historical frontier of India has been associated with India's culture and tradition for the last two thousand years, or so, and has been an intimate part India's life and thought 'and therefore would resist by all means any infringement to its independence and integrity.[77]

These exciting and passionate words of Nehru should be viewed from an angle of his internal political mileage, as well as to win over the ardent pro-Rightist propagandists against him and his policies, rather than being due to his own conviction.

---

[74] CIA, *The Sino-Indian Border Dispute Staff*, Section II (1959–1961), 15.

[75] Ibid.

[76] Statement, 10 September 1959, *Rajya Sabha Debates* 26, cols. 3895–3915.

[77] *Letter Government of India to Government of China 4 November 1959* (White Paper II), 20–24.

The Kongka Pass tragedy, in which India suffered human casualties, had actually compelled Chou to be mild and to stand up for further talks.[78] Subsequently, on 7 November, in his letter to Nehru, Chou wished for an immediate premier-level meeting to hold talks in the immediate future.[79] But 'the Indian leaders did not accept Chou's proposals for Prime ministerial-level talks and they suggested a new set of pre-conditions for negotiations'. Nehru had to respond by stating that 'the atmosphere in India was not ripe for bargaining, nor were his advisers disposed to do so'.[80] The reply to Chou's letter was basically drafted by Home Minister G. B. Pant with a set of preconditions.[81] The letter underlined that a prime ministerial-level meeting must be for 'fruitful discussion' not to get lost 'in a forest of data'.[82] But Peking

---

[78] CIA, *The Sino-Indian Border Dispute Staff*, Section II (1959–1961), 4.

[79] *Letter from the PM of China to the PM of India 7 November 1959* (White Paper III), 44–45. Chou Enlai suggested that for an amicable settlement, both Indian and Chinese troops should withdraw 12.5 miles from the McMahon Line in the east and the LAC in the west. This suggestion, he asserted, was merely an extension to the entire border of an earlier Indian proposal (note of 10 September 1959) that neither side send its troops into Longju. Actually, Chou's suggestion that troops withdraw, leaving a demilitarized zone under 'civil administrative personnel and unarmed police' was a refinement of his own 8 September proposal for a return to the 'long-existing status quo' under which the Chinese accepted the McMahon Line de facto while retaining unchallenged possession of north-eastern Ladakh. Chou's view of military disengagement along the border included no real Chinese concessions. CIA, *The Sino-Indian Border Dispute Staff*, Section II (1959–1961), 5.

[80] Cabinet members at 'the 9 November Congress Working Committee meeting recorded their opinion that adequate steps should indeed be taken to prevent further clashes, but these steps should not affect India's security or involve any acceptance of Chinese aggression'. CIA, *The Sino-Indian Border Dispute Staff*, Section II (1959–1961), 5.

[81] (a) Chinese withdrawal from Longju ensuring that it will not be re-occupied by Indian forces; (b) mutual Indian and Chinese withdrawal from the entire disputed area in Ladakh. The Indian troops would withdraw south and west to the line which China claimed on its 1956 maps and the Chinese troops would withdraw north and east to the line claimed by India on its maps; (c) personal talks with Chou Enlai are acceptable, but 'preliminary steps' should first be taken to reach an 'interim understanding' to ease tensions quickly and (d) a mutual 12.5-mile withdrawal all along the border is unnecessary, as no clashes would occur if both sides refrained from sending out patrols. Letter by Indian Prime Minister on 16 November to the Chinese Premier. CIA, *The Sino-Indian Border Dispute Staff*, Section II (1959–1961), 8.

[82] *Letter from the PM of India to the PM of China 16 November 1959* (White Paper III), 46–50.

was unwilling to abide by the clause for mutual withdrawal in Ladakh as suggested by India. They insisted on meeting with Nehru either in China or in Burma.[83] This seemed to be with the purpose of avoiding the anti-China lobbyist pressure on him in Delhi. But New Delhi insisted on a reply from the Chinese premier to his earlier detailed letter dated 26 September and the note dated 4 November 1959 before any discussion.

The eagerness of Peking for negotiations is explained in the context of an emerging US factor in between. An 'encirclement' theory that the USA was trying to capture or influence countries of Asia around China and Russia was quite persistent in Chinese thinking at this time. Once General Thimayya's discord with Menon on the issue of the former's demand for a joint Indo-Pak defence against China[84] became apparent, it caused a level of apprehension in Peking. In the event of a suspected 'Rightist' General's attempt to remove Krishna Menon as defence minister (September 1959), a real fear was felt among the Chinese leaders that India was on the brink and 'must be snatched away from going into the US imperialist camp'.[85] In this context, Mao is reported to have told Ghosh on 5 October that he understands the difference between Nehru and his 'Rightist' advisers 'in the Ministry of External Affairs including General Thimayya, who wanted to exploit the border dispute to help the US and to isolate China'.[86] Liu Shao-chi even advised Ghosh on 8 October that Nehru might decide in favour of these Rightists, and hence all efforts should be directed towards preventing him from doing so.[87] It was due to this deterioration in ties that the Chinese premier on 17 December 1959 suggested a personal interaction with Nehru and expressed that Peking would be willing to exchange its claim to the south of the McMahon Line in exchange

---

[83] *Letter from the PM of China to the PM of India 17 December 1959* (White Paper III), 51–55.

[84] Pakistan had already endeared to the USA and the overwhelming interest of the USA to stake claim in South Asian and Southeast Asian affairs was found to be disturbing to New Delhi. Thimayya had strong differences with Menon which resulted in the submission of his resignation to the prime minister in September 1959. It is also alleged that Thimayya was one of the American favourites among Indian bureaucrats.

[85] CIA, *The Sino-Indian Border Dispute Staff*, Section II (1959–1961), 2.

[86] Ibid.

[87] Ibid.

for Aksai Plain. But he was under tremendous pressure from the opposition in the Parliament and the press and, therefore, Nehru was reluctant to meet with Chou. However, even when he later agreed, he raised several preconditions for talks. This created an impression that China stood for dialogue, while New Delhi refused.

The discussion for a Nehru–Chou meeting was held on 2 February 1960 in the Foreign Affairs subcommittee meeting, but Home Minister Pant objected. Therefore, Nehru's letter to Chou on 5 February 1960 was about agreeing to meet, but 'there can be no negotiations' based on the Chinese view that the entire boundary had never been delimited,[88] and the later communiqué dated 12 February affirmed that the Sino-Indian boundary 'does not require formal definition',[89] which sounded like a negotiation was unwelcome to New Delhi. Nehru subsequently said in the Parliament that there would be no negotiations with China until it withdrew from Aksai Chin. This attitude ultimately led to an 'interminable series of "talks" between the two countries with no results'.[90] It was a decision taken against his will and his convictions. But the change in his stance seemed to calm the clamorous internal atmosphere, especially in the Parliament and the press. This tough stand from Nehru was unexpected to Chou Enlai, who yet again suggested talks in New Delhi. This time, Nehru could not decline and finally agreed to meet in March 1960 without making it public.

The decision was to remove a possible misconception among world leaders about New Delhi's stand on 'no negotiation'. On 9 February 1960, Ambassador Parthasarathy was deputed with the task of carrying a carefully worded note[91] along with a personal letter from Nehru to the Chinese premier. The note implied that New Delhi was not against a premiers-level meeting, and it neither insisted on the earlier preconditions of the Chinese withdrawal from Ladakh, nor did it

---

[88] Letter from Nehru to the Government of China, 5 February 1960.

[89] *Note from the Government of India to the Government of China 12 February 1960* (White Paper III), 82.

[90] Subramanian, 'Looking Back to the Future'.

[91] *Note from the Government of India Dated 9 February 1960 in Response to the Chinese Note Dated 26 December 1959* (White Paper II; New Delhi: MEA).

persist on an explicit acceptance of the McMahon Line. But prior to conveying his invitation to Chou, as an effort to conceal it from an 'aroused sentiment' among the Indian public, Nehru displayed an anti-China hard line in his words in the Parliament. On 12 February, therefore, he responded to opposition questions in the Parliament to create the impression that he was against even meeting with Chou. Actually, this was a tactful move. He said, 'I see no ground whatever at present, no bridge between the Chinese position and ours.... There is nothing to negotiate at present. Whether that will arise later I cannot say'.[92] This firm line of 'no negotiation' was largely intended to pacify the opposition, which cheered him up in the Parliament. In contrast to an unwilling New Delhi, Peking's overwhelming enthusiasm to come to the negotiation table scored in favour of China. China disarmed its critics from the West and the USSR, who had levelled charges at an unwilling Peking to settle its border disputes amicably.

But on 15 February, when the government released the texts of Nehru's letter of 5 February inviting Chou to meet in India, the opposition was agitated and the Parliament witnessed an unprecedented uproar. The Indian press had already smelted the news and had inflicted maximum damage on the efforts of the Government of India. With a scathing attack on the government, *Hindustan Standard* considered it an 'insult' to the Parliament and the country. On 10 February, *the Times* characterized Nehru's reversal as 'astonishing' and 'nourishing dangerous illusions'. These attacks no doubt disturbed Nehru and were reliably reported to have influenced his future actions on China.[93]

In the midst of all this, Chou made a tactical move and Peking signed a deal to settle the historical border dispute with Burma and agreed for a survey and demarcation on 28 January 1960.[94] Peking 'apparently calculated that a speedy border agreement with Prime

---

[92] Quoted in CIA, *The Sino-Indian Border Dispute Staff*, Section II (1959–1961), 37.

[93] Ibid., 37–39.

[94] In May 1960, the China–Burma border was surveyed for demarcation and in October the same year Chinese Premier Chou Enlai signed a border treaty with the Burmese Premier U Nu. Richard Michael Gibson, *The Secret Army: Chinag Kai-Shek and the Drug Warlords of the Golden Triangle* (Hoboken, NJ: John Wiley & Sons, 2011), 171–172.

Minister Ne-Win would make it more difficult for Nehru to reject similar talks'.[95] Nehru now could not insist on this 'no-talk' attitude and agreed to drop his preconditions on the advice of his ambassadors and certain cabinet members.[96] He wrote, 'I would be glad if you could take the trouble to come to Delhi…and you will be our honoured guest when you come here'.[97] Chou accepted the invitation to Delhi. In the meantime, in March 1959, Peking quickly reached another border agreement with Nepal, which brought further pressure on Nehru from the international community and gave China the upper hand. Taking the cue from the Sino-Burmese agreement, the Chinese won against the propagandists who criticized Communist China's belligerence. The *People's Daily* stated, 'Surely what has happened between China and Burma can take place between China and other countries'.[98] However, the prime minister struggled to find a balance between an inflexible opposition and a persistent Communist China. Finally, the Chinese team was welcomed to Delhi for a proposed meeting in April 1960.

[95] CIA, *The Sino-Indian Border Dispute Staff*, Section II (1959–1961), ii–iii.

[96] Ibid.

[97] *Letter from the PM of India to the PM of China 4 March 1960* (White Paper III; New Delhi: MEA, Government of India, Nov. 1959–March 1960).

[98] *People's Daily*, 1 February 1960, quoted in CIA, *The Sino-Indian Border Dispute Staff*, Section II (1959–1961), 37.

The Road to Border War (1959–1962): II

On 19 April 1960, Chinese Premier Chou Enlai and Foreign Minister Chen Yi, accompanied by a large delegation, arrived in Delhi for a six-day official visit. Although the reported cold feet were not that apparent in the official Indian attitude, 'not much hope was entertainment in India'.[1] The Chinese, reportedly, were looking forward to a concrete settlement of the border issue, and there were vague reports in the press[2] about China proposing an 'overall settlement on the basis of present actualities' and mutual accommodation and the constitution of a joint boundary commission.[3] The prime minister, the defence minister and their close aides also kept their hopes high on the outcome of the proceedings. Nehru had already prepared enough for further discussions with Peking, and as part of his preparedness he had deputed S. Gopal, a historian and director of the Historical Division, MFA, to London for the purpose. To study and report on archival documents preserved in the Indian Office, Gopal visited London in November 1959. But it seems that Gopal had 'failed to do his homework on both the Aksai Chin and the McMahon line issue and briefed Prime Minister Nehru poorly on India's border claim which led to rigidities on his part in expounding'[4] Indian arguments. Nehru's advisors were actually expecting nothing out of the sittings and maintained a pessimistic posture. Before the Chinese team arrived, when Nehru had discussed with his colleagues and advisors the strategy and the

[1] Mankekar, *The Guilty Men of 1962*, 31.

[2] *The Times of India*, 21, 23 and 24 April 1960.

[3] Sinha and Athale, *History of the Conflict with China 1962*, 55.

[4] Subramanian, 'Looking Back to the Future'.

line of discussion to be followed in a possible bargaining with Chou, 'the advice he received from all sides was to be adamant'.[5] President Rajendra Prasad repeatedly counselled against giving Chou any concessions, and Ambassador Parthasarathy suggested to Nehru that India's policy can only be to reject firmly all Chinese territorial claims.[6] The leaders in India had already prepared their arguments for confronting the Chinese team, which they expected to be prepared for a tough negotiation on terms dictated by Mao and the CCP leadership. Moreover, the Indian propositions to be placed during the deliberations had already been aired in public by senior Indian politicians in their conversations with Western diplomats. This was reflected in the words of Vice-President Radhakrishnan who, on 1 April, reportedly told British High Commissioner Malcolm MacDonald that there would be 'a breakdown' in the talks between Nehru and Chou 'on the second day'.[7] On 5 April, Morarji Desai is reported to have informed MacDonald that the Indian government appreciated the importance of the 'Aksai Chin road to the Chinese and were prepared to assure them use of the area, but this would have to be done without any surrender of Indian sovereignty over the region'.[8] Ambassador Parthasarathy implied to American officials in Hong Kong on 12 April that he was concerned that Nehru might be taken in by Chou.[9] Vice-President Radhakrishnan also stated that Nehru could not cede territory 'because Indian public opinion will not tolerate that'.[10] Naturally, this confrontational attitude could not provide any desired outcome in the Delhi talks.

---

[5] CIA, *The Sino-Indian Border Dispute Staff*, Section II (1959–1961), iv.

[6] Ibid., 45.

[7] Record of the conversation with the vice-president by MacDonald, 1 April 1960, FO 371/150440, TNA, quoted in Srinath Raghavan, 'Sino-Indian Boundary Dispute, 1948–1960: A Reappraisal', *Economic & Political Weekly* 41, no. 36 (2006): 3882–3892. Available at https://www.jstor.org/stable/4418679 (accessed on 8 September 2020).

[8] Report of conversation with Secretary-General, N. R. Pillai, 17 March 1960; Finance Minister, Morarji Desai, 5 April 1960, UKHCI to CRO, DO 35/8822, TNA, quoted in Raghavan, 'Sino-Indian Boundary Dispute'.

[9] CIA, *The Sino-Indian Border Dispute Staff*, Section II (1959–1961), 45.

[10] Record of conversation with Radhakrishnan by MacDonald, 12 April 1959, DO 35/8822, TNA, quoted in Raghavan, 'Sino-Indian Boundary Dispute'.

Chinese Delegation in Delhi Encounters Resistance

During the dialogue at Delhi, Chinese negotiators proposed a 'barter deal'—China's acceptance of the McMahon Line as the border of the NEFA and, in Ladakh, India's acceptance of the LAC accommodating China in Aksai Chin. This meant that China would not make any claim in the eastern sector to the areas south of the McMahon Line, over which it had proposed an extended claim in 1959, but India had to accept the Chinese occupation of Aksai Chin, where it had built a road. But in New Delhi, it was construed that this was an attempt to maintain the status quo after taking hold of substantial territory in Ladakh. The talk, which initiated on the afternoon of 20 April at the residence of the Indian prime minister between Nehru and Chou, went on for several sessions until 24 April without reaching any breakthrough.[11] The two major conditions that Chou put forth were that (a) the entire boundary had to be negotiated and (b) the status quo had to be maintained. India did not agree to the proposal for the bartering of Aksai Chin, but insisted on withdrawal of the PLA from Aksai Chin. According to Noorani, India should have considered the mutual barter proposal as a realistic option, but it did not. Mankekar also opined that 'it was most unfortunate that Nehru at this moment felt impelled to reject' Chou's proposal, 'a proposal that should have made sense to any realist'.[12]

Several rounds of talks went on over 22 and 23 April between the leaders from both sides, but without any breakthrough. Peking wanted to consider all three sectors together, but New Delhi's approach was radically different, as they insisted on treating each sector separately, because of which the talks once again failed. The collapse of the dialogue was highly disheartening to the peacekeepers on both sides of the border. Chou even departed from the diplomatic protocol and talked to Nehru and his top advisors, including Krishna Menon, in separate private sessions. But all of these were stonewalled by the

---

[11] *Record of Talks between PM Nehru and Premier Chou Enlai Held between 20 and 24 April 1960* (History and Public Policy Program, Digital Archives, Nehru Memorial Museum and Library, P. N. Haksar Papers, File #24), 69–85. Available at http://digitalarchive.wilsoncenter.org/document/121124 (accessed on 8 September 2020).

[12] Mankekar, *The Guilty Men of 1962*, 32.

opposition. But by now, news of the proceedings was debated in public and in the media. This brought the

> pressure of Indian public opinion, particularly of the opposition in parliament, which had driven Nehru into a corner, with no room left for a manoeuvre. While the Chinese Premier was still in New Delhi, a mass demonstration was staged in front of Nehru's house 'demanding not to "succumb" to the Chinese. Nehru came out and addressed the crowd and assured them that not an inch of Indian soil would be yielded to China'.[13]

This rejection of all the proposals made Peking realize India's tough stand on the issues. Chou finally went back from India 'disappointed, embittered and in a rage' and gave a vent to his feelings during a midnight press conference in Kathmandu.[14]

Other issues that invited displeasure of the guests in Delhi cropped up as well. China was of the view that the manner in which the Chinese premier was addressed to in Delhi by top officials was not as per international diplomatic standards. Chou's separate talk with Home Minister G. B. Pant on 21 April was a disaster, as the latter spoke bluntly stating 'We feel betrayed'. Chou's talk with Finance Minister Morarji Desai on 22 April was no different as Desai did not mince words in addressing the premier. When Chou criticized New Delhi for granting asylum to the Dalai Lama, Desai was reported to have replied, 'You should be the last person to object to political asylum. Where would you be today if political asylum had not been given to Lenin?'[15] In Chou's talk with Vice-President Radhakrishnan, a similar instance of a blunt response was reported. In an argumentative temper, Radhakrishnan reportedly told Chou that if the Chinese believed that Aksai Chin is theirs, 'on such a basis India could claim Kandahar, Kabul, and many other areas including parts of China'.[16] These words and deeds seemed to be a desperate attempt to defeat the diplomatic effort of 'Socialist Nehru', who they suspected to be lenient with Communist China.

---

[13] Ibid., 31–32.

[14] Ibid., 33.

[15] *Minister Morarji Desai's Discussions with Chou Enlai, April 1960 (Extract)* (White Paper; New Delhi: MEA).

[16] CIA, *The Sino-Indian Border Dispute Staff*, Section II (1959–1961), 47.

In this atmosphere, Chou rejected Nehru's suggestion for withdrawal of the Chinese troops from the occupied areas. The only point on which they agreed was that the talks would continue. So a temporary, informal 'understanding' was reached to halt patrolling and turn the talks over to subordinate officials who would meet to collate historical evidence from each side and draft a joint report,[17] but were not empowered to recommend a solution. The Chinese had never anticipated this adamant attitude from Delhi, and what they had experienced from Nehru was a real shock. After the collapse of the talks, in a press conference on 25 April 1960, while responding to a question from K. Rangaswami, *The Hindu* correspondent, Chou commented that 'there exists a relatively bigger dispute' in the western sector.[18] Political analysts suggest that it was most unwise for Nehru to have insisted on China's withdrawal from Aksai Chin, which caused the talks to collapse. Later, China reversed its suggestion of recognition of the McMahon Line and strengthened its previous position in the eastern sector.

Since the failure of the 1960 talks, even when there was an understanding, at least verbally, to reduce forward patrolling, there was a persistent demand to arm the border. During the long conversations in Delhi in 1960, at one point, Chou reportedly offered to withdraw the Chinese troops from Longju as a friendly gesture, and Nehru responded by offering a withdrawal of some Indian forces at one point in Ladakh, but this was dropped out during the final drafting of the communiqué.[19] However, China ceased regular patrolling activities in its self-imposed demilitarized zones and only sent out occasional reconnaissance parties with the aim of reducing the possibility of armed clashes. All border troops were instructed to exercise extreme restraint and this was 'approved by party Central Committee and Chairman Mao'.[20]

[17] Joint communiqué of the Prime Ministers of India and China, 25 April 1960, quoted in Jain, *China–South Asian Relations*, 171.

[18] *Premier Chou Enlai's Visits to Burma, India and Nepal* (Information Office, Embassy of the People's Republic of China), 25–26, quoted in A. G. Noorani, 'Truth & Tawang', *Frontline* 25, no. 25 (2008): 6–19.

[19] CIA, *The Sino-Indian Border Dispute Staff*, Section II (1959–1961), 49–50.

[20] Ibid., 53.

It was meant to silence Russia and India for criticizing China for its aggressiveness.[21] Similarly, an informal mutual understanding was also reached to suspend forward patrolling by both sides, and the nations agreed to avoid clashes on the frontiers. This was indicated in the formal statement of 25 April; Nehru agreed to this but 'this had not been written into the 25 April communiqué'.[22]

But the day after the talks ended (26 April), the DMI told the American Military Attaché that Chinese forward patrolling had ceased and that the Indians would take no action that might provoke border incidents.[23] An apparent informal oral understanding to temporarily cease sending out forward patrols did not affect New Delhi's programme of reinforcement in Ladakh. Nehru reportedly told President Prasad on 25 April 1960 that, regardless of the outcome of his talks with Chou, police constabulary units would be replaced by regular army units and that the government would press forward with the development of the entire border area and the construction of communication lines and new roads.[24] However, after the deadlock in Delhi, the official teams of both nations again met for a series of talks during three sessions in Peking, New Delhi and Rangoon[25] between June and December 1960. On the basis of these deliberations, a comprehensive report was later prepared by each side and brought together for publication. These reports were published by New Delhi (February 1961) and Peking (April 1962). On 14 May 1961, India took the initiative to further break the ice. It sent a note to the Chinese government urging it to consider the proposal (India withdrew from the Chinese claim line and China from the Indian claim line) of Nehru on 16 November 1959 and, as a matter of courtesy, 'pending negotiation and settlement

---

[21] Ibid., 53, 60.

[22] This reminds one of the talks between Vajpayee and Musharraf at Agra, and at the final stage of drafting of the communiqué, certain imports outcomes of the agreements were dropped.

[23] CIA, *The Sino-Indian Border Dispute Staff*, Section II (1959–1961), 50.

[24] Ibid., 51.

[25] Ministry of Information & Broadcasting, *China's Betrayal of India: Background to the Invasion* (New Delhi: Ministry of Information & Broadcasting, 1962).

of the boundary question, permit the continued use of Aksai Chin road for Chinese civilians' traffic'.[26] This meant that the disputed territory in the western sector would be free from both sides until a solution was reached. As both militaries vacated to distant lines, there was no possibility of clashes, and China could use the road it had constructed in the territory claimed by the Indian side for civilian purposes. China now adopted a tougher posture and posed a question—was it a defeated country to follow the dictates of the other? [27] China now began to be emphatic on the NEFA. This, of course, was nothing but an argumentative proposition, in which both parties did not budge from their stand. After the failure in Delhi, Peking was generally found to be less enthusiastic about initiating talks. The defeat of the April 1960 talks by the Delhi *junta* was a severe blow to the peace initiative. On his way back from Mongolia in July 1961, the Secretary General of the MEA, R. K. Nehru, visited China again and met Chou Enlai but for no avail.

For Peking, the McMahon Line was a negotiable one, as in the case of Burma. On 28 January 1960, in an agreement with the country, Chou accepted the McMahon Line as the recognized boundary between Myanmar and China.[28] Actually, a reasonable question can be raised here—how was it that China was able to recognize the McMahon Line in its agreement with Myanmar, while it could not reach any such settlement with India?[29] China had shown willingness in the case of India as well in 1960, but it was a trump card for China to bargain for Aksai Chin. They were ready for a 'give and take' proposal, but for India, the Aksai Chin area was considered a matter of prestige and, therefore, remained a factor beyond the reach of negotiations.

[26] *Note Given by the MEA to the Embassy of China in India, 14 May 1962* (White Paper VI), 43.

[27] *Note Given by the MFA to Embassy of India in Peking, 2 June 1962* (White Paper VI), 57.

[28] Noorani, 'Truth & Tawang'.

[29] Myanmar was part of India until 1937 and also at the time the Simla Agreement was concluded.

All Roads Lead to Military Face-off

After the Delhi session, except for a few minor efforts, the peace initiatives were not getting adequate attention in mending bilateral relations. India refuted the charges of China (1 March) that it was unwilling for negotiation, and on 13 March proposed its readiness for negotiation on the condition that China would withdraw from the area that it had 'encroached' upon since 1957. The precondition for negotiations, from both sides, was about maintaining the status quo, which, according to India, was the withdrawal of the Chinese troops from Aksai Chin, while for Peking it was its occupation in Aksai Chin. India categorically stated that it was always ready for negotiation with China, but could not compromise on aggression along any part of its territory. This escalating tension on the frontiers, where both sides had already mobilized forces, prompted Nehru to propose on 26 July, a couple of months before the war, a positive gesture to make way for negotiation, even at the cost of relaxing its stand. Allowing China to continue to possess territory up to its first claim (1956) until a final settlement was reached was considered a reasonable proposition.[30] But once news came out, it invited severe criticism from the Indian press and the Parliament against the government. Parliamentary debates described the move as being most disgraceful and shocking to the nation.[31] *Hindustan Times* wrote an editorial on 9 and 10 August 1962, titled 'The Road to Dishonour'.[32] This closed all the doors to further negotiations.

By mid-1962, the escalation in the border had reached a crescendo, with all the roads leading to a military encounter, and even a small level of friction was sufficient to start a conflagration. In a radio broad-cast on 3 August 1962, the Chinese Foreign Minister Chen Yi declared that it was 'impossible for Chinese troops to withdraw from its own

---

[30] *Note Given by the MEA to the Embassy of China in India, 26 July 1962* (White Paper VII), 34.

[31] *Lok Sabha Debates* (3rd series, vol. 6. 1962/1884); Sinha and Athale, *History of the Conflict with China 1962*, 89.

[32] *Hindustan Times*, 9 and 10 August 1962; Sinha and Athale, *History of the Conflict with China 1962*, 89.

territory, which will be against the will of its 650 million people and no force in the world could oblige us to do something of this kind'.[33] China once again rejected the proposal and, in its reply note, dated 4 August 1962, insisted that India should come to the negotiation table without any conditions.[34] There was no sign of negotiation in the near future. Now the rigour was not confined to words, but hectic armed mobilization on the frontiers. The New Delhi's FP in late 1961, though marked by several inadequacies, had already brought a larger part of its border under the control of the armed forces. Similarly, Peking mobilized enormous military strength on its side. This created a highly volatile situation. The Henderson Brooks and Bhagat Report has shed light on border situations that led to an escalation, resulting in armed encounters, even when the report was silent on certain areas to shield certain 'interests'.

Forward Policy, A Misguided Strategy to the Warfront

India's FP, introduced between late 1961 and early 1962, is considered to be one of the decisive factors that escalated the situation leading to a border war in October 1962. Neville Maxwell tries to project that Nehru's FP was the fundamental reason for the 1962 war.[35] But Maxwell's unabashed view that India's guilt was total[36] cannot be taken at face value. FP alone cannot explain the reason that led to war. When Maxwell presents his thesis on the basic premise that the border war erupted solely from Nehru's FP, he fails to take into account the factors behind the introduction and the situation under which Menon and Nehru were compelled to give the directive. If the FP (1961) was the sole reason for the provocation, who was behind the 1959 mishaps

---

[33] Quoted from *Italian-Swiss Radio Broadcast in a Note by the MEA to the Embassy of China in India 22 Aug 1962* (White Paper VII), 36.

[34] *Note Given by the Ministry of Foreign Affairs to Embassy of India in Peking, 4 August 1962* (White Paper VII), 18.

[35] Maxwell, *India's China War*, 171–257.

[36] Parshotam Mehra, 'India–China Border: A Review and Critique', *Economic & Political Weekly* 17, no. 20 (1982): 834–838. Available at http://www.jstor.org/stable/4370923 (accessed on 8 September 2020).

at Longju and Kongka Pass that opened the door to the armed clash? Pressure tactics for military border movements against China since 1959 were not taken into account. Maxwell not only does not count Peking's belligerent militarism since 1960, which was far higher than New Delhi's, but also his all-out attack on Nehru is totally blind of the US factor, which was a propelling force behind the curtains, pushing India towards a military encounter. However, despite these aspects, one can agree that the FP had aggravated the situation, finally leading to the outbreak of the war in 1962.

Had the introduction of forward posts been adopted with an aim of protecting borders and with the intention of strengthening frontiers, without provoking the neighbour, those who had advised this policy and implemented the same should have taken enough precautionary measures to avoid any such adverse eventualities. Once this was decided, there were several other prerequisites to be completed before venturing into such a decisive step: (a) establishment of a minimum basic infrastructure like a road and communications network connecting remote areas where jawans were deployed; (b) actual topographical specifications of the terrain for the correct perception of border alignments, maps, etc., which should have been the essential prerequisite and (c) establishment of contact with the people on the border to learn about the alignment from them. But above all, before the FP was implemented, the following should have been considered: (a) the actual strength and capacity of the armed forces and their commands on ground zero should have been evaluated; (b) a proper understanding of the strength and weaknesses of the border forces, on the other side, and the possible eventuality of such large armed mobilization, etc., should have been strictly assessed. The fact was that there was neither proper direction to the forces, nor were the field commands provided with any kind of proper maps or other devices. The FP was, therefore, introduced in a haphazard way in a short time frame, with the least respect to the facts mentioned earlier; (c) when these existing inadequacies were added to the lack of coordination between the various agencies in defence, which was an integral part of the policy, there was no doubt that it created more hazards than its targeted objectives. These disadvantages might have invited attention for immediate action by a well-coordinated, properly reinforced stronger armed mobilization on the other side and (d) above all these disorders, a more serious fault line was that it was introduced on the incorrect and misconceived illusion that China would not react strongly, and that it would retreat at the sight of a strong Indian force in Ladakh. This was built on a misconstrued and misguided narrative by vested interest groups within government establishments. In addressing these issues, the policy should have been able to attain the desired objective. But personal ego clashes and factional feuds between agencies badly affected the policy. The central commands in both the defence and the political circles were ill-advised. On closer observation of all these irregularities, it was apparent that the FP was implemented to achieve certain desired negative ends.

Operation Onkar

The operative principles for the implementation of the policy suggested the following: (a) to patrol as forward as possible from the present Indian position in Ladakh, with a view to establish posts to prevent the Chinese from advancing further without getting involved in clashes unless it becomes necessary for self-defence; (b) to move forward as far as possible for the effective occupation of the whole frontier in the central and eastern sectors as well. Wherever there was any gap which had to be covered, either by patrolling or by posts, efforts had to be made to position a major concentration of forces along the Indian border behind the forward posts to provide reinforcements at short notice.[37] The Brooks and Bhagat Report stated that 'with the meagre force in Ladakh, there was no question of being major bases worth to withstand any sizeable attack, and western command had already reported a paucity of force and other logistic support for effective defence of Ladakh'.[38]

The History Division of the Ministry of Defence suggested that 'the basic assumption behind the FP decision was no longer valid'.[39]

---

[37] Sinha and Athale, *History of the Conflict with China 1962*, 68.

[38] Government of India, 'The Henderson Brooks–Bhagat Report (NM)', 8.

[39] B. N. Prasad, 'Introduction', in *History of the Conflict with China*, ed. B. N. Prasad (New Delhi: Ministry of Defence, 1962), 20.

The Brooks and Bhagat Report stated that the real background for a decision regarding the introduction of the policy by the Government of India was not known.[40] The Commission pointed out that the minutes of the meeting, laying down the FP, held on 2 November 1961 in the Prime Minister's Office were not available—they were either missing or not maintained to keep secrecy.[41] The meeting chaired by the prime minister was attended by Defence Minister V. K. Krishna Menon, Foreign Secretary M. J. Mathai, COAS Gen N. Thapar, Lt Gen and Chief of the General Staff (CGS) B. M. Kaul, Director of IB, B. N. Mullik, and his Deputy Hooja, DMO Brigadier D. K. Palit and other officials.[42] In the meeting, the director of IB expressed his opinion that 'the Chinese would not react to our establishing new posts and that they would not likely to use force against any of our post even if they were in a position to do so'.[43] This was contrary to the military intelligence appreciation, which clearly indicated that the Chinese would resist by force any attempt to take back the territory held by them.[44] Despite the army headquarters' reservations in its implementation, why did the director of IB push for it?[45] Before its implementation, General Thapar had also written to the defence minister warning against Chinese reaction to the policy in Ladakh and other issues of inadequacy of troops and logistics.[46]

Whatever might have been in the minds of the officials who argued for introduction of such a policy, they should have anticipated the repercussions that it would have brought upon the armed forces sent to the borders. Those officials who advised the government on

---

[40] Government of India, 'The Henderson Brooks–Bhagat Report (NM)', 8.

[41] Ibid.

[42] Sinha and Athale, *History of the Conflict with China 1962*, 85; Mullik, *My Years with Nehru*, 314.

[43] Army HQ Letter no. 71939/GS/MO1 dated 20 Dec 1962, Para 7, Annexure 10 of Government of India, 'The Henderson Brooks–Bhagat Report (NM)', 8.

[44] Army HQ's Annual Intelligence Review: China–Tibet 1959–1960, Annexure 9 of Government of India, 'The Henderson Brooks–Bhagat Report (NM)', 8.

[45] Army HQ Annual Intelligence Review: China–Tibet 1959–1960, Annexure 9 of Government of India, 'The Henderson Brooks–Bhagat Report (NM)'.

[46] Sinha and Athale, *History of the Conflict with China 1962*, 86.

establishing posts as forward as possible to the frontiers or, in certain cases, even beyond the posts that the Chinese had already occupied, should have had enough awareness about the situation that forces at ground zero could face. They were also aware of the situations faced by the Indian Army, for example, the inadequacy of basic requirements and other logistics, the lack of accurate maps about the actual boundary, etc. They should also not have failed to appraise the real strength of the enemy forces on the other side. They had either not assessed the situations in which the commands and the jawans were in the forward, or they had purportedly neglected such aspects which amounted to a serious offence. This shows that the force was directed to move without awareness about the possible eventualities of such an adventure. This was the case in Longju and Kongka Pass in 1959 or more visibly in Dhola in 1962. The Henderson Brooks–Bhagat Report has pointed out a number of such cases.

Justifying the introduction of the FP, the official version of the history states that, in eastern Ladakh, a wide corridor of empty areas was lying unoccupied, separating the Chinese and Indian forward posts into which the Chinese were steadily pushing forward. The Indian force also therefore moved forward to leave the empty areas to be occupied.[47] The 'so called Forward policy, therefore, appears fully "justified", but it went too far, got too reckless and lost its balance in its later stages'.[48] The assumption behind the FP was the belief of the IB that the Chinese were unlikely to use force against India, even if they were in a position to do so. Militarily, the posts established as part of the FP were done hurriedly and were too small to withstand any attack, established in highly ill-advised locations. They were not adequately reinforced on advance requests of exigencies nor responded to even on emergencies. These situations clearly showed that 'the basic assumption behind the FP decision was no longer valid'.[49] It is suggested that reappraisal of the new situation and the feasibility of this policy were done neither by the army headquarters nor by the Government

[47] Prasad, 'Introduction', 20.

[48] Ibid.

[49] Ibid.

of India. It was largely implemented under the misguided advice of the IB and Home Ministry officials with specific interests in the army headquarters. Although the initial intention behind introducing the FP was to prevent the Chinese forces from advancing further, later the aim became to push the Chinese back from the posts they had already occupied, as in Namkha Chu in Tawang (the NEFA), which ultimately led to the border clash.

In addition to the fault lines that existed, political pressure was the dominant factor behind the policy. According to Lt Gen B. M. Kaul, who was present in the initial meeting, 'Nehru framed the FP principally for the benefit of the parliament and Public and also perhaps as a strategy of beating the Chinese at their own game'.[50] This statement points to the fact that the mounting pressure from the Parliament, the press and the public was strong on Nehru and his government to take a strong proactive or provocative step on the border issue. Even his own colleagues and 'trusted' advisors in the IB and other defence establishments and the Home Ministry pressed for military action. As regards the implementation of the policy, the army headquarters had shown little interest and therefore had not taken any immediate action until 5 December.[51] New posts near the McMahon Line were set up under 'Operation Onkar' by the Assam Rifles under the supervision of the army. In the western sector, it was actually implemented in April 1962 due to the harsh winter. When 36 new posts were established there by the end of September 1962, it was reported that the Chinese had already established 47 posts in this area. In Chushul, both forces had come closer face to face and in Demchok the Indian forces had almost reached the international border.

Low-key Reaction of China, an Ill-advised Proposition

The introduction of the FP was based on the firm belief of the political leadership, but the same view was shared and guided by the bureaucrats in the IB and the Home and Defence Ministries. They 'believed'

---

[50] Kaul, *The Untold Story*, 281.

[51] Government of India, 'The Henderson Brooks–Bhagat Report (NM)', 8.

that, except for small skirmishes or isolated clashes, there would be no large-scale armed conflict and, to avoid a nuclear war, China would not escalate them into a full-scale war.[52] But many experts in the military as well as in the defence circles suggested that the FP was against all sound military advice. A few higher officials in the armed forces warned against the indiscriminate forward movement of the army. Lt Gen Daulat Singh, in his memo to the government on 17 August 1962, criticized this policy and suggested, 'It is imperative that political direction is based on military means'.[53] The director of IB and Lt Gen B. M. Kaul, with Nehru's permission, had pushed for the move.[54] But it is largely noticed that the blame was invariably mostly pinned on the political authority, with scant consideration of reality. Maxwell grossly put the blame on Nehru.[55] But a review of the situations that led to the recommendation of the policy by the experts in the defence and intelligence establishments and the subsequent direction by the political leadership would reveal the real motives of the policy.

There were strong differences of opinion between the army and the IB over the implementation of the FP and the likely response of China in the event of its introduction.[56] Despite the Indian Army's objections due to logistical difficulties, Mullik enthusiastically took up the task with the paramilitary forces under the Union Home Ministry. When the Indian Armed Forces viewed that it would be disastrous for the country due to possible armed action by China, 'a group of so-called "nationalist" faction within the army led by General B. M. Kaul blindly took the advice of the IB under B. M. Mullik'. So a split in the Indian Army between the 'professionals' and the 'nationalists' was quite evident.[57] Even when the Indian Army was short-staffed and poorly equipped, it blindly began to set up forward posts along the

[52] Sinha and Athale, *History of the Conflict with China 1962*, 414.

[53] Neville Maxwell, 'Henderson Brooks Report: An Introduction', *Economic & Political Weekly*. Available at https://www.epw.in/journal/2001/14-15/perspectives/henderson-brooks-report-introduction.html (accessed on 8 September 2020).

[54] Guruswamy, 'Peace with China'.

[55] Maxwell, *India's China War*, 129–143.

[56] Palit, *War in High Himalaya*, 231.

[57] Subramanian, 'Looking Back to the Future'.

unoccupied borderlands with China, especially in the disputed areas. So a large number of small forward posts were set up with inadequate resources, poor communications and extremely vulnerable supply lines.[58] B. N. Mullik, a confidant of Nehru, kept informing him that the Chinese would not use force against these Indian posts. D. K. Palit reveals that B. M. Kaul, CGS, another confidant of the prime minster, had accepted Mullik's assertion that China would not go to war with India on the border issue. Palit added that the 'IB had failed to warn Nehru about possible Chinese attack across the border in the North and the East'.[59] It either had no intelligence on the 'political intentions' of the enemy, or it seemed to have concealed the available intelligence report from the political leadership. Mullik's FP was mooted since 1959, but was stalled after the Kongka Pass disaster. However, it was resumed by the army in 1961. The Henderson Brooks–Bhagat Report reveals that Mullik stuck to his view even in 1961, when the possibility of a violent response from the Chinese was not much in doubt. Presumably, 'Mullik had briefings from the CIA, which had extensive covert operations in Tibet'.[60] Mullik never revealed the source of his information on what he considered would be the Chinese response to India's FP.[61]

V. K. Krishna Menon is reported to have said that 'there would be no war between India and China and in the most unlikely event of there being one, Menon was quite confident of fighting it on the diplomatic level'.[62] On 10 January 1960, speaking at Tezpur, Menon categorically stated that 'the Indo-China border dispute was not of such magnitude as could precipitate a war'.[63] B. M. Kaul had stated that, in a number of meetings held by the defence minister, the general view was that the Chinese would not provoke a showdown.[64]

---

[58] Guruswamy, 'Peace with China'.

[59] Palit, War in High Himalaya, 231.

[60] Shakya, The Dragon in the Land of Snows.

[61] Subramanian, 'Looking Back to the Future'.

[62] Thorat, From Revival to Retreat, 191.

[63] A PTA report quoted in Bhargava, The Battle of NEFA, 67, in Sinha and Athale, History of the Conflict with China 1962, 428.

[64] Sinha and Athale, History of the Conflict with China 1962, 428.

Within the political and military circles, it was a regular feature to blame Krishna Menon those days, and there was a strong Western lobby against him in politics. Actually, the order to 'throw the Chinese out' in Dhola was not directed by Menon, but was given by K. Raghuramaiah, Minister of State for Defence, on 22 September 1962, who was in charge when Menon was in New York. The Army Chief General K. N. Thapar gave his appreciation of the situation in the Dhola area, and the foreign secretary presumed that the Chinese were unlikely to react strongly.[65]

Similarly, in 1961, during his visit to Bomdila, Nehru was confident of a political solution to the border issue and, in response to a question, he firmly said, 'There will be no war with the Chinese. There will be a political solution to the problem'.[66] These words of confidence from the defence minister and the prime minister were largely based on the advice of the IB and the army officials. In June 1962, Lt Gen B. M. Kaul, CGS, in his report to the COAS, stated, 'It is better for us to establish as many posts as we can in Ladakh, even though in penny-pockets, rather than wait for a substantial build up, as I am convinced that the Chinese will not attack any of our positions'.[67] In September 1962, Gen J. S. Dhillon said, 'Experience in Ladakh had shown that a few rounds fired at the Chinese would cause them to run away'.[68] Relying on these bureaucratic propositions, on 8 November 1962, a few days before the real war began, Nehru stated in the Lok Sabha, 'Even the Chinese aggression on our border during the last five years,…hardly has led us to the conclusion, though it troubled us greatly, that China would indulge in a massive invasion of India'.[69] It is generally alleged that the officials in the military shared this view because they were not bold enough to go against the assertive opinion

[65] Guruswamy, 'Peace with China'.

[66] Interview of Lt Col Shamshersingh (Retd), quoted in Sinha and Athale, *History of the Conflict with China 1962*, 429.

[67] Quoted in Sinha and Athale, *History of the Conflict with China 1962*, 415.

[68] Ibid., 430.

[69] Jawaharlal Nehru's 'We Accept China's Challenge' speeches in the Lok Sabha on India's resolve to drive out the aggressor, quoted in Ministry of Information & Broadcasting, *China's Betrayal of India*, 6.

of V. K. Krishna Menon as he was strongly supported by Nehru.[70] But Nehru might have erred from his overdependence on confidants such as B. M. Mullik and Lt Gen B. M. Kaul.

It seems that a possible reason for the Chinese aggressive response to these border posts, turning into a full-scale war on 20 October 1962, might have been prompted from their awareness of the weaker positioning of the forward posts, with little backing from any immediate military base. The espionage system of China was so effective and active within the territorial limits of India and even among the forces that it could easily measure the depth of chaos and confusion, as well as weakness and discord among the defence officials of India.[71] On account of improper intelligent inputs and faulty implementation of military preparedness, the Indian Armed Forces were virtually provoking the enemy to storm into its exposed loopholes.

'Government of India was under tremendous pressure from the parliament, the press and the public'.[72] With limited knowledge of the situation at the borders and military issues, the three Ps (press, Parliament and public) accused the government of lack of will, and vociferously and stridently demanded military action on the borders. Parliamentary documents of debates in both houses and newspaper headlines over 1960–1962 prove the role of the three Ps in the border war. Due to the mounting pressure and the misguided version of the IB input, the government ordered for moving the force on to the borderlines, ultimately leading to heavy casualties.[73] At the same time, many officers in the army, like Lt Gen Daulat Singh, General Officer Commanding (GOC)-in-Charge, suggested that the Chinese be left in possession of the Indian territory they had grabbed, for the time being, and consolidate the area by pushing the roads ahead, building strong bases equal to that of the Chinese. Since 1961, negotiation had virtually come to a standstill. By mid-1962, Peking came out with more

---

[70] Sinha and Athale, *History of the Conflict with China 1962*, 415.

[71] China was able to take part in espionage activities, taking advantage of the Tibetans fleeing to India. The Chinese mingled with the Tibetan refugees to enter the NEFA and Assam.

[72] Prasad, 'Introduction', 23.

[73] Ibid.

stringent action, presumably in response to the FP. Adding fuel to the fire, China established a few more posts on 12 July, and the process continued in August and September 1962 within the 'Indian territory' beyond what it claimed in 1956.[74]

What Happened at Dhola?

What triggered the winter war of 1962 was the hostility over the Dhola post in the NEFA. On 8 September 1962, the Chinese troops marched across the international boundary in the eastern sector. In the presence of a large troop of soldiers on both sides of the border, a spark was enough to set off a massive encounter. Even when Indian leaders, time and again, reiterated that China would not attack on any massive scale leading to a war, it did finally happen on 20 October 1962. The first shot was fired by China. It was never an unexpected or unprovoked war forced upon New Delhi. There were enough provocations on both sides of the border after 1959. The large-scale armed clash in the eastern sector had begun with the Indian Army's establishment of the Dhola post and their efforts to evict the Chinese Army from the location. The proper location of the post that was to be established was not clear to even those who did the work. The Chinese Army surrounded and stormed the post and wiped out India's 7th Infantry Brigade.

When the Indian Armed Forces were instructed to push forward and open up new posts, it included the 'controversial' one post in the western China–Bhutan–India tri-junction in Dhola as well.[75] The location of the post was contested even by those forces which were involved in its establishment. Until the introduction of the FP in December 1961, no patrolling was permitted within 2–3 miles of the McMahon Line other than for the purpose of defence,[76] and most of

---

[74] Note Given by the MEA to the Embassy of China in India, 12 July 1962 (White Paper VI), 83.

[75] Government of India, 'The Henderson Brooks–Bhagat Report' (Annexure 35 para 8 [b]), 48.

[76] Headquarters to Eastern Command Letter No. 120901/20/A/GS (O) dated 9 June 1960, Annexure 40, quoted in Government of India, 'The Henderson Brooks–Bhagat Report (NM)', 51.

the forward posts in the Siang and Lohit frontier divisions were some distance from the border. Indian patrols and posts were also instructed not to cross the border at any point of time. The actual establishment of this post at Dhola, the location of which was not as per the watershed principle, was carried out on 4 June 1962 under Captain Mahabir Prasad.[77] When it was implemented, as the border on the map did not run along the watershed and was running due west from Khenzamane, and the watershed tri-junction was 4 miles north of the one on the map, the post was not established at the old tri-junction, but at Dhola MM 8316.[78] The post should have been a little south of Namkha Chu at the tri-junction. But the actual tri-junction, covered heavily with snow, Che-Dong, was selected a few kilometres north of Dhola. Major General Niranjan Prasad, GOC, 4th Infantry Division, questioned the propriety of establishing posts there and suggested that the post be withdrawn or moved to a tactically sound position on the Thagla Ridge. But he was instructed from above, 'the line drawn in the map, because of its thickness, misrepresented the boundary', which actually should be along the Thagla Ridge to the north.[79] The Henderson Brooks Commission states that 'implementing of posts in the Kameng Frontier Division was carried out without reference to Eastern Command. The XXXIII Corps in May 1962 on their own initiative ordered the establishment of the tri-junction Post (Dhola)'.[80]

Finally, the post was established at a wrong location and 'to avoid alarm and queries from all concerned, it was proposed to continue

---

[77] In pursuance of the FP, on 10 January 1962, the Eastern Command issued instructions for forward movement. Subsequently, on 24 February 1962, the Tezpur-based XXXIII Corps under the command of Lt Gen Umrao Singh recommended establishing nine more additional posts, which included the one at the tri-junction at Dhola, in Kameng frontier division. In March 1962, the Eastern Command obtained permission from the army headquarters to patrol the area of the McMahon Line west of Khenzamane, and the permission was accorded on 27 April for patrolling as well as establishing new posts, without prior permission. Government of India, 'The Henderson Brooks–Bhagat Report (NM)', 50–52.

[78] Originally, the location for the intended post was at the China–Bhutan–India tri-junction as given in the map existing in May 1962 and the map showed the tri-junction at MM 7914. Government of India, 'The Henderson Brooks–Bhagat Report (NM)', 52.

[79] Sinha and Athale, *History of the Conflict with China 1962*, 88.

[80] Government of India, 'The Henderson Brooks–Bhagat Report (NM)', 49

using the present grid'. However, later in August 1962, the XXXIII Corps brought to the notice of the Eastern Command the discrepancy between the arbitrary line drawn up on the map and the line as it should be according to the watershed principle. 'The boundary line printed on the map had considerable inaccuracies'.[81] The Henderson Brooks–Bhagat Report suggests that 'this in effect, meant that the post was actually north of the McMahon Line', and the IB, in the meantime, on 23 May 1962, also traced the area as under the claim of the Chinese. This was a typical example to show that in many instances this kind of disparity among the real topographic specifications, the cartographic perceptions in mind and the actual maps in hand always existed. The establishment of the Dhola post at a controversial location was either due to a discrepancy in the documents at hand or due to an incorrect implementation of the order. It is also significant to note that the army headquarters neither knew the local topographical specifications nor the practical difficulty in executing their order. In many instances, the army headquarters in their orders for the implementation of the FP by the lower formations were provided without adequate preparation, including specific maps and other specifications.[82] Meanwhile, in August, China issued diplomatic protests and, on 8 September, a strong team of the PLA occupied the top of the Thagla Ridge. Soon came the directive on 18 September to repulse the Chinese from the Thagla area, called 'Operation Leghorn', which was planned by Lt Gen B. M. Kaul. But the Chinese stormed the Indian post on 20 September, resulting in severe casualties on both sides. Brigadier Dalvi, who commanded the forces at Thagla, also considered that the location was on an incorrect assumption.[83]

The Chinese storming in Thagla, however, caused severe criticism of the government. The media described incident as illegal Chinese encroachments on Indian territory, which enraged the public and the mood was reflected in the Parliament clamouring for immediate action on the border to repulse the Chinese from the Thagla Ridge area. This persistent clamour in the Parliament and the press was

---

[81] Ibid., Annexure 42, 52.

[82] Ibid., 50.

[83] Dalvi, *Himalayan* Blunder, 22–23.

taken up by the political parties in the opposition, as well as by all those against Nehru's policies, and demanded action against China. Finally, the government instructed the army to get Thagla Ridge vacated by the Chinese as early as possible, with least possibility of a strong retaliation from the other side. The result was a high casualty to the Indian Army. It appears that the political leadership was misled into believing that everything in Ladakh was in favour of China, while the Indian Army in the NEFA was capable of 'throwing out' the Chinese. The reality, however, was entirely different. In fact, in many forward locations, army personnel were sent despite knowing the eventuality that they might face a strong attack from Chinese forces. The fact was that they were, in effect, scapegoats of the ego clash among the higher bureaucrats in the Defence and Home ministries. The role of the IB in indiscriminately pushing the jawans to far-off locations is an area that demands further enquiry, which would be a learning. It is reliably presumed that the chief of the IB for ulterior motives had insisted for such hasty and blind actions. It was in such contexts that the Commission observed that 'no troop placed in the circumstances as they were, could be expected to obey orders, let alone fight'. This 'changed disciplined men in to a rabble, an Army into a mob'.[84]

Who Directed the 'Eviction' of the Chinese from Dhola?

On 8 September 1962, when about 600 Chinese soldiers surrounded the post, the Indian Army, which was in a totally disadvantageous position, was asked on 12 September to evict the Chinese from Dhola. Lt Gen Umrao Singh and Maj Gen Niranjan Prasad, who were deputed for the task, soon expressed that it was beyond their capacity, considering the troops available to them and the inadequate logistical support.[85] But a pertinent question arises here. On 18 September, when the prime minister, the defence minister and the finance minister were abroad, who asked the government spokesperson to announce during

---

[84] Government of India, 'The Henderson Brooks–Bhagat Report (NM)', 54.

[85] Mankekar, *The Guilty Men of 1962*, 46.

a press conference that the army had been instructed to drive the Chinese from Dhola?[86] What was the logic behind announcing such a military strategy in public? On 20 September, there was a short exchange of fire between the two forces in which two Chinese were killed and two wounded.[87] On 22 September 1962, a crucial meeting was convened in the Defence Ministry's room, when Menon was in New York, to review the border situation. But the details of the meeting were not available to the Commission, which was appointed to enquire about the whole episode of India's debacle in 1962.[88] This crucial meeting was chaired by the Deputy Minister of State for Defence K. Raghuramaiah. As reported, for political reasons, it was insisted in the meeting that there was no alternative but to evict the Chinese from Dhola.[89] The COAS 'Thapar refused to authorise an attack without a written directive from government'.[90] He warned of possible Chinese retaliation in Ladakh in the event of Indian action in Dhola. But the foreign secretary was of the opinion that the Chinese were unlikely to react strongly. An order was issued to evict the Chinese from Dhola, even at the expense of losing some territory in Ladakh.[91] The government order was issued under the signature of H. G. Sarin, the joint secretary to the Defence Ministry, which read 'the Chinese should be evicted from the Thagla-Dhola area. The chief of army staff should take necessary action'.[92]

What was the compelling factor to take such a disastrous decision? Who were the people who were insistent on pushing the nation into a

[86] Ibid., 47.

[87] Ibid.

[88] The commission had noted from other sources that, in the meeting, the army staff had done an appraisal of all the possible eventualities in the case of an eviction order, such as (a) a possible Chinese armed reinforcement to Dhola; (b) retaliation in Ladakh and (c) a strong Chinese move elsewhere. Government of India, 'The Henderson Brooks–Bhagat Report (NM)', 63.

[89] Mankekar, The Guilty Men of 1962, 47.

[90] Dalvi, Himalayan Blunder, 427.

[91] Government of India, 'The Henderson Brooks–Bhagat Report (NM)', 17.

[92] Dalvi, Himalayan Blunder, 427.

border war? Was it a political compulsion, or was it in the interests of the arms lobby? Only classified documents in sealed vaults can provide the final verdict on such speculations. However, the government was not 'in a position to resist, any more, the pressure of the public opinion demanding action against Chinese provocations'.[93] In this situation, according to Nirad C. Chaudhuri, 'The political authorities had asked the soldiers to open an offensive without giving them a chance to win. The contemplated offensive was never approached as a military measure. It was insisted upon in the most frivolous manner out of a sense of political expediency'.[94] Both Lt Gen Daulat Singh from the Western Command and Lt Gen Sen from the Eastern Command had expressed concern at possible casualties, and they opined that, in the case of a Chinese attack, they would annihilate the Indian Army, but the government 'being driven to it by the pressure of public opinion' was now all for action at any price.[95]

The Dhola mishap was the real beginning of the armed encounter that came up a couple of weeks later. No sound advice was taken nor adequate preparation was ensured, but the Indian force was instructed to take Dhola. Tactical retreat was no way an unsound decision on the battleground, but such sound decisions always cannot easily win public applause. It was common sense that, in the case of an action against the enemy in one sector, one has to expect a retaliatory military action in both theatres (western and eastern). The incident of the Galwan post in Ladakh shows that such a precaution also was not taken. The Brooks and Bhagat Commission reported that it was the responsibility of the army headquarters that 'no army should be placed at the mercy of the enemy, on the off chance that the latter would not react'.[96] It further reported that the orders of the army headquarters were 'tactically unsound' and 'unrealistic', and 'it appeared that events controlled actions, rather than actions events'.[97]

---

[93] Mankekar, *The Guilty Men of 1962*, 45.

[94] Dalvi, *Himalayan Blunder*, 438.

[95] Mankekar, *The Guilty Men of 1962*, 46.

[96] Government of India, 'The Henderson Brooks–Bhagat Report (NM)', 18

[97] Ibid.

Committed Force but Command-less

As we have already found, it was at the efforts of General Kaul and the director of IB with the Home Ministry officials that the political leaders were advised that China would not react even at the show of strength by India.[98] General Kaul, as CGS and DGMO, had time and again pushed for the implementation of the FP. Even when the Defence Ministry had directed for armed action, it was the responsibility of the army headquarters to apprise the higher authorities in the political circle of the reality in which the latter had failed. Brooks and Bhagat say, 'Militarily, it is unthinkable that the General Staff did not advise the government on the weakness and inability to implement the FP'.[99] The Chinese had already strengthened their borders in the name of suppressing the Tibetan uprisings and the rebels' crossing of the borders. But when the Indian FP was introduced at the end of 1961, sufficient military preparedness should have been taken before pushing inadequate armed forces to the border where a strong enemy force was stationed. Absolute failure in this was evident from the incidents over August–September 1962 in Galwan post (Ladakh) and Dhola post (the NEFA). Such 'lapse in staff duties on the part of the Chief of the General Staff, his deputy the DMO, DMI and others was inexcusable'.[100] They observed that the mistakes and lapses of the staff sitting in Delhi, without considering the stress and strains of the command and its forces in the actual field, were 'more heinous than the errors made by commanders in the battle field'.[101] There was also 'an attempt to under-play the valour of the jawan'.[102] But the Commission's report emphatically says that

it was a junior leaders' and jawans' battle and there is no doubt they acquitted themselves well from the crime of their superiors[103] because they fought under grave handicaps and in face of defeat, yet there was no sign

[98] Ibid, 30.

[99] Ibid.

[100] Ibid., 32.

[101] Ibid.

[102] Dalvi, *Himalayan Blunder*, 377.

[103] Government of India, 'The Henderson Brooks–Bhagat Report (NM)', 32.

of undue panic and never a rout because they fought under commanders they trusted.[104]

Hence, the good name of our army was not marred.

The essential requirements, such as boots and warm clothes, were highly inadequate for the survival of the forces in the Himalayas. An overwhelmingly enthusiastic Kaul, who was promoted to overtake several in the line of promotion, had failed to assess the actual situation on the border, but had ordered the troops to move forward wildly. General Chaudhuri blames Kaul for planning the NEFA battle without any backing and hurriedly jumping to the task. Once appointed as the GOC, Kaul reached the headquarters at Tezpur and was carried to the frontier on a palanquin by his jawans. But soon, Kaul was flown back to New Delhi for 'treatment' and 'the Indian forces found themselves leaderless, with their corps commander lying "ill" in faraway New Delhi'.[105] He flew back to Delhi on 11 October, leaving his force 'command-less' and it was widely rumoured within the defence circles that he was bedridden due to panic. When the Chinese launched their massive attack on the Indian Army on 20 October, the Indian forces had no corps commander to direct and coordinate their operations. He had not entrusted anyone with this task, and to everyone's surprise he was alleged to have been directing the forces from Delhi. Chaudhuri is quoted saying, 'Hardly had Kaul gained his feet as corps commander than he fell "seriously ill", but even before he fully recovered hurriedly he was again sent to the frontiers'.[106] Brigadier John Dalvi, who was destined to witness the fate of the forces, narrated the alarming situation on the frontier when Kaul was commanding IV Corps from a sick bed in Delhi. On 19 October, the evening before the Chinese attacked across the Namkha Chu and swept away his brigade, Dalvi told his divisional commander, 'I am not prepared to stand by and watch my troops massacred. It is time someone took a firm stand. If

---

[104] Ibid., 33.

[105] Mankekar, *The Guilty Men of 1962*, 75–76.

[106] It is reported that on 29 October 1962 when the radio news broadcasted the return of Gen Kaul to resume charge of IV Corps after his short rest for illness in Delhi, the officers expressed shock at their fate under him. Mankekar, *The Guilty Men of 1962*, 104.

the higher authorities want a scapegoat, I am prepared to offer myself and put in my papers on this issue'.[107] Henderson Brooks says, 'The Brigade Commander had represented almost daily before this, but by 19 October, he had reached the end of his tether' until the Chinese struck the next morning.

Warmongers Attain Their Objectives

The war that began on 20 October 1962 lasted only until 21 Nov 1962. It was a full-scale military encounter spread over both the theatres of the western and the eastern sector. The war brought large casualties on both sides and, sometimes, more casualties among Indian soldiers on account of severe weather and inaccessible terrain during their retreat. In the initial days of the war itself, India lost a force of more than 2,500 soldiers, listed as dead and missing. Disorganized activities and absence of coordinated efforts, rather than lack of men and material, marked the closing phase of the military operations in the NEFA. The 4th Infantry Division was disintegrated in the NEFA jungle and the 2nd Infantry Division was severely bruised.[108] China took over an additional 3,000 square miles of Indian territory in Ladakh, more than what it possessed in Aksai Chin before the war.

But what was more embarrassing in the country, immediately after the debacle, was that the army officers were freely airing their criticism of developments in the border to the media. Resentment was mounting against the defence minister and officials in the army and civil sectors. This was actually the 'targeted outcome' of the US and the Western imperialist powers against Menon and Nehru. Under pressure from all quarters, in the middle of the war, on 30 October 1962, the defence minister resigned. It was also the end of all his efforts for defence production within the country, which was the ultimate aim of the Anglo-American lobby. In terms of the pressure exerted on the government for the expulsion of Menon, the Congress party members went ahead and placed the portfolio on the Deputy Minister of Defence

---

[107] Dalvi, *Himalayan Blunder*, 165–221.

[108] Government of India, 'The Henderson Brooks–Bhagat Report (NM)', 172–189.

K. Raghuramaiah, who had ordered the controversial 22 September force movement to Dhola. On 8 November 1962, an emergency committee was constituted within the cabinet and several committees within the Defence Ministry. On 26 October, in the middle of the war, an urgent appeal was made to the USA and the UK for military aid and New Delhi now 'feverishly negotiated with Washington and London' to face the looming Chinese threat further. This was the objective of the so-called Anglo-American power axis, which was dominant in the region and dominated Indian politics. The first consignment of US arms arrived on 3 November, even before a formal pact was signed on 14 November 1962.[109] Immediately after the war, there was a series of dismissals and reshuffling of officers in the defence sector.[110]

On 20 November 1962, Peking declared a unilateral ceasefire and said that, from 1 December 1962, the frontier guards would withdraw 20 km behind the LAC as on 7 November 1959.[111] The defence correspondent of *London Times* wrote that the Chinese were 'demonstrating to India and the world that they were able to make any border adjustments which they may think necessary whenever they desire and they can now retire to conduct negotiations from strength'. But it seems more appropriate to say that Peking was demonstrating its military capability to the whole world, by which it wanted to send a powerful message to Washington for its surreptitious activities on the borders and in its Tibetan region, and also to warn those who were trying to leverage New Delhi to the Washington axis.

According to sources in the Defence Ministry, Maj Gen A. S. Pathania and Lt Gen B. M. Kaul share the maximum blame for the mishaps to the military.[112] Gen Thapar and Lt Gen Sen were also guilty

---

[109] Mankekar, *The Guilty Men of 1962*, 64.

[110] The Divisional commander Niranjan Prasad was replaced by A. S. Pathania, but Lt Gen Kaul who was accused of several irregularities continued to resume his job after his leave on 'sickness' during the first phase of the war. The COAS Gen Thapar resigned and was replaced by Gen J. N. Chaudhuri, and Lt. Gen Manekshaw displaced Lt Gen Kaul as Corps Commander.

[111] It was after November 1959 that India had established a number of extended border posts far into the frontiers.

[112] Prasad, 'Introduction', 19.

of abdicating responsibility by refusing to issue orders to Pathania in the absence of Lt Gen Kaul in the troop headquarters. The military debacle was certainly due to tactical failure.[113] But the failure was not merely military and was more of a political one, as the political party had to take a decision under pressure from the Parliament and the public, with irrational and un-militaristic demands by the opposition. V. K. Krishna Menon was blamed for the debacle to the maximum extent. His errors were of policies with no respect for service rules and hierarchy, which, no doubt, invited displeasure and rivalry within the military. But when Menon found the officer cadre as a divided house steeped in rivalry, he sidelined the old guards and posted a band of his trusted and committed army officers in key positions. However, Menon's major 'guilt' was of inviting the displeasure of the USA. He tried to revamp the Indian military and stood for self-reliance on arms production without being dependent on the West.[114] Even when Menon got ample political support from the prime minister, the existing rift and widespread frustration in the armed forces, because of differences between Menon and COAS Gen K. S. Thimayya, crippled his control on the forces. India failed to avoid a war and was dragged into it due to incorrect intelligence, faulty political assessments and pressure from within to initiate military action.[115] It seems that this was what some of his adversaries within the country wished to see. In the end, India faced a humiliating defeat not only on the battleground, but more on the international arena. This had an adverse impact on Nehru and India, which had gained considerable respect and reverence world over from the West to the East, through the charismatic personality and intelligent statesmanship of Nehru. It would not be completely incorrect if anyone were to believe that Nehru failed to visualize the politically polarizing developments within his government because he was preoccupied with maintaining his image in the international community.

---

[113] Ibid.

[114] Menon was frequently vilified in the Western press, which often described or depicted him as a 'snake-charmer', *Time magazine's* 1962 cover portrait. Shashi Tharoor, 'An Unusual Life', *The Hindu*, 29 April 2007.

[115] Prasad, 'Introduction', 23.

Conclusion

9

Wars have not settled disputes and, in fact, have only further aggravated situations and deteriorated bilateral relations. The deployment of armed forces to a volatile border cannot buy peace and resolve any issues. Bilateral border disputes should be settled through diplomatic dealings. Those especially of a sensitive and eruptive nature cannot be resolved through bipartisan debates within domestic politics. It needs determined interventions by a resolute leadership. Border disputes that are left unresolved are like dormant volcanoes that can erupt at any moment. The winter war of 1962 fought in the Himalayan mountains is no way different.

Military encounters have in no way helped to mitigate or resolve disputes. Instead, they have only led to distrust and disquiet in the region, disrupting peace-building processes, as in the case of Sino-Indian relations. The 1962 Indo-China war had adversely impacted the whole process of building Asian unity and also significantly weakened the move for strengthening Afro-Asian unity through the Non-Aligned Movement, in which India held a pivotal position. The war had had an immense impact on relations among Asian nations, which had been divided, though it was not that apparent, on ideological and other grounds. The war did not serve any purpose to the resolution of the dispute, other than militarizing the frontiers and thereby increasing the tension in the region. The war further strengthened the influence of the Anglo-American powers in the area. The affinity of Peking towards the cause of Pakistan intensified the tension, especially between India and Pakistan. The role that the USA played in dictating terms to these three powers in the South Asian region brought further distrust between Peking and New Delhi. Defence and military procurements from the West multiplied year after year. The funds from the public exchequer began to be used up for the purpose of defence. India and Pakistan got extensive support to militarize the region and came face to face in a military encounter in 1965. The Sino-Indian borders got advanced military attention and sophisticated armaments. Recurrent rifts and a military stand-off led to much apprehension among the public. The neighbours India and China, two ancient civilizations that had maintained harmony and cooperation for millennia, are now two of the leading nuclear powers with the two largest armed forces in the world. The world expects not enmity but amity among this 40 per cent of the world's population.

The present position of the dispute between these two nuclear powers is nothing like how it has been so far. Since New Delhi and Peking are two dominant powers in the world economy with both trying to position themselves as future 'superpowers', in the newly emerging geopolitical situation where the focus is shifting from the West to the East, both nations have a larger say in the global world. In this environment, the nations of the world are looking at developments in the region and some are showing interest in getting involved in the complexities of the border dispute, which could further aggravate differences and lead to a deterioration of relations. The June 2020 escalation of the border dispute in the Galwan Valley which culminated in bloodshed, the last such instance being 45 years ago, should be seen from a broader perspective. Despite earnest efforts for de-escalation, again lives have been lost on both sides and a tense environment continues to exist at multiple other points on the frontier. This is a warning to both nations about the gravity of the dispute.

The fundamental reasons that prompted Mao's China to adopt a belligerent attitude in its relations with India in the late 1950s stem from three aspects. First, the active intervention of the USA in the dispute with an extended arm of the CIA providing military training to the Tibetan rebels, in addition to arms, ammunitions and other logistical support, had no doubt aggravated the border situation. The US factor is still a persisting issue as far as China is concerned. Sino-Indian relations since 1949 have always been intricately intertwined with the active presence of the USA in between. The covert or overt operations of the CIA along the border regions, colluding with agencies like the anti-PRC Taiwan cliques, had been active on Indian soil. Hence, discussions on armed Sino-Indian conflicts would be incomplete without reference to the USA. the interventions of the USA had turned the border dispute into a military conflict.

Second, an overwhelming interest in the Tibet issue prevailed in India, beyond the standards of international refugee norms. The Indian stand on the Tibetan issue and the passion and enthusiasm it had showed in accommodating the Tibetan rebels on the grounds of human rights played a role in worsening bilateral relations. When the Dalai Lama became a favourite in Western and Indian media and was accorded reverence on Indian soil with state honours at the cost of portraying China as a belligerent undemocratic country, the friendship that India and China shared gave way to mutual distrust. Nehru's efforts to attain Asian unity, by extending support to new Communist China in the face of a hostile Western world, had gone in vain. The Chinese government accused India, stating that Tibetan rebels were working at the behest of India's instigation. They propagated the idea that the expansionist policy of certain neighbours caused tension in the Tibetan region. In this effort, China unsuccessfully tried to win over the allegiance of various tribes inhabiting the border areas which, no doubt, encouraged disruptive elements in the north-eastern states and other border regions. After several decades, when the Tibetan community assimilated to the Indian society and was accommodated even in the Indian military and government, Peking continued to allege that New Delhi was taking political advantage of the internal affairs of China.

Third, the efforts of Indian 'reactionaries' in colluding with the Western imperialists for anti-China propaganda, which was an active component of Indian politics, played an auxiliary role in this Sino-Indian issue. All of Nehru's detractors, among various parties, rallied in the name of Tibetan sympathy for active anti-Peking rhetoric which, with US backing, got strengthened in India. The covert relations of Indian bureaucrats, press and political leaders with the USA and other external forces strengthened the anti-China debate not only in India but also in world fora. Unless the border dispute is permanently resolved, the present diplomatic proximity of New Delhi to the 'Washington Axis' would further harm relations with its neighbours. A strong anti-Nehru faction, not only in the opposition but also more powerfully within his own party, had been active in New Delhi. While parliamentary debates and the Indian press could devote considerable space for anti-China propaganda and were involved in creating communist phobia among the Indian public, the Chou–Nehru diplomacy could not win over Mao's militaristic mind. When Mao Zedong's hopes in Moscow for an anti-Western comradeship were also shattered, the PLA ventured out to give a military shock to Nehru by which the CCP and Mao intended to send a strong message to the world.

While taking stock of evidence regarding the border dispute, the arguments of India seem to be stronger in the western sector, but they are legally not sound. As far as the eastern sector is concerned, China has no supporting documents, while India has its historical and administrative background for reference. Hence, neither China's claim to an extended Ladakh in the Galwan Valley nor India's claim for the whole region of Aksai Chin up to the Kunlun range can be justified by foolproof documentary evidence or any legality. In fact, proper and naturally defined border alignment within the western sector would not have provided any scope for dispute in the post-colonial Sino-Indian relations if it had been adopted as the norm. From very early on, the region had been divided between both nations on the basis of their natural delimitation as well as their usage and requirements. In fact, there were two areas of Aksai Chin, dividing the entire plateau into two regions, the north-eastern side of the Laktsang ridge under China, and the south-western Aksai Chin as part of the Ladakh region of Kashmir for India.[1] A feasible settlement allowing China to retain the north-east Aksai Chin in the Laktsang range through which its Sinkiang-Tibet road traverses, and the part of Ladakh that China now holds after September 1962 would be the final solution.

As regards the eastern sector, there is a definite border in theoretical and practical terms which both nations observe and respect.

---

[1] Refer to Figure 2.2 in Chapter 2.

China has recognized the nature of Indian possession of this region, but still holds on to it as a tactical trump card to bargain with for its claim in the western sector. Here, other than rhetoric, both nations, in principle, follow the LAC as the international territorial borderline. The alignment of the McMahon Line, no doubt, is in consistency with historical and geographical facts, with the exception of deviations in a few locations, including the Tawang region. China would also agree to this line, but pushes this argument only as a strategy for its claim on the western sector. In addition to these two major sectors, a few minor issues remain in the central and eastern sectors, which can be resolved if the political leadership of both nations is determined to seek a lasting resolution.

Until 1960, Peking was eager to negotiate a settlement over the border dispute. It seems that, while demonstrating their claims on the basis of evidence, Peking was not equipped with sufficient documentary evidence in both sectors and, therefore, China seems to have shown more enthusiasm for a mutual settlement. But New Delhi had been demonstrating its claims on the basis of documented proof from the pre-colonial days and, therefore, the argumentative posture of China was found to be in a disadvantageous position. Although it was vocal about the boundaries handed down through traditions and customs, Peking's approach was fundamentally different towards the debate. For the Chinese, the treaties and agreements executed by local officials in Tibet regarding frontiers were not ratified with the PRC. They argued that the colonial imperialist devices were not in consensus with the Chinese authorities and that a sovereign Chinese Republic was not bound by those treaties. Moreover, most of these pre-colonial treaties and engagements were not related to territorial jurisdictions and no specific delimitations or demarcations were part of these documents. The Chinese officials, therefore, dismissed the bulk of the evidence that India provided for its territorial claims.

New Delhi had missed out on opportunities to resolve the dispute, as the internal political atmosphere disallowed the government to push through for a viable solution. China was prepared for an exchange settlement of Aksai Chin for Chumbi Valley, a vitally strategic and important area for India. This proposal for mutual exchange was considered by some war strategists as a missed opportunity that could have avoided conflict.[2] As per the 'Krishna Menon Plan', it was suggested that India would lease the Aksai Chin area to China and, in return, China would lease the strategic Chumbi Valley, which is like a pointed dagger near the narrow passage of India with its north-eastern states. But Nehru was forced to drop the idea as an 'ignorant and vociferous media and opposition parties played a disastrous role in forcing a reluctant Nehru on a confrontation course'.[3] Michael Bercher says that Nehru was forced to take a strong stand due to pressure from some of his cabinet colleagues, such as Pant and Shastri, and public opinion.[4] The plan was dropped because the 'Rightist' opposition and some members of the Congress Party, along with the media, portrayed it as being submissive to Communist China. The rejection of such a reported practical offer, however, was looked at by China with suspicion, and Peking believed that Indian plans were aggressive.[5]

India's FP, on the advice of the IB and the Home Ministry in late 1961, had no doubt worsened the relationship at the border. Even though the objective of the FP was an effective mechanism for border defence and was completely devoid of any expansionism, it became a correct deed that was implemented in a wrong manner. Even when China had mobilized a large force on the frontiers in the context of crushing the Tibetan rebels, Peking considered India's FP as 'bourgeoisie expansionism' with Western support. But Peking's timing of the winter strike coincided with the Cuban crisis. The two superpowers, the USA and the USSR, had locked horns in the Pacific region. This provided the right opportunity for China. China cannot be absolved from the fact that it struck first on 20 October 1962. However, there is no merit to the argument that the winter strike of 1962 was totally unexpected in Delhi, because armed preparations had been underway

---

[2] Anil Athale, 'Remembering a War, The 1962 India–China Conflict' (2002). Available at http://www.rediff.com/news/india-china-1962-war-50-years-2012.html (accessed on 9 September 2020).

[3] Sinha and Athale, *History of the Conflict with China 1962*, 412.

[4] Michael Bercher, *India and World Politics: Krishna Menon's View of the World* (Bombay: Oxford University Press, 1968), 145.

[5] Ibid., 145–154.

at the frontiers since 1961. But it is also illogical to assume that a militarily superior nation would not dare to strike any time to score points in national or international politics. But those who appraised the political authority about an unreal situation in the border were responsible for the debacle. Contemporary China's recurring military muscle-flexing and belligerent attitude in the border region is also a concern in this context. What was surprising was that Peking had raised objections on several occasions when Indian official dignitaries had visited the NEFA. The infrastructural development activities of the Border Roads Organisation had also been objected to by Peking. At the same time, China was suspected of encouraging subversive activities in the region.

More than 21 rounds of formal talks have been conducted so far to resolve the tussle, most of which have been inconclusive. These unending dialogues might have satisfied political interests and would have yielded electoral dividends, but would have contributed nothing towards national interests. No talks can be fruitful or lead to any conclusion without a readiness for negotiations. Since there is no documentary evidence to prove the claims of both parties, the dialogues will remain in limbo until both sides decide to make compromises. The solution of militarizing the border with advanced arms and ammunitions, and frequent military face-offs in the border, might have provided political mileage for Mao when he failed to make the *Great Leap Forward*. Mao's dream of seeing the Red Flag fluttering the whole 'Middle Kingdom' and its peripheries, however, would not provide any lesson for the present-day China.

Bibliography

I. Reports/Official Files/Government Documents, etc.

Academy of Military Science. *The History of Counter Attack, War in Self Defense Along Sino-Indian Border*, 1st ed. Beijing: Beijing Military Science Publications, 1994.

CIA. 'Abraham Michael Rosenthal to Mr Salisbury, Undated, Box 159' (Raw Data, Harrison Salisbury Papers). In *The Sino-Indian Border Dispute Staff*, Section II (1959–1961), edited by CIA. New York, NY: Butler Library, Columbia University, 1961.

MEA. *The Parliamentary Debates*, part 2, vol. IX, Col. 5320. New Delhi: Government of India, 1951.

———. *Rajya Sabha Debates*, vol. 36, col. 2281–2287. New Delhi: Government of India, 1959a.

———. *Rajya Sabha Debates*, vol. 26, cols. 3895–3915. New Delhi: Government of India, 1959b.

———. *Rajya Sabha Debates*, vol. 26, cols. 2288–2292, nos. 14–24. New Delhi: Government of India, 1959c.

———. *Nehru's Speech in Parliament on November 25, 1959*. New Delhi: MEA, Govt. of India, 1960.

———. *Prime Minister on Sino-Indian Relations*, vol. 1. New Delhi: Government of India, 1961.

Nehru, Jawaharlal. *Selected Works of Jawaharlal Nehru* (Second Series [1955], Vol. 29), edited by H. Y. Sharad Prasad and A. K. Damodaran, 257. New Delhi: Oxford University Press, 2001.

Tibet Justice Center. *Agreement of the Central People's Government and the Local Government of Tibet on Measures for the Peaceful Liberation of Tibet*, 1951. Available at https://www.tibetjustice.org/materials/china/china3.html (accessed on 9 September 2020).

Xinhua, A. *A Selection of Documents and Materials Concerning the Tibet Issue*. Beijing: Xinhua News Press, 1959.

II. Newspapers/Magazines/Periodicals

Cowell, Adrian. 'I Saw the Secret Shooting War with China'. *Argosy* 364, no. 5 (1967): 29–33.

Gupta, Shekhar. 'National Interest: Once Upon a Spooky Time, Why US Spy Planes Loved Orissa and How They Took Me for a Ride'. *The Indian Express*, 2 May 2019. Available at https://indianexpress.com/article/opinion/columns/national-interest-once-upon-a-spooky-time/ (accessed on 9 September 2020).

Noorani, A. G. 'India's Forward Policy'. *The China Quarterly* 43 (1970): 47–80.

———. 'Nehru's China Policy'. *Frontline* 17, no. 15 (2000). Available at https://frontline.thehindu.com/other/article30159538.ece (accessed on 9 September 2020).

———. 'U.S. Espionage in India'. *Frontline* 23, no. 16 (2006). Available at https://frontline.thehindu.com/other/article30210577.ece (accessed on 9 September 2020).

———. 'Jingoism—From Jana Sangh to BJP'. *Frontline* (2014). Available at https://frontline.thehindu.com/the-nation/jingoismfrom-jana-sangh-to-bjp/article5847744.ece?test=1&textsize=large (accessed on 9 September 2020).

Outlook. 'China Declassifies Files; "Kashmir Princess" Incident'. 20 July 2004. Available at https://www.outlookindia.com/newswire/story/china-declassifies-files-kashmir-princess-incident/236591 (accessed on 9 September 2020).

Patterson, George. 'Ambush on the Roof of the World'. *Reader's Digest* (1968): 59–64.

People's Daily. 31 March 1959.

———. 23 April 1959.

———. 28 April 1959.

———. 6 May 1959.

———. 1 February 1960.

———. 25 October 1962.

———. 27 October 1962.

Ramakrishnan, Venkitesh. 'An Insider's View'. *Frontline* 22, no. 5 (2005). Book Review of *Open Secrets: India's Intelligence Unveiled* by Maloy Dhar, Manas Publications, New Delhi, 2005. Available at https://frontline.thehindu.com/other/article30203781.ece (accessed on 9 September 2020).

Subramanyam, K. 'Neville Maxwell's War'. *Hindustan Times*, 18 and 25 October 1970. Available at http://mps100428.nevagroup.com/system/files/K.Subrahmayam%27sBook%20Review.pdf (accessed on 9 September 2020).

The Diplomat. 22 May 2020. Available at https://thediplomat.com/2020/05/amid-dispute-with-india-nepal-publishes-new-political-map-what-now/ (accessed on 20 October 2020).

The Economic Times. 1 August 2018. Available at https://economictimes.indiatimes.com/news/defence/no-border-dispute-between-india-and-myanmar-states-government/articleshow/65229882.cms?from=mdr (accessed on 20 October 2020).

The Indian Express. 17 April 1955.

The Print. 21 May 2020. Available at https://theprint.in/diplomacy/nepal-halts-distribution-of-new-text-book-with-revised-map-incorporating-indian-areas/508293/ (accessed on 20 October 2020).
The Times. 25 April 1955.
———. 2 September 1959.

III. Online Articles

Arpi, Claude. 'The Himmatsinhji Committee Report' (2012). Available at http://claudearpi.blogspot.com/2012/08/the-himmatsinghji-committee-report.html (accessed on 9 September 2020).
Burgess, David S. 'Foreign Affairs Oral History Project' (1991). Available at https://www.adst.org/OH%20TOCs/Burgess,%20David%20S.toc.pdf (accessed on 9 September 2020).
Davar, Praveen. 'How 1962 War Cut Short 2 Brilliant Careers'. *The Asian Age*, 1 December 2017. Available at https://www.asianage.com/india/all-india/011217/how-1962-war-cut-short-2-brilliant-careers.html (accessed on 9 September 2020).
Gupta, Karunakar. 'The McMahon Line 1911–45: The British Legacy'. *The China Quarterly*, no. 47 (1971): 521–545. Available at http://www.jstor.org/stable/652324 (accessed on 9 September 2020).
Historic Wings. 'Assassination via the *Kashmir Princess*' (2013). Available at http://fly.historicwings.com/2013/04/kashmir-princess/ (accessed on 9 September 2020).
Masani, Zareer. 'No Accident India Forgot Swatantra Leader'. *The Print*, 16 June 2019. Available at https://theprint.in/opinion/no-accident-india-forgot-swatantra-leader-my-father-minoo-masani-the-beef-eating-parsi/250483/ (accessed on 9 September 2020).
Office of the Historian Department of State, USA. *Memorandum of Conversation* (no. 162; 1971). Available at https://history.state.gov/historicaldocuments/frus1969-76v17/d162 (accessed on 9 September 2020).
Phanjoubam, Pradip. 'How McMahon Drew His Line, and Why China Wants It Changed'. *The Wire*, 20 May 2015. Available at https://thewire.in/diplomacy/how-mcmahon-drew-his-line-and-why-china-wants-it-changed (accessed on 9 September 2020).
Pubby, Manu. 'Nehru Okayed US Spy Flights to China from Orissa Base: CIA Files'. *The Indian Express*, 17 August 1913. Available at http://archive.indian-express.com/news/nehru-okayed-us-spy-flights-to-china-from-orissa-base-cia-files/1156448/ (accessed on 9 September 2020).
Ratu Ngawang, interview, Delhi, 5 December 1997, in *Journal of Cold War Studies* 8, no. 3 (2006): 102–130. Available at https://www.colorado.edu/anthropology/sites/default/files/attached-files/mcgranahantibetscoldwar.pdf (accessed on 9 September 2020).

Yadav, R. K. 'Remembering the Legendary Kao'. *Canary Trap*, 15 January 2009. Available at http://canarytrap.in/2009/01/15/remembering-the-legendary-kao/ (accessed on 9 September 2020).

IV. Books

Barron, John. *KGB Today: The Hidden Hand*. London: Hodder and Stoughton, 1984.

Baxter, Craig. *The Jana Sangh*. Philadelphia, PA: University of Pennsylvania Press, 1969.

Bunker, Ellsworth. 'Oral History, Interview'. New York, NY: Butler Library, Columbia University, 18 June 1979.

———. 'Oral History, Interview'. New York, NY: Butler Library, Columbia University, 17 July 1979.

Christopher, Andrew. *Defence of the Realm, the Authorized History of MI5*. Bristol: Allen Lane, 2009.

Christopher, Andrew, and Vasili Mitrokhin. *The KGB and the World: The Mitrokhin Archive II*. Bristol: The University of Michigan, Allen Lane, 1999.

Clark, Gregory. *In Fear of China*. Manchester: Lansdowne Press, 1967.

Damodaran, A. K. 'Foreign Policy in Action'. In *A Century History of the Indian National Congress (1885–1985)*, vol. 4. New Delhi: Vikash Publishing House Private Limited, 1990.

Deendayal Upadhyaya in S. L. Poplai, ed., *1962 General Election in India*. Bombay: The Hindu Archives, 1962.

Galbraith, John Kenneth. *A Life in Our Times: Memoirs*. London: Andre Deutsch, 1981.

Galiullin, Rustem. *The CIA in Asia: Covert Operations against India and Afghanistan*. Moscow: Progress Publishers, 1988.

George, Francis Stevens. *China and Africa Love Affair*. Scotts Valley, CA: CreateSpace Independent Publishing, 2014.

Haas, Elizabeth, Terry Christiansen, and Peter Haas. *Projecting Politics: Political Messages in American Films*. Abingdon: Routledge, 2015.

Jhangiani, Motilal A. *Jana Sangh and Swatantra*. Bombay: Manaktalas, 1967.

Kalugin, Oleg. *Spymaster: My Thirty-Two Years in Intelligence and Espionage against the West*. New York, NY: Basic Books, 2009.

Kumar, Satish. *CIA and the Third World: A Study in Crypto-Diplomacy*. New Delhi: Vikas Publishing House, 1981.

Kux, Dennis. *India and the United States: Estranged Democracies*. Washington, DC: National Defence University Press, 1993.

Li Ping et al., ed. *A Chronological Record of Zhou Enlai, 1949–1976*, vol. 1. Beijing: Zhongyang Wenxian, 1997.

Lyall, Sir Alfred. *Rise of British Dominion in Asia*. London: John Murray, 1894.

Mathai, M. O. *Reminiscences of the Nehru Age*. New Delhi: Vikas Publishing House, 1978.

Maxwell, Neville. *China's Borders: Settlements and Conflicts.* Sydney: Maxwell Publications, 2012.

MEA. 'The Revolution in Tibet and Nehru's Philosophy', *People's Daily*, People's Republic of China Office of the Charge d'affaires. New Delhi: MEA, Government of India, 1959.

Mehta, Jagat. *Negotiating for India: Resolving Problems through Diplomacy.* New Delhi: Manohar Publishers, 2006.

Mishra, D. P. *The Post Nehru Era Political Memoirs.* New Delhi: Har-Anand Pub. Pvt Ltd, 1993.

Moynihan, Daniel Patrick. *A Dangerous Place.* Norwalk, CA: Secker and Warburg, 1979.

Nehru, Jawaharlal. *Selected Works of Jawaharlal Nehru* (Second Series [1955], Vol. 35), edited by Mushirul Hasan, H. Y. Sharad Prasad and A. K. Damodaran, 352–361. New Delhi: Oxford University Press, 2005.

Patterson, George. *A Fool at Forty.* Waco, TX: Word Books, 1970.

Peissel, Michel. *The Secret War in Tibet.* Boston, MA: Little, Brown and Company, 1972.

Reid, Sir Robert. *History of the Frontier Areas Bordering on Assam.* Shillong: Government of Assam Press, 1942.

Sandhu, P. J. S., R. S. Kalha, and Vinay Shankar. *1962: A View from the Other Side of the Hill.* New Delhi: Vij Books India Pvt Ltd Delhi, 2015.

Yajee, Pandit Sheel Bhadra. *CIA: Manipulating Arm of U.S. Foreign Policy: 40 Years of CIA Manoeuvres against Freedom and Dignity.* New Delhi: Criterion Publications, 1987.

About the Author

Ismail Vengasseri is Assistant Professor in the Department of History, Lady Shri Ram College (LSR) for Women, University of Delhi. As a teacher for the last three decades in central government institutions and formerly HOD of the Department of History, LSR, he is presently engaged in teaching and research on modern Indian history, the history of China and Japan, and issues in world history. His doctoral thesis was on 'Revenue Administration in Malabar under English East India Company'. He has also published articles and books, the recent being a co-edited book entitled *Gandhian Thought: Different Perspectives*.

Index